The following alphabetical lists include the names of the 600 or more persons w[...]
edition of The Honourable Balmoral Her Peers and Piers, by subscribing for [...]

SUBSCRIBERS Abraham - Downie.

Abraham, K.E.	Barton, R.A.	Brown, H.	Clammer, B.	Dalgoutte, D.
Adam, G.M.	Bassett, C.S.	Brown, K.J.	Clammer, T.	Danielson, I.G.
Adam, S.	Bawden, M.	Brown, S.	Clare, R.D.	Danielson, J.D.
Adams, F.	Beeney, D.	Brown, T.	Clark, A.	Danielson, J.M.
Adams, J.M.	Bell, T.W.	Brown, T.H.	Clark, J.K.L.	Danielson, M.R.
Adams, K.	Bennett, A.E.	Bryant, A.B.	Clark, P.	Danielson, R.E.M.
Alderman, K.	Berry, I.	Bryant, G.T.	Cleary, R.	Dark, R.B.
Alexander, C.	Biddle, M.	Budd, G.	Clements, J.R.	Darlaston, R.H.
Allen, H.	Bigmore, R.A.	Bullock, N.K.	Clemow, V.S.	Davies, I.
Allen, R.	Birchenough, J.A.	Bullock, P.L.	Cole, A.	Davies, M.F.
Allwright, K.	Booth, D.	Bungard, R.	Collard, C.	Davis, J.
Anderson, D.	Boswell, G.	Burgess, W.H.	Colledge, S.	Davis, J.E.
Anderson, D.J.	Boulter, R.L.	Burke, S.	Collier, A.	Dawson, J.
Anderson, J.	Bowker, M.F.	Burrough, R.J.	Collins, J.	Day, D.C.
Anderson, R.S.	Boyd, D.	Burrows, D.	Connett, R.E.	Day, E.T.
Andrews-Horrigan, P.T.	Boyt, M.	Butterworth, S.	Cook, D.C.	Day, S.
Angell, A.J.	Bradford, P.W.	Buttivant, D.	Cook, L.	Dell, R.P.
Antill, C.	Bradley, T.F.	Cade, L.	Cooke, C.	Dempster, R.M.
Appleyard, I.S.	Braisted, D.	Cairns, L.	Coombes, N.	Denby, S.
Arnold, J.	Breeze, G.	Cameron, A.R.	Coucill, P.	Dennison, P.R.
Atrill, S.M.	Brennan, W.J.	Camm, C.A.	Coucill, T.	Dewar, I.
Austin, G.M.	Bridges, A.J.	Campbell-Platt, G.	Coyler, H.G.	Dickman, D.A.
Badger, D.	Bright, C.G.	Carn, J.	Cozens, J.	Digby, G.
Baker, A.	Broad, D.	Castle, G.D.	Creasley, P.	Ditchfield, G.
Balfe, T.	Brockie, B.	Chalk, D.L.	Cripps, B.M.	Dixon, B.T.
Ball, D.	Brocklesby, P.	Chambers, P.D.	Cronin, J.E.	Dolbear, P.
Banham, J.A.	Brookes, M.	Chaplin, D.	Croucher, A.	Donaldson, J.
Banyard, F.	Brown, A.	Cheverton, K.	Crowhurst, K.M.	Donne, G.L.
Barford, V.E.	Brown, A.J.	Child, G.J.	Cruickshank, A.F.H.	Douglas, D.
Barton, D.J.	Brown, D.	Clammer, R. & C.	Crump, I.	Downie, E.

SUBSCRIBERS Downs - Lane.

Downs, A.	Free, K.	Grainger, P.	Hilling, D.	Johnson-Allen, B.
Draper, K.	Freeman, E.	Grant, D.J.	Hillman, N.	Johnston, B.
Drewett, G.D.	Freeman, J. & D.	Gray, V.	Hinton, C.	Johnston, R.
Duncan, D. & N.	Fricker, P.	Green, B.	Hitchman, P.	Jonas, L.P.
Dunckley, B.	Fry, N.H.J.	Green, K.J.	Hithersay, A.I.	Jones, A.W.
Dunkinson, R.	Fryer, S.	Green-Price, R.	Hobbs, J.L.	Jones, C.
Dutfield, S.J.	Fynn, L.	Greenway, P.A.	Hodges, K.	Jones, D.K.
Eadie, A.W.	Galanos, S.	Gregory, D.	Hodgskin, J.W.	Jones, G.J.
Ebsworth, P.W.	Galley, W.F.	Gregory, D.S.	Hogan, M.K.	Jones, H.
Edlin, R.F.V.	Gallie, D.R.	Gresley, R.R.	Hogg, A.F.	Jones, J.
Edney, E.	Gamblin, A.P.	Griffin, N.	Holden, C.	Jones, N.
Edwards, G.J.	Gardiner, L.G.	Griffiths, C.	Homer, P.	Jones, P.F.
Edwards, J.A.	Garner-Richards, P.	Gully, A.	Hood, G.J.	Jones, R.F.
Edwards, K.	Garth-Thornton, M.J.	Gutteridge, K.C.	Hopwood, S.	Jones, R.N.H.
Ellis, R.H.W.	Gaskell, B.	Haddleton, D.S.	Horan, J.	Jones, S.J.
Elsworth, B.E.	Gawn, D.	Halcrow, M.J.	Horn, A.M.	Kay, P.J.
Entwistle, N.	Gellatly, G.	Hall, P.	Horsham, M.J.	Kells, R.J.
Evans, J.	Gentry, R.	Hamilton, R.	House, J.	Kelly, I.L.
Evans, L.	Gibbons, P.	Harker, R.	Howard, D.W.	Kelly, J.
Evans, P.	Gill, A.	Harverson, R.	Howarth, D.	Kelly, J.R.
Evans, P.C.	Gillard, E.	Hatch, J.	Howell, K.	Kendrick, J.R.
Fairbairn, G.W.	Gladwell, A.	Hatcher, J.	Howells, J.T.	Kent, W.J.
Fay, R.C.	Glanville, R.	Haydon, R.	Hughes, A.	Kibby, N.G.P.
Fielder, J.	Glendinning, E.H.	Haynes, F.A.	Hull, G.	Killip, R.A.
Figg, M.J.	Glenister, J.	Hayward, D.A.	Hull, J.	King, M.D.
Fillis, E.	Godeck, J.W.G.	Hayward, P.	Hunter, H.	Kirk, E.A.
Fisher, M.J.	Gold, J.M.	Henderson, M.G.	Hurr, B.	Kirkham, J.
Fleming, R.	Goldsmith, R.J.	Henton, C.	Jackson, B.G.	Kitchenham, E.
Flux, K.F.	Goldwater, D.	Herington, O.E.	Jamieson, S.	Knowlden, N.J.
Forster Brown, J.	Gosling, A.	Hewitt, J.A.	Jeffrey, A.G.	Korman, D.
Foster, P.A.	Gosling, P.D.	Hewlett, B.W.	Jenkins, D.	Lambie, R.C.
Fraser, K.	Graham, D.	Heyes, J.M.	Jenkins, P.M.	Lane, E.C.
Fraser, T.	Graham, I.	Heyes, R.	Johnson, P.	Lane, E.J.

The Honourable
Balmoral
Her Peers and Piers

THE STORY OF BRITAIN'S MOST WIDELY-TRAVELLED EXCURSION SHIP

by Richard Danielson

Published by Maritime Publications, Laxey, Isle of Man, IM4 7JT
and produced on behalf of Waverley Excursions Ltd., operators of the *Balmoral*.

Text origination and design by
Keith Uren Publishing, 12 Manor Lane, Douglas, Isle of Man, IM2 2NX

Printing, reprographics and binding by
The Bath Press Ltd., Lower Bristol Road, Bath, BA2 3BL.

ISBN 0 - 9513155 - 8 - 7

*If there were ever a competition to find the smallest pier visited by the **Balmoral**, surely Carrick Castle (on the west side of Loch Goil) must be amongst the likely contenders, closely followed by the Raglan Pier at Port Erin in the Isle of Man. Here we see the **Balmoral** at Carrick Castle on 27th September 1998.*   Photo: Joe McKendrick.

South Coast ports, including Southampton, the Isle of Wight and thereabouts with my father, George, were very frequent and looked forward to with eager anticipation.

A little later in life, after I had met and married Pat in 1969, I found her father, Donald Hoskin (a former sea-going man just like my own father) to be an enthusiastic follower and supporter of the **Balmoral**, the **Waverley** and other small craft. Pat's family had run the village shop and Post Office at St. Mabyn in Cornwall for well over half a century and the only time I could easily prise Donald away from his emporium, was with the promise of a visit to the **Balmoral** or, later, the **Waverley**.

Almost everywhere as the years have gone by, slowly but inexorably, the larger excursion steamers and pure passenger ferries have been phased out. If they were succeeded at all and many were not, in their place the now ubiquitous, shapeless, characterless (but no doubt thoroughly efficient and economic) car ferry arrived. In strict commercial terms, we are expected to believe that this is progress. However, that is the whole point of our story as the **Balmoral** now operates everywhere purely for the pleasure of her passengers and not on one particular money making route.

By and large, their disappearance was true, not only of the ships that are the subject of this book, but of most around our shores. It is therefore perhaps hardly surprising that there remains a large number of us (not enough, the ship operators would say) who feel that so much went out of our lives when, one by one, the pleasure steamers and many of their once proud owners retired.

Happily, as the story unfolds, readers will be able to follow the events which finally led to the **Balmoral** escaping oblivion on more than one occasion and being saved to operate in support of the world's last sea-going paddle steamer, the **Waverley**.

It is a fact that when the **Balmoral** was built some 50 years ago, almost every seaside town in Britain had a pleasure boat operating off its beach or a fleet of steamers large or small. They probably also had one or more piers or a jetty or harbour wall from which an excursion steamer could safely ply its business.

Around our shores nowadays, the would-be day sailor can still find short boat trips to go on and a few vessels still put to sea on coastal sailings between various estuaries, ports and harbours. The requisite Class III passenger certificate (technically for short excursions to sea) is now quite rare whereas, not so long ago, ships so licensed were to be found lying gunwale to gunwale awaiting their human cargoes every day throughout the summer months.

Today the Paddle Steamer Preservation Society is responsible for the regular operation of the last two traditional British paddle steamers, namely the well known **Waverley** dating from 1947 and the smaller river paddle steamer, the **Kingswear Castle**. She was built in 1924 with engines taken from an earlier ship of the same name built in 1904. The third ship of the fleet, the subject of this work, is the 50-year-old motor vessel **Balmoral** and she is a joy to behold. Like the paddle steamers, despite a permanent shortage of money, she too is maintained in pristine condition and sails thousands of miles every year. Using the peculiar language of the ship operator (wherein one round trip counts as two passengers) between the three ships, they carry well over 300,000 passengers every season. The fixing of fare prices is a delicate juggling act designed to maximise numbers of passengers yet at the same time make a modest profit. The whole operation is a Registered Charity.

This then is the golden jubilee story of Britain's most widely-travelled excursion ship, the **Balmoral**. And widely-travelled she certainly is, visiting hundreds of ports and harbours and sailing the equivalent of three-quarters of the way round the whole world each year. But this has been no ordinary period of 50 years, looked at in terms of mankind's achievements good, bad and indifferent.

In 1948, whilst the **Balmoral's** design was being finalised and her construction commenced, Britain's railways were nationalised only to be privatised again, half a century later, having thereby gone the full circle! In private homes, gas lighting was still very common at the close of the 1940s, whilst public television broadcasting and the use of the family car had by then barely begun. With both of those came the inevitable pollution, not only of the atmosphere.

In 1969, twenty years after the **Balmoral** was launched, but still over thirty years ago, the Americans led by Neil Armstrong took one giant leap for mankind, straight onto the moon. Even then, most of the world had to wait another decade or more for the home computer, the microwave oven and the pervasive mobile 'phone which, nowadays at the turn of the Millennium, we take for granted.

Yet all the while, the **Balmoral** has remained true and constant - a benchmark by which all other things can be reliably calibrated.

This then is the **Balmoral's** Millennium and golden jubilee celebration and I am sure you will enjoy the **Balmoral** experience, now and well into the future.

Richard Danielson,
Laxey, Isle of Man.
September 1999.

The paddle steamer **Balmoral** (I) was the last of the Red Funnel ships to operate excursions across the Channel to France. This atmospheric photograph of her, out of the water and undergoing refit and survey at Northam, shows her just before the War complete with short mainmast and wireless aerial. She was never refitted after the War and was broken up at Northam in 1948/49; thus her name became available for the new ship. *Photo: Red Funnel archives.*

*The **Balmoral** is seen here in all her considerable glory. Within the limiting confines of designing a ship to be principally an Isle of Wight ferry, a more handsome and pleasing looking vessel it would be difficult to imagine. This photograph was taken on 17th August 1968 in Southampton Water and her full height mainmast, added in 1954 to meet the new lighting regulations, is clearly visible. Also, by the time this photograph was taken the paintwork surrounding her bridge and wheelhouse had reverted to cream, it having been cream originally but was later given a wood finish for some years.* Photo: John Edgington.

Setting the Scene for the Red Funnel Era

The story of our ship, the **Balmoral**, begins rather earlier than the year 1949 when she was launched and first entered service. Even the period between late 1947 and early 1948 when she was actually conceived, designed and ordered, is far from being the true beginning of how her whole fascinating history evolved.

To see the picture in perspective it is helpful first to look briefly at the state of relevant local ferries and excursion shipping services in the South and around Southampton Water, Spithead and the Solent to see how they were emerging as, thankfully, the Second World War was coming to an end.

Then the story will turn upon the steps that Red Funnel Steamers (and the various other operators) were taking to rebuild their war-torn fleets and how they were meeting all the business opportunities and challenges arising in the first few years after the end of the War.

Subsequent chapters will follow the **Balmoral's** career and all her vicissitudes during the next fifty years. During this splendid period, others around her have come and mostly gone but the **Balmoral** has remained at the very heart of her time-honoured trade - the passenger-moving business.

The population's sense of relief and new found feeling of freedom after the long dark years of war was great. The urge to escape and the arrival of the family car (although petrol rationing was still a big problem) were all suddenly to play a major part in shaping the whole of Britain's coastal passenger shipping operations. All this applied equally to those serving the South Coast and sea area around Southampton and the Isle of Wight, as anywhere else.

The economics of running propeller driven motor ships rather than using steam power delivered through paddles or screws, or raising that steam through burning oil not coal, were dawning upon ship operators.

Also, further advances in naval architecture were beginning to be responsible for the emergence of an improved breed of vessel capable of combining several functions and operating throughout the year.

Certain of the larger local shipping operators, including The Southampton, Isle of Wight & South of England Royal Mail Steam Packet Company Limited (latterly known as Red Funnel Steamers) and the Southern Railway, at the time not yet nationalised, were able to begin to take advantage of these innovations as they renewed or replaced their fleets. Even between these two main contenders, their respective approaches to the challenges that lay ahead were really quite different for many years to come.

Fortunately for them, neither had to rely to a great extent on summer-only excursion trade, attractive though it might have seemed. Both had significant year-round ferry services operating between two or more ports, thus substantially underpinning their businesses. In Red Funnel's case, they had their very significant fleet of tugs too but as our story is about passenger vessels, mention of the tugs will be confined to any detail vital to the text.

The passenger ships of the Southern Railway fleet were in many ways seaborne trains and much of their ferry trade centred upon serving the needs of the railway passenger and connecting with train timetables.

In the fo'c's'le of their ships, forward of the main superstructure, there was a hold into which passenger baggage was stowed for the crossing. At Portsmouth Harbour railway station (and many other railway connected harbours round the coast) travellers had only a few short paces to take them from the railway carriage to the gangway of the steamer waiting to carry them across the water, in this case to Ryde.

However, train passengers were by no means the exclusive preserve of the railway-owned ferries. Passengers for Isle of Wight destinations travelling by train via Southampton Central railway station would be sold a through ticket from their local station (maybe hundreds of miles away). In this case, a connecting Hants & Dorset bus would convey them from the station down to the Royal Pier for the voyage to Cowes by a ferry belonging to Red Funnel Steamers.

On the other hand, operators of pure excursion craft including Cosens & Co. Ltd. and P. & A. Campbell Ltd. were, as we shall see, very much subject to the vagaries of the weather. Also, apart from the fickle weather, to some extent the success of these operations relied on public nostalgia and perceptions of how things were immediately before the War.

Profitable seasons for some of the operators of these 'summer butterflies' as they were euphemistically called, were from now on to be few and far between and the years of plenty had to be good enough to try to make up for all the poor ones. To add to the difficulties straight after the War, Campbell's suffered relatively more than the others on account of war time cross-Channel sailing restrictions remaining in force and the fact that some piers had been deliberately disabled to stop any possibility of their being used by foreign invasion forces.

The old paddle steamer **Balmoral** *has really got the 'bit between her teeth' in this classic photograph. Heeling well over to port, the raw power she is exuding as she speeds away from the Royal Pier gives this photograph great atmosphere.*
Photo: H.A. Allen collection.

The handsome, single-funnelled **Lorna Doone** *(I) dating from 1891 (but not acquired until 1898) had been a most popular mainstay of Red Funnel Steamers' excursion fleet until the outbreak of the War. Sadly, and much to many people's distress, when she returned after the hostilities, she was deemed to be too dilapidated for economic repair.* Photo: Keith Adams coll'n.

During the War, the Isle of Wight had been a restricted area for national security purposes open only to residents, service personnel and a small number of other permitted persons.

As finally the War ended and the local travel restrictions were lifted, the operations of the relevant passenger shipping services within (or along the South Coast towards) Spithead and the Solent area began to return to normality. However, there were considerable delays in restarting some of the excursions on account of the ships and piers having to be reconditioned after the War.

Southampton lies at the head of the eponymously named waterway upon which it stands. Gosport, Southsea, Portsmouth and Brighton lie to the east, whilst to the west, the area relevant to this book covers Hythe and Fawley, Lymington, Bournemouth, Poole, Swanage and Weymouth. The Isle of Wight, locally known as the 'Garden Isle', nestles close to the adjacent mainland county of Hampshire, separated by the Solent on its north and north-west flanks and by Spithead on its north-east flank.

Unlike most of Britain's coastline, estuaries and ports, which have two, distinct high and low tides each day, the tides at Southampton are quite different. At Southampton, where the tidal range is only some 13 feet compared with an average of 30 feet elsewhere, the water level remains high for about two hours before beginning its ebb. After slack water around low tide, the flow begins to rise again but at about half tide, there is a further period of slack water and this interruption to the normal tidal rise is called the 'Young Flood Stand'. In any given day, Southampton enjoys a far longer than typical period of relatively high, slack water during which the manoeuvring and handling of ships in the port can be more easily managed. These phenomena are not, as was originally thought, due to the proximity of the Isle of Wight causing water to flow up

Above: The railway-owned, 1948-built **Brading** *was fitted with radar from inception. By comparison, the* **Balmoral** *did not have radar until 1964.*

Right: The coal-fired paddlers **Ryde** *and* **Sandown** *are moored at the coal-hulk just off the ferry berths at Portsmouth Harbour. The hulk used to be replenished periodically, originally by towing it into dock where the Southern Railway had a rail-connected jetty and coaling facilities. Later, a coal supply ship would come alongside the hulk.*

Photos: Author's collection.

the Solent and down Spithead and vice versa. The same conditions are known to prevail on the Normandy coastline of France too and tidal experts continue to spend a long time theorising about the various possible causes.

As this is the history of the motorship named **Balmoral**, built for Red Funnel Steamers in 1949 (and her immediate peers), the main thrust of the narrative will start by being confined to those vessels serving the Isle of Wight area and having a direct bearing on her rationale, construction and delivery.

Nevertheless, wherever the context allows us to do so a little, the opportunity will be taken to digress and mention will certainly be made of other excursion ships and ferries whose operations had an impact or were 'special', one way or another. Hopefully, the adroit excursion shiplover will appreciate these deviations that will permit the inclusion of a range of fascinating vessels.

So, we start on England's south coast, the Solent, Spithead and Isle of Wight area, with a general synopsis of the prevailing picture at around the end of the 1939-1945 War and a little of what went on before and during the War.

The Southern Railway, which became British Railways' Southern Region from 1st January 1948, operated Isle of Wight services from Portsmouth and Lymington. At Portsmouth, the Southern Railway, which came into existence following the grouping of various separate railways in 1923, operated their main ferry service for passengers between Portsmouth Harbour and Ryde on the Island's north-east coast.

The ferry connected with trains (electrified since 1937) running from London's Waterloo and Victoria stations or elsewhere and with local rail services on the Island. In many ways, the Isle of Wight could be regarded as 'London-on-Sea'. Additionally, in the summer season, extra sailings from Portsmouth went via Southsea to Ryde whilst others sailed direct from Southsea's Clarence and South Parade piers. Until the War, they also operated their traditional passenger vessels, all of which were coal-fired, steam powered, paddle steamers, on a variety of cruises, some of which

used to sail as far afield as Weymouth and right round the Isle of Wight. Sadly, after the War, the long day excursions became a thing of the past and thereafter the railway steamers no longer ventured far beyond their immediate environs.

In addition since 1927, they operated a separate vehicular service with some passenger accommodation from Portsmouth to Fishbourne (Wootton Creek) using purpose built motor ferries with ramps fore and aft. Before this, vehicles and livestock were carried in barges, towed behind the passenger boats, later by tugs.

In 1938, the Southern Railway fleet at Lymington comprising two paddle steamers, both coal-fired and one brand new diesel powered vehicular ferry, operated a service for passengers and vehicles to Yarmouth near the western end of the Island.

Just a year later, at the start of the hostilities, the Admiralty

The railway-owned paddler **Sandown** *was built by Wm. Denny & Bros. Ltd. in 1934 and operated the Portsmouth to Ryde ferry and summer excursions until she was withdrawn at the end of the 1965 season. Both the* **Sandown** *and her sistership the* **Ryde** *remained coal-fired throughout their lives.*

Photo: T. Rayner.

quickly called up the three newest Portsmouth vessels namely the large **Southsea** and the newer sisters **Sandown** and **Ryde**. This left the main passenger service to Ryde Pier initially in the hands of the three old steamers, **Shanklin**, **Merstone** and **Portsdown** that was later sunk. They also had on loan from Lymington the very elderly paddle steamer **Solent**. In addition there was also at least one of the Portsmouth-Fishbourne vehicle ferries running and, with the much reduced traffic then on offer, this was normally adequate.

The other large paddle steamer **Whippingham** was held in reserve initially but was at Dunkirk with the **Sandown** and the **Portsdown** in May/June 1940, where they helped with the evacuation. The vehicle ferries **Fishbourne** and **Wootton** were at Dunkirk, but were not able to give much assistance. Towards the end of the War, in connection with the all important Normandy landings in 1944, even the remaining elderly paddle steamers, **Solent**, **Merstone** and **Shanklin**, were pressed into service in readiness for the landings by helping to load the assault craft.

Portsmouth lost two of its Isle of Wight vessels during the Second World War.

Firstly, whilst on war service in February 1941, the large paddle steamer **Southsea** (the sistership of the **Whippingham**) built by Fairfield Shipbuilding & Engineering Co. Ltd at Govan, was mined off the north-east coast near the mouth of the River Tyne and was subsequently beached and abandoned as a result.

Then the paddle steamer **Portsdown**, whilst making a scheduled island crossing in September 1941, was unlucky enough to hit a mine off Southsea as a result of which she sank. She was a sistership of the **Merstone**, which was laid-up from 1948 but remained available for service for a while and was then finally scrapped in 1952.

By the end of the hostilities, the remaining Portsmouth based paddle steamers were the **Shanklin** (built 1924, which was later sold to Cosens & Co. Ltd. in 1951 and became the **Monarch**); **Merstone** (built 1928); **Whippingham** (built 1930); **Sandown** (built 1934) and the **Ryde** (built 1937).

Campbell's magnificent oil-fired paddler **Cardiff Queen** *spent the 1952 and 1953 summer seasons, for which she was rather unsuitably named, on Campbell's South Coast (otherwise known as their English Channel) services. Whilst there, she served Hastings, Eastbourne, Newhaven, Brighton, Worthing and ran cruises up Southampton Water to view the liners and visited the Isle of Wight piers at Ryde, Sandown, Shanklin and Ventnor. Unlike the* **Glen Gower**, *the* **Cardiff Queen** *had no certificate for cross-Channel trips. There were no Campbell's sailings from Sussex in 1951 but the big, turbine-powered* **Empress Queen** *was based at Torquay that year.* Photo: Bristol Evening Post.

*This is Lymington Harbour in July 1957. The lovely old paddle steamer **Freshwater** lies at the pier and the diesel-electric paddle vehicle ferry **Farringford**, is unloading on the slipway.*   *Photo: John Edgington.*

Soon after the War, the Southern Railway ordered two substantial new passenger ferries from Wm. Denny & Bros. Ltd., at Dumbarton. Named **Southsea** and **Brading** they were launched contiguously from the same slipway on 11th March 1948. They could each carry 1,331 passengers and had a gross tonnage of 837 tons. Their length was fairly typical at 200 feet but with a beam of 47 feet, they were very wide and roomy, clearly emulating the old paddle steamers whose extreme breadth across the paddles was similar to the two new motorships'. A third near sister ship from the same shipyard, again named **Shanklin** (as the name was available following the sale of the earlier ship to Cosens & Co. Ltd.) was launched on 22nd February 1951. By the time the first two were launched, the railways had been nationalised.

At the same time, the Portsmouth based, double-ended vehicle ferries were the **Fishbourne** (built 1927); **Wootton** (built 1928) and the **Hilsea** (built 1930).

At Lymington, the fleet then comprised the **Solent** (built 1902, which was later beached near Portchester for static use in 1948, and was scrapped in 1958); **Freshwater** (built 1927) and the **Lymington** (built 1938).

Unlike Portsmouth which had the two, later three, pure passenger vessels built soon after the War, the need on the Lymington - Yarmouth crossing was for another vehicle ferry (with more accommodation for passengers too). Named **Farringford** when launched at the Wm. Denny & Bros. Ltd. Dumbarton, shipyard in 1947, this ship was at first sight, a practical, innovative and far larger version of the older **Lymington**. Technically she was something rather different and, put politely, it would be difficult to imagine a more functional, less attractive looking ferry than the new utilitarian, diesel-electric paddle steamer **Farringford**.

Under The Transport Act 1947, Britain's separate railway companies, the Southern Railway included, were nationalised. From 1st January 1948 they were thereafter arranged as the six regions of British Railways namely the Southern, Western, London Midland, Scottish, North-Eastern and Eastern Regions.

At the same time, the many railway-owned shipping operations around our shores were also grouped together and passed to the Railway Executive. Whilst some vessels, such as those of the former LMS Railway controlled Caledonian Steam Packet Company Ltd., remained registered in the individual shipping subsidiaries' names, ownership of the others was transferred direct to the British Transport Commission, set up for the purpose.

The former Southern Railway's shipping services from Dover, Folkestone, Newhaven and Southampton to the Continent and the Channel Isles and their Isle of Wight routes and excursion business to which this book refers particularly, all then came under the aegis of the Southern Region and the ships became owned by the British Transport Commission.

In common with most of the railway-owned ships (but there were some notable exceptions that kept their own individual colours) upon nationalisation in 1948, the Isle of Wight fleet retained the black hulls, white superstructures and buff funnels with a black top. These it had acquired when the combined Southern Railway first emerged back in 1923 and would remain thus until 1964/65. For the railway-owned ferries and cross-Channel boats, the brand name Sealink came into use by British Railways around this time, mainly for marketing purposes. Later the vessels were registered in the name Sealink (U.K.) Ltd., prior to its sell-off.

The Portsmouth Harbour ferry operated the cross harbour ferry service between Gosport and Portsmouth. It was operated initially by three separate organisations of which two were later to merge becoming the Portsmouth Harbour Ferry Company PLC and the last, the floating bridge chain ferry company, was wound-up. In the summer season, their vessels also ran popular excursions in Spithead and the Solent as required. Later some surplus ferries

*The **Hotspur IV** dating from 1946 has been superficially modified (and sometimes brightly painted) on various occasions in her 53 or more years of service on the Hythe Ferry and local excursions. She was re-engined in 1968 and her original single funnel was removed and replaced with twin exhaust pipes. At the time of writing, the author having crossed to Hythe in her in May 1999, she remains in relief service with a red hull bearing the legend Hythe Ferry down each side.* Photo: Author.

were sold off to other operators who then used them as trip boats and on short excursions. With their green funnels, they were later dubbed 'Green Funnel Cruises'.

At Southampton, General Estates Co. Ltd. ran the ferry from Town Quay across Southampton Water to Hythe and they also operated docks cruises and other short excursions. At the end of the War, their fleet of small motor vessels comprised the ***Hotspur II*** (built 1936, later sold in 1978 to work on the Clyde and renamed ***Kenilworth*** and still in service); ***Hotspur III*** (built 1938, scrapped 1981) and finally the ***Hotspur IV*** (built 1946 and still in reserve service). The full history of that service is amply told in Alan Titheridge's excellent book entitled *Hythe Pier and Ferry* (Itchen

Printers, 1981) Today, the ferry is operated by White Horse Ferries who also run the Tilbury to Gravesend ferry and other services on the Thames.

P. & A. Campbell Ltd. were better known in their main area of operations in the Bristol Channel area where they had been established since 1888. In 1947 they re-started excursions along the South Coast from Brighton in both directions, to destinations quite far afield, including the Isle of Wight. Their South Coast operations lasted ten years more. They were known as the White Funnel Fleet. Their principal post-war operations are described in more detail in subsequent chapters.

Arguably the finest pleasure steamer of all time. The splendid turbine steamer **Empress Queen** *built for P. & A. Campbell Ltd. in 1940 was simply too big, too fast and too expensive for the available business after the War. This early, post war photograph of her leaving Ryde shows the* **Empress Queen** *before her French grey paintwork was brought down one strake lower, in which condition she may be seen in the photograph on page 100.* Photo: Author's negative library.

The ships used by Campbell's from time to time at Brighton and other South Coast piers, in the period 1947 to 1957, were the **Glen Gower** (built 1922); the splendid **Empress Queen** (built 1940); **Britannia** (built 1896); **Cardiff Queen** (built 1947) and finally, the chartered **Crested Eagle** (built 1938 as the **New Royal Lady**).

At Weymouth, Cosens & Co. Ltd., widely known as the Buff Funnel Fleet, became a majority-owned subsidiary of Red Funnel Steamers in 1946 and consequently suffered no competition from them after 1951. They operated paddle steamer excursions to and from nearby resorts including Portland, Lulworth Cove, Swanage, Poole, Bournemouth, Yarmouth and mostly the westerly piers of the Isle of Wight. Occasionally they sailed further afield too. They also had a busy marine engineering workshop business that was used extensively and universally by small ship operators from near and far. Even Campbell's used to send their paddle steamers down from Bristol to Weymouth for specialist treatment.

The Cosens & Co. Ltd. fleet after the War comprised the **Monarch** (built 1888); **Empress** (built 1879); **Victoria** (built 1884); **Emperor of India** (built as **Princess Royal** in 1906, bought in 1908); **Consul** (built as **Duke of Devonshire** in 1896, bought in 1938); **Embassy** (built in 1911 as **Duchess of Norfolk**, bought in 1938).

Until succeeded by Croson Ltd. in 1958, J. Bolson & Son Ltd., the well-known and respected Poole based shipbuilder, operated an interesting fleet of pleasure and excursion vessels on trips between Bournemouth, Poole, Swanage, Yarmouth and occasionally further up the Solent into Red Funnel Steamers' territory.

Immediately after the War, J. Bolson & Son Ltd. were considered to be emerging as a threat to Red Funnel's excursion ship business, especially on account of six landing craft support ships, which they bought from the Admiralty in 1946. According to Mr. David Chalk's interesting work entitled *Any More for the Skylark*, they converted three of these to become the rather unusual-looking 'Bournemouth Skylarks' and with them did some useful extra business for the next two years whilst other services were getting back to normal. Of

*Cosens & Co. Ltd. were renowned for running veteran paddle steamers. Here we see their **Empress**, dating from 1879, going astern out of Weymouth. She was withdrawn in 1955.* Photo: Author's negative library.

*Cosens & Co. Ltd. bought the former **Duchess of Norfolk** from the Southern Railway at Portsmouth in 1938 and renamed her **Embassy**. She is seen here at Totland Pier where she is coming alongside, her paddles having just been put astern to bring her to a halt. Note the bathers in the sea. She was thoroughly reconditioned after the War in 1946 when she was converted to burn oil fuel and Cosens & Co. Ltd. themselves became a majority-owned subsidiary of Red Funnel Steamers in the same year.*

Photo: Author's negative library.

the remainder, one such vessel was rebuilt beyond all recognition by Bolson's and sold by them to the New Medway Steam Packet Co. Ltd. to become their **Rochester Queen** from 1948.

There was even talk that J. Bolson & Son Ltd. had planned to buy the **Queen of Kent** and the **Queen of Thanet**, which were actually, as we shall read shortly, bought by Red Funnel Steamers. Other commentators, somewhat uncharitably, say that Red Funnel's aims might have been furthered much more quickly by letting Bolson's buy them and suffer the problem of sorting out and paying for all their defects!

In the last half-century, Favourite Boat Cruises, Star Boats, Solent Boating Company (or Wight Line Cruises as they were also known), Blue Funnel Cruises and many more have all in their time operated trips in the sheltered sea area around Southampton, the Isle of Wight, Spithead and the Solent. Mergers, partnerships and operational associations were fairly common and some were more formal than others. Additionally, there were very many other individual operators too numerous to mention separately but all doing a wonderful job providing a huge variety of local trips in their boats.

Mr. Bill Hogg (now in his 70s and one of the longest serving boat operators of the area) has written to the author recently explaining the origins of the operations of some of those small excursion vessels. He says that he and two partners founded Blue Funnel Cruises out of Favourite Boat Cruises, which began in 1950 using the former Portsmouth Harbour steam ferry **Varos**. His main partner (the other retired soon after) was Mr. Horace Barkham whose father had run an engineering and boating business before the War. Blue Funnel Cruises are now based at Southampton's Ocean Village.

Southampton Pleasure Cruises Ltd. was formed by Favourite Boat Cruises and Star Boats together but this arrangement only lasted for a relatively short time after which they went their separate ways. At the time Favourite Boat Cruises had three passenger launches each capable of carrying over 50 passengers.

For a very long time past, right up to the present day, spare Portsmouth to Gosport ferries have often operated short excursions and trips to the Isle of Wight. Here we see the coal-fired single screw **Verda** *(dating from 1929) crossing Portsmouth Harbour in May 1958. In the end, soon after this photograph was taken and like so many of her consorts, she was sold to Solent Boating Co.*   *Photo: Phil Fricker.*

Another former Portsmouth Harbour ferry was the coal-fired **Vesta II** *dating from 1909. She became redundant following the arrival of the new ferry* **Venus** *in 1948 and was sold a year later for further service on the Thames under the name* **Kingston Belle**. *A few years later she was back near her old haunts and was renamed* **Southampton Belle** *running for Star Boats and under the Southampton Pleasure Cruises flag.*   *Photo: Author's negative library.*

As Southampton Pleasure Cruises Ltd., they bought the **Kingston Belle** from Hastings Steamers on the Thames and operated her as the **Southampton Belle**. Originally she had been the Portsmouth Harbour steam ferry **Vesta II** dating from 1909. Another of their ships was the **Shamrock** (II) but later in 1972 she was renamed **Southampton Star**.

Mr. Bill Hogg (who with his daughter still works the pleasure cruiser **Favourite Lady 2** from Town Quay) says in his letter that over the years, Star Boats then ran independently and Favourite Boat Cruises became Blue Funnel Cruises. Blue Funnel then merged with the Solent Boating Company (Wight Line Cruises) from Ryde. In the end, they had acquired many of the old Portsmouth Harbour steam ferries, had them converted to diesel and ran them on trips throughout the Southampton and Solent area.

On Isle of Wight ferry routes, the popularly named Red Funnel Steamers of Southampton were the Southern Railway's main rival. The Company had been formed in 1861, but can clearly trace its origins back to the Isle of Wight a further 40 years. Since that time, it has continuously served the Island's passenger, cargo and vehicle shipping needs with its main service from Southampton to Cowes (later East Cowes also). In addition, the Company was a major operator of seasonal excursion ships and until the Second World War had even carried day-trip passengers across the Channel to Cherbourg, France and along the South Coast as far as Brighton and Eastbourne in the east and Torquay and Dartmouth in the west. Whilst they would dearly have liked to return to those halcyon days, the intervention of the War put an end to the international and longer trips. In addition, their fleet of harbour and general towage tugs was impressive but, like their ferry business, it was in need of further capital investment. Until the War, they also used to run the cross-river service between Cowes and East Cowes (the former often referred to as West Cowes to avoid confusion).

Throughout the Company's long and proud history, their passenger ships have carried a number of different liveries and until about 1935, funnels were variously red, white or buff, with or without a black top at different times. Since then, the funnels have been dark red with a black top, the hulls black with a thin white or yellow line and for the most part the superstructure was cream. From this, they were known as the 'Red Funnel' steamers but it was to be some years later that any strict corporate use of the name was formally adopted.

Before the advent of the now common, often large, high-speed craft, there were a number of attempts to run fast services to the Isle of Wight, amongst the first of which Red Funnel operated for several years immediately before the Second World War and then ceased. Save for small operations using prototype hovercraft, there was then a long period without substantial regular fast craft until 1966 at which time the main operators took another look at high-speed vessels for the Isle of Wight. The operation of these craft is really beyond the scope of this book but let it suffice to say a few words here, for the sake of completeness.

British Rail Hovercraft Limited, or SeaSpeed as it was branded, then experimented for a while using various types of fast craft (of hovercraft origin) but in the end the service was withdrawn, the residue having been transferred to Hovertravel's

At the time this photograph was taken, Star Boats' **Shamrock II** *was running a docks cruise whilst operating under the banner of Southampton Pleasure Cruises Ltd. She was typical of the large number of trip boats of the 1950s and 1960s offering short excursions (completely open to the elements) around the Solent and docks cruises. She was renamed* **Southampton Star** *in 1972.*

Photo: Author's collection.

Solent operation based at Southsea. It was not until 1986 that the two new high-speed catamarans **Our Lady Patricia** and **Our Lady Pamela**, both built in Tasmania, came permanently onto the Sealink service between Portsmouth and Ryde virtually replacing the remaining traditional passenger boat service provided by the **Southsea** and the then near-defunct **Brading**.

At Southampton in 1969, using the original **Shearwater** hydrofoil, Red Funnel Steamers became the first operators of sustained hydrofoil ferry services anywhere in United Kingdom waters and in this they certainly were the bellwether of the ferry industry. They developed the hydrofoil principle fully, right up to the powerful **Shearwater 6**. Their fleet of high-speed vessels has now evolved into today's three magnificent fast craft named **Red Jet 1, 2** and **3**, with which catamarans Red Funnel maintain the

Seen here off Hythe, the Red Funnel hydrofoil **Shearwater 2** *was an unreliable craft, which in the end was cannibalised to help keep the original* **Shearwater** *in active service. In the event,* **Shearwater 2** *only operated for Red Funnel Steamers for 1970 and 1971 before being sold for further conventional boat service with her foils removed.* Photo: Author's negative library.

fast (22 minute) Southampton to West Cowes service.

From the scene-setting perspective of this chapter, the current high-speed services were still well in the future.

During the War, Red Funnel Steamers lost three ships - two paddle steamers and a tug. In David Divine's two important books, the benchmark on their subject, entitled *Dunkirk* and *The Nine Days of Dunkirk*, we read that the Southampton paddle steamer **Gracie Fields** was attacked at Dunkirk on 29th May 1940 and sank in the early hours of the following day.

The reasoning behind the rather old-fashioned design of the **Gracie Fields**, built in 1936, is difficult to understand but it does perhaps help to put the later passenger vessels, namely the **Vecta** and our **Balmoral** into perspective. Although the **Gracie Fields** came five years after the diesel-engined, twin screw, **Medina**, she was actually an improved version of the 1927-built **Princess Elizabeth**, complete with coal-fired boilers, paddles and a square fronted, open bridge, initially with no wheelhouse at all!

It was as if the great steps forward, made with the building of the motorship **Medina** in 1931, had been expunged from their directors' minds and the clocks had been turned back years.

Certainly, especially as she was to be a near copy of an existing ship (the **Princess Elizabeth**) the capital cost of the **Gracie Fields** would have been much less than an all-new, diesel-powered ship. But beyond that, the overall costs of burning coal were far greater than oil, irrespective of whether the oil is burnt to raise steam or in a marine diesel engine. Stand-by costs, time wasted bunkering, disposing of ash and soot have all to be taken into account too.

There were also aspects of fleet flexibility of which to be cognisant. A diesel-powered ship can be activated almost immediately, always provided starting air reservoirs are kept topped up by running a simple compressor periodically. However, unlike the diesel engine, a steamship requires some 24 hours or more to enable boilers to be gently heated through from cold before she can come on service.

The most likely answer to the question of the design of the

The attractive but rather old-fashioned **Gracie Fields** *was the last paddle steamer built for Red Funnel Steamers and was delivered by J. I. Thornycroft & Co. Ltd. in 1936. Her wheelhouse was added a year later. Sadly, she was lost at Dunkirk on 30th May 1940.*

Photo: F. Plant/ Richard Howarth collection.

This photograph of the **Medina** *dates from February 1953, just prior to the fitting of new Crossley diesels designed to give her 13 knots, being an extra 3 knots over her then unsatisfactory maximum speed. She also received a new, larger funnel that, unlike the previous one, needed no guys to support it. She was never a fast ship and could roll unmercifully in any beam sea she encountered, especially when out beyond Calshot. The photograph has been inserted in the book here, slightly out of chronological sequence, so as to enable a comparison to be made between the 1931-built* **Medina** *and the old fashioned, coal-fired paddler* **Gracie Fields** *built five years after the* **Medina**.

Photo: Phil Fricker.

Gracie Fields seems to be that she was something of a compromise. The Red Funnel directors and management (not all of whom were as progressive as others) clearly had an eye to the then buoyant local excursion side of the business around the mid-1930s. Therefore the growing age of their ships mainly engaged in that side of their trade, appears to have been the reason upon which they decided that a dual role ship of traditional design should be constructed.

Quite separately, on 1st December 1940, the old Red Funnel paddle steamer **Her Majesty** was bombed and sunk in an air raid on Southampton. She dated from 1885 but had been altered in 1927 to carry more cars. 1927 was also the year their new paddler, the **Princess Elizabeth,** entered service.

In the Company's centenary book by G.W. O'Connor, entitled *The First Hundred Years, 1861-1961*, we are told that whilst stationed at Plymouth, on 20th March 1941, their tug the **Sir Bevois** was bombed and sunk whilst on war duty.

The Red Funnel Fleet at the end of the War consisted of the following passenger vessels: The **Lorna Doone** (I) (built 1891, acquired 1898); **Balmoral** (I) (built 1900); **Lord Elgin** (built 1876, acquired 1908); **Duchess of Cornwall** (built as the **Duchess of York** in 1896, scrapped 1949/50); **Princess Helena** (built 1883); **Solent Queen** (I) (built 1889); **Bournemouth Queen** (built 1908); **Princess Elizabeth** (built 1927); **Calshot** (tug/tender built 1930); **Medina** (built 1931) and the **Vecta** (built 1938).

At a meeting of the directors of Red Funnel Steamers held on 5th February 1945, at Bugle Street, Southampton, where the Company maintained its head office, it was agreed to appoint Captain W.V.J. Clarke D.S.C. as the general manager of the Company with effect from 12th February 1945. This, we shall see, proved to be a very important appointment having far-reaching consequences for the Red Funnel Fleet in the following seven vital years.

Soon after the main War ended and following the appointment of Captain Clarke, Red Funnel Steamers had some important decisions to make and time was of the essence. The broad choices included the following in various combinations. Firstly, trying to

The tug/tender **Paladin** *was the first of the second-hand vessels bought by Red Funnel Steamers after the War in 1946, to help restore their fleet to pre-war strength.*

Photo: Richard Howarth collection.

repair and recommission all the aged paddlers when they returned from their wartime duties with the Admiralty. Secondly, making some stop-gap arrangements in the hope that shipbuilding prices would fall after the War. Thirdly, going ahead and building at least one new vessel immediately and, in which case, they had to decide quickly on the design parameters for any such new ship.

Following much deliberation, the Company decided to build up its fleet and this they achieved initially by making purchases of second-hand ships. The board meeting held on 1st April 1946 approved the purchase of the first two such ships. As a result, the **Paladin** (tug/tender, built 1913) was purchased for £5,500 and

almost immediately put on charter to Cunard *'for not less than five weeks at a fee of £500 per week'*. She was followed by the former Birkenhead ferry **Upton** (built 1925) which vessel Captain Clarke was authorised to purchase *'at the lowest possible price'*. A month later, on 20th May 1946, it was reported that Captain Clarke had been able to secure the purchase of the **Upton** for £15,000.

The **Norris Castle** came next (built 1942, ex-Admiralty tank landing craft bought for conversion to passenger and vehicle ferry in 1947) and the old **Bournemouth Queen** was completely refurbished in time to re-enter service for the summer of 1947.

The first **Balmoral** and the **Lorna Doone** were in such poor condition when they returned from war service in January 1947, that it was questionable whether either of them could be repaired economically. Nevertheless, there was a faction within the board of directors and management at Red Funnel Steamers who wished to see money spent on these two old favourites in order that they might be brought back into service, presumably fairly quickly.

This beautiful, almost ethereal photograph of the **Vecta**, *gliding along in flat calm water, disturbed only by the passing steamer on which the photographer was travelling, was taken in June 1952.*

Photo: Phil Fricker.

In addition to running the main all-year-round passage route to Cowes, Red Funnel Steamers served the resorts of Ryde, Southsea, Sandown (after its pier was rebuilt in 1954), Shanklin, Ventnor, Bournemouth, Swanage and ran sailings right round the Isle of Wight. They also ran popular dock cruises and innovative trips designed to meet up with and escort ocean liners arriving at or departing from the docks.

Whilst the Red Funnel board were still deliberating over the precise course of action to pursue, the one thing that did unite them was the knowledge that they needed to act as quickly as possible to ensure that no competitors encroached on their territory. They were concerned too about the situation at Bournemouth where the other main operator, Cosens & Co. Ltd., appeared to be about to be swallowed-up by one of the national outfits or another interested party represented by Charterhouse Trust, an offshoot of the famous merchant bankers. By August 1946, Red Funnel Steamers found themselves successfully bidding for Cosens & Co. Ltd. against Charterhouse Trust.

From the author's appreciation of their financial statements, it appears that in addition to Cosens' goodwill, its extensive marine workshop facilities and its elderly fleet of excursion paddle steamers, they had a mostly positive cash-flow, assets to be realised and tax benefits to enjoy. In autumn 1946, Red Funnel Steamers were reported to have paid the sum of £170,000 for some 70% of Cosens & Co. Ltd.'s shares, thereby crystallising the

Red Funnel's answer to the new breed of vehicle-carrying ferries built for the railway-owned service from Lymington to Yarmouth was the acquisition and conversion of a former tank landing craft, which they renamed **Norris Castle***. She was very slow which was a drawback. After the building of the 'buffer pontoon' (constructed from parts of old wartime Mulberry Harbour sections) seen here on 10th July 1950, she became a particularly useful member of the fleet and could even embark single loads of up to 40 tons over her bow ramp.*
Photo: Southern Daily Echo.

The old paddler **Princess Helena** *was finally able to take semi-retirement as soon as the new* **Balmoral** *entered commercial service in December 1949. She was kept in reserve and was scrapped at Northam in the summer of 1952. In this lovely photograph may be seen the ropeman, standing in the bows, ready to make fast alongside imminently and her bulwark doors have already been swung open ready for unloading.*   Photo: H.A. Allen/ K. Adams and R. Howarth collections.

financial position very much to their mutual convenience and seeing off the potential opposition at a stroke.

In the Red Funnel Company's Directors' Report for the period ended 31st December 1947 it was stated by their Chairman that *'The acquisition of a controlling interest in Cosens & Co. Ltd. of Weymouth was a very important step in the history of both* companies. *Here are two companies, pioneers in providing pleasure steamers on the South Coast which by coming together are ensuring a co-ordinated service to the public which it is hoped will result beneficially to all concerned'.*

However, despite the considerable enthusiasm demonstrated by all involved, Red Funnel Steamers were bound to remain vulnerable. They were a relatively small, local public company now competing with the nationalised body that ran Britain's railways and its ferry fleets. In direct contrast with the railways, whose pockets were ultimately very deeply lined, Red Funnel Steamers' resources were strictly limited and were certainly then fully deployed.

After the War, such as they then were, Red Funnel's reserves were stretched to the absolute limit. Times were hard, competition was tough and their shareholders were unkindly reported as investing for the travel concession thereby obtained, as much as for capital growth. Fortunately for Red Funnel Steamers, their bankers appear to have been willing to help them through the worst difficulties. There was always the threat of take-over or even possible nationalisation, which was very much the vogue at that time and had been the subject of letters between Red Funnel Steamers and J. I. Thornycroft & Co. Ltd. previously. Nationalisation was a threat not to be taken lightly and contingency plans had been discussed in detail between the two entities. But, remaining solidly independent, Red Funnel Steamers were, for the most part, an astute outfit, they did provide a very important, alternative route to the Island and thereby gave effective competition for all the Southern Railway's Isle of Wight shipping operations.

Some of the main decisions affecting the immediate and medium-term future of the Company were taken in October 1947. Previously, there had been much discussion between the new general manager Captain Clarke, his Red Funnel board and also with J. I. Thornycroft & Co. Ltd. as to how best they should move forward and with what ships. They had already started with some second-hand purchases mentioned above.

According to Mr. Bob Willatts' extracts from the Thornycroft Papers housed at the National Maritime Museum, Captain Clarke had issued his routine general manager's report dated 29th September 1947. In this he says:

'The important matter of the replacement of the two old

*ships **Solent Queen** and **Princess Helena** and the question of whether to recondition the (old) **Lorna Doone** and **Balmoral** or build new tonnage fall to be decided in the near future. After mature consideration, I have come to the conclusion that the wisest course would be to replace the two excursion ships with a new ship of the **Vecta** type which could be used either on the Cowes run or on excursions and to purchase another motor vessel for service on the Cowes run principally, but available for other work if required'.*

He then went on to say that he was giving some consideration to two available ships, namely the 248 gross ton, previously Scarborough-based **New Royal Lady** and to a ship named **Laurana** then operating between Malta and Sicily.

More importantly to our book, about the new **Balmoral** Captain Clarke reported:

*'So far as new building is concerned, I have asked Thornycroft's to let us have figures for a ship of the **Vecta** type, diesel propulsion, twin screw and when this is available the Board will no doubt come to a decision generally'.*

Presumably by discussing matters with J. I. Thornycroft & Co. Ltd. direct, he was able to explain the sort of ship he (personally) was really hoping for. This will account for various significant alterations to her design being called for, prior to contract and building.

From research in the vaults of 12, Bugle Street, Southampton, we read the reciprocal information from the board minutes of their meeting held on 27th October 1947 that, having considered Captain Clarke's routine report, the directors discussed the **New Royal Lady** mentioned above and noted that she had now been sold to General Steam Navigation Co. Ltd. (shortly to become their **Crested Eagle**). They did not consider the **Laurana** again formally. However, they did briefly consider the **Thane of Fife** that was the former Wallasey ferry **Snowdrop**, which had been adapted for car-carrying from Granton across the Firth of Forth to Burntisland.

However, as director Mr. Redman pointed out, the ship had been visited at Alloa but was found to be too deep-drafted to be of full use at Southampton and Cowes.

Captain Clarke's commercial philosophy was for Red Funnel Steamers to try to re-establish its business on all fronts, including the long distance and cross-Channel excursions; but times had changed and perhaps this was not then fully appreciated. Whilst at first sight that philosophy might have seemed a good one, from the modern-day perspective, it can be shown that many of those areas of business were doomed, never to fully re-materialise. It only took a few short years for the apparent futility of some of the early post-war acquisitiveness to manifest itself.

If the two old paddlers **Balmoral** (I) and **Lorna Doone** (I) were not to be recommissioned, Captain Clarke argued that he would need other (not necessarily new) vessels capable of running excursions and also suitable for use on the service route between Southampton and Cowes.

At the board meeting held on 27th October 1947, under the heading NEW TONNAGE, COMPANY'S FUTURE POLICY, several interesting resolutions were passed.

Firstly, it was finally agreed not to go to the expense of reconditioning the old paddle steamers **Balmoral** (I) and **Lorna Doone** (I) on account of their age and the amount of work needed to be done on them. In fact, since their meeting in July 1946, Red Funnel Steamers' directors had been in negotiations with the War Ministry regarding these two old ships, having been offered £65,000 in reparations as a lump sum to cover their refurbishment after war service. Reasonably enough, Red Funnel had wanted rather more and something extra to cover the cost of chartering alternative tonnage whilst the reconditioning was taking place.

Secondly, it was further resolved that *'The most suitable vessel for the present needs of the Company was an improved **Vecta** with a Class III passenger certificate and capable of about 15 knots'.*

Thirdly, interestingly, the same board meeting agreed *'That Messrs Thornycroft's should provide suggestions for another*

*additional boat of an intermediate type, between the **Vecta** and the **Medina** which would be economical in running costs and be capable of doing the Southampton to Cowes passage in under the hour'.* This last resolution was vaguely redolent of the design anomaly of the old **Gracie Fields** mentioned earlier.

At a subsequent meeting of the Red Funnel directors, held on 2nd February 1948 under the heading NEW VESSEL, it was resolved that *'The latest estimates for the cost of the ship submitted*

*The little **Crested Eagle** was one of several vessels that Red Funnel Steamers had briefly considered buying in 1947 when it was looking to rebuild its fleet after the War. The same vessel was actually bought by the General Steam Navigation Co. Ltd. who in turn, later chartered her to P. & A. Campbell Ltd. for (only) their 1957 South Coast season in a vain attempt to keep alive their Sussex based presence.*   Photo: Peter Taylor, Australia.

by J. I. Thornycroft & Co. Ltd. Engineers and Shipbuilders be agreed and that subject to contract they be instructed to proceed with the building of the new vessel forthwith'.

On the 15th March 1948, again under the heading NEW PASSENGER VESSEL, the directors of Red Funnel Steamers resolved that *'Contracts for the building of a new passenger vessel having been submitted by J. I. Thornycroft & Co. Ltd., and approved, the same were ordered to be signed and sealed'.*

The estimated cost of the new ship was £154,750 and she was to become Yard No.4120, for delivery in 1949.

Other commentators have generally accepted that the order for the new **Balmoral** was placed with J. I. Thornycroft & Co. Ltd. on 11th December 1947. Certainly this was the date upon which the minutes of the directors' meeting held on 27th October 1947 were confirmed and signed. However, from the wording of the minutes of the subsequent meetings held on 2nd February 1948 and 15th March 1948 (reproduced above) it would appear that the date of the final contract was somewhat later.

The same meeting also stated that the old paddle steamer, **Balmoral** (I), should be handed over to *'Messrs Thornycroft and that Red Funnel should be credited with any arisings therefrom'.* By now, things were happening very quickly.

Surprisingly, the **Robina** (built 1914) was bought at short notice by Red Funnel in1948, when the original little **Solent Queen** failed with boiler problems.

From the time the new **Balmoral** was envisaged, a number of major changes were made to her design to take into account the duties she was expected to be able to perform.

By the time the final design and specification for the new **Balmoral** had all been determined and fully six months before her launching, two further grand old excursion ships had been bought up by the Company and come into operation. These were to be renamed by Red Funnel Steamers as the **Lorna Doone** (built 1916, ex-**Queen of Kent**, ex-H.M.S. **Atherstone**) and **Solent Queen** (built 1916, ex-**Queen of Thanet**, ex-H.M.S. **Melton**).

The acquisition of these two charismatic former New Medway Steam Packet Co. Ltd. paddlers took place in December 1948 with delivery in early January 1949. Originally Naval coastal minesweepers, they had been regular pioneers in the excursion cross-Channel trade from the Thames coastal area to Calais, Boulogne and Dunkirk. Both had been rendered redundant and laid-up in 1938, with the expected arrival of the splendid **Royal Daffodil** for the parent company, General Steam Navigation Co. Ltd. as it happens, just before the War.

Captain Clarke had been authorised by his board to pay up to £30,000 in order to purchase the two ships and if successful, their new names were agreed to be as above. In fact, he paid rather less than this figure. Their purchase by Red Funnel Steamers was seen by many as an act worthy of considerable applause. These 33-year-old ships were very popular with the excursion public at Chatham, Margate and Southend and quickly won the hearts of ship-lovers (if not always the captains, management and accountants) at Southampton and Bournemouth when they came to Red Funnel.

With the exception of the **Norris Castle** and the **Paladin**, the already elderly ships, bought second-hand, only lasted a comparatively short time with the Company. As it happens, the whole nature of the business was changing to the extent that many excursion steamers (not just those belonging to Red Funnel Steamers) were fast becoming redundant anyway.

The well thought-out and planned acquisition of the former tank landing craft **Norris Castle** was to prove pivotal to the Company's success and facilitated their breakthrough into the carriage of large numbers of cars, lorries, heavy and outsize vehicles. Previously they had been limited to what could be accommodated on the deck of the service passenger vessels, or on one or other of the Company's previous freight and cargo ferries, universally converted from retired, old coal-fired paddle steamers. This was a quantum leap for Red Funnel Steamers, which had previously not had a real answer to the purpose-built, railway-owned vehicle ferries serving the Isle of Wight from Portsmouth and Lymington.

The relationship between Red Funnel Steamers and J. I. Thornycroft & Co. Ltd. was historically very close and these days such an association would probably even be described as 'cosy' in terms of corporate governance. Directors and shareholders were common to both companies and nothing significantly competitive appeared to be required to go on between them. Red Funnel ships usually came from Woolston and were overhauled at Northam, with little in the way of outside tendering going on. That is not to suggest that either company suffered from the arrangements; indeed that synergy was clearly a workable arrangement, at least for those days.

In the intervening years, between then and now, both companies lost their original independence when they became respective parts of other, much larger groups and any relationship now, would clearly have to be at arm's length.

Back in the closing years of the 1940s where our story presently rests, Red Funnel Steamers had to be content to await the delivery of their latest progeny from the Woolston shipyard of J. I. Thornycroft & Co. Ltd. This was to be our **Balmoral**.

Seen here in May 1937 travelling at speed with a good complement of passengers aboard, Red Funnel Steamers' magnificent paddle steamer **Balmoral** *(I) was the first ship of the name and dating from 1900, was one of the relatively few 20-knot pleasure steamers ever built. She also ran long day trips across the Channel to Cherbourg. The old* **Balmoral** *was finally disposed of for breaking-up after a career spanning 48 years including valiant war service in two World Wars. The name* **Balmoral** *became her legacy to the new motorship that is the subject of this book.*   *Photo: Tim Cooper collection.*

"RED FUNNEL" STUFF

The Story of the
RED FUNNEL STEAMERS

6d.

Written by ⌐ E. P. LEIGH-BENNETT
Decorated by ⌐ HELEN McKIE
AND ILLUSTRATED WITH NUMEROUS PHOTOGRAPHS.

RED FUNNEL
Steamers

Illustrated Brochure

RED FUNNEL STEAMERS
EASTER HOLIDAYS, 1950
MARINE ATTRACTION
SPECIAL CRUISES by the
NEW M.V. "BALMORAL"
From SOUTHAMPTO
(Weather and circumstances permitting)

EASTER SUNDAY
April 9th

To RYDE, SOUTHSEA and SHANKLIN
Leaving the Royal Pier at 10.45 a.m. (by M.V. "Bal
Returning from Shanklin 4.30, Southsea (S
Pier) 5.40, Ryde 6.10 p.m.

SPECIAL TRANSPORT TO THE ROYAL PIER.
From Burgess Road (Stile Inn),
" Swaythling,
" Peach Road (via Warren Avenue)
" Shirley (High Street),
" Portswood Junction,
" Bassett (Cross Roads)

Buses connecting with this Steamer will leave
10.9 & 10.16 a.m.
10.3 a.m.
10.9 a.m.
10.7 a.m.
10.9 & 10.24 a.m.

From Woolston (Floating Bridge) (via Sholing)
" Woolston (Floating Bridge) (via Heath Road)
" Bitterne Church
" Bullar Road (via Northam)
" Bullar Road (via Portswood)
*Connecting with buses at Civic Centre.

Afternoon Trip to COWES
Leaving the Royal Pier 2.30 p.m. Returning from Cowes 4.0 and 6.
RETURN FARE - 5s. 6d.

EASTER MONDAY
April 10th

To RYDE, SOUTHSEA and SHANKLIN
Leaving the Royal Pier at 10.45 a.m. (by M.V
Returning from Shanklin 4.30, Southse
Pier) 5.40, Ryde 6.10 p.m.

Afternoon Trip to COWES
Leaving the Royal Pier 2.30 p.m. Returning from Cowes 4.
RETURN FARE - 5s. 6d.

FARES (including Embarking and Landing Tolls)

	SINGLE	RE
To RYDE	4s. 3d.	5s.
To SOUTHSEA	4s. 6d.	6s.
To SHANKLIN	6s. 3d.	8s.

Children between Three and Fourteen Years, Half Fares

THESE CRUISES ARE ADVERTISED SUBJECT TO ALTERATION OR CANCELLATION W
The Company will not be liable for delays, accidents, personal injury, or sea risks of any ki
the Company be responsible for the loss of or damage to, any passenger's luggage while using
upon any Pier not belonging to the Company, whether or not the toll in respect of the use of suc
Tickets will not be issued in excess of the number of passengers the Vessels are allowed to carr
Ministry of Transport.
The Company reserves the right to close any booking office so long before the stated time of
opinion of the Company is necessary to secure punctuality of departure and also reserves the
than the stated time if the full number of passengers is on board.
The Vessels are equipped with large, well-appointed Dining Saloons where Meals and Refreshm

SOUTHAMPTON, ISLE OF WIGHT AND SOUTH OF ENGLAND
ROYAL MAIL STEAM PACKET COMPANY, LIMITED,
12 BUGLE STREET, WESTERN ESPLANADE, SOUTHAMPTON.
CAPTAIN W. V. J. CLARKE, D.S.C., A.M.Inst.T., Assoc.

DAILY STEAMER CRUISES

September 1st—18th 1952 (inclusive)

From RYDE and SHANKLIN PIERS

(Weather and circumstances permitting and subject to the
Conditions published in the Company's Time Tables)

RED FUNNEL STEAMERS
SOUTHAMPTON
CLOSING TRIPS OF THE SEASON

From RYDE

At 10.15 a.m.	**MONDAY, SEPTEMBER 8th** SEA CRUISE ROUND THE ISLAND. Back about 3.15 p.m.	FARE 11/6
At 3.20 p.m.	Non-Landing CRUISE to SHANKLIN. Back about 6.45 p.m.	FARE 4/-
At 10.15 a.m.	**TUESDAY, SEPTEMBER 2nd** SEA CRUISE ROUND THE ISLAND. Back about 3.15 p.m.	FARE 11/6
At 2.0 p.m.	To SOUTHAMPTON WATER to view R.M.S. "QUEEN MARY" at Southampton Docks. Back about 5.25 p.m.	FARE 5/-
At 3.20 p.m.	Non-Landing Cruise to SHANKLIN. Back about 6.45 p.m.	FARE 4/-
At 2.0 p.m.	**TUESDAY, SEPTEMBER 9th** To SOUTHAMPTON WATER to view R.M.S. "QUEEN ELIZABETH" at Southampton Docks. Back about 5.25 p.m.	FARE 5/-
At 2.0 p.m.	**WEDNESDAYS, SEPT. 3rd and 17th** To SOUTHAMPTON WATER to view R.M.S. "QUEEN MARY" at Southampton Docks. Back about 5.25 p.m.	FARE 5/-
At 2.15 p.m.	**WEDNESDAY, SEPTEMBER 10th** To SOUTHAMPTON WATER to meet R.M.S. "QUEEN ELIZABETH" on route to New York and to see S.S. "UNITED STATES" approaching Southampton. Back about 6.30 p.m.	FARE 5/-
At 11.45 a.m.	**THURSDAY, SEPTEMBER 4th** CRUISE through SPITHEAD to meet the R.M.S. "QUEEN MARY" on route to New York. Back about 2.0 p.m.	FARE 3/-
At 11.45 a.m.	**THURSDAY, SEPTEMBER 11th** CRUISE through SPITHEAD to meet S.S. "UNITED STATES" en route to New York. Back about 2.0 p.m.	FARE 3/-

For Particulars of Reduced Return Fares for Parties of not
less than 12 Adults (Two children under fourteen counted
as one), apply to the General Manager, Red Funnel
Steamers, 12 Bugle St., Western Esplanade, Southampton.

SEASON TICKETS AVAILABLE FOR SEVEN DAYS.
Between Ryde and Southampton 22/- per ticket, or to include
all excursions (except Special Trips where notified) 33/- per
ticket, exclusive of all Pier Tolls. Obtainable at Shanklin Pier
Booking Office, on board the Steamers, and at I.W. Tours, Ltd.,
67 Union Street, Ryde.

For Times of SINGLE TRIPS to SOUTHSEA or
SOUTHAMPTON, see Cruise pamphlets available at
Ryde and Shanklin Piers.

From SHANKLIN

At 2.15 p.m.	**SUNDAY, SEPTEMBER 7th** CRUISE towards the Needles. Back about 5.15 p.m.	FARE 5/-
At 2.15 p.m.	**MONDAY, SEPTEMBER 1st** CRUISE TOWARDS THE NEEDLES. Back about 5.15 p.m.	FARE 5/-
At 12.5 p.m.	**MONDAY, SEPTEMBER 8th** SEA CRUISE ROUND THE ISLAND. Back about 5.10 p.m.	FARE 11/6
At 12.5 p.m.	**TUESDAY, SEPTEMBER 2nd** SEA CRUISE ROUND THE ISLAND. Back about 5.10 p.m.	FARE 11/6
At 12.30 p.m.	**TUESDAYS, SEPTEMBER 9th and 16th** To SOUTHAMPTON WATER to view R.M.S. "QUEEN ELIZABETH" or R.M.S. "QUEEN MARY" at Southampton Docks. Back about 6.15 p.m.	FARE 8/-
At 12.30 p.m.	To SOUTHSEA. Returning from SOUTHSEA (South Parade Pier) 5.0. Back about 6.15 p.m.	FARE 4/6
At 12.30 p.m.	**WEDNESDAY, SEPTEMBER 3rd** To SOUTHAMPTON WATER to view R.M.S. "QUEEN MARY" at Southampton Docks. Back about 5.15 p.m.	FARE 8/-
At 12.30 p.m.	**WEDNESDAY, SEPTEMBER 10th** To SOUTHAMPTON WATER to witness departure of R.M.S. "QUEEN ELIZABETH" for New York and to see S.S. "UNITED STATES" approaching Southampton. Back about 6.15 p.m.	FARE 8/-
At 12.5 p.m.	**THURSDAYS, SEPTEMBER 4th and 11th** CRUISE to SPITHEAD to meet R.M.S. "QUEEN MARY" or S.S. "UNITED STATES" on route to New York. Back about 3.30 p.m.	FARE 5/-
At 12.5 p.m.	**THURSDAY, SEPTEMBER 18th** CRUISE to SPITHEAD to meet R.M.S. "QUEEN MARY" on route to New York. Back about 4.0 p.m.	FARE 5/-
At 2.15 p.m.	**FRIDAY, SEPTEMBER 5th** CRUISE TOWARDS THE NEEDLES. Back about 5.15 p.m.	FARE 5/-

Children between three and fourteen years, Half Fares.

The above Fares include Embarking and Landing Tolls at Shanklin, Southsea and Southampton Piers, and Landing Tolls only at Ryde Pier.
Tickets for Cruises from RYDE may be obtained in advance at the Office of Isle of Wight Tours, Ltd., 67 Union St., Ryde, and from SHANKLIN at Shanklin Pier Booking Office
In the event of the Company being unable to embark passengers at any pier for the return journey, owing to stress of weather or other causes, passengers will be
entitled to return by train on exchange of the return half ticket at the station to which they are directed.
THESE CRUISES ARE ADVERTISED SUBJECT TO ALTERATION OR CANCELLATION WITHOUT NOTICE.
The Vessels are equipped with large, well-appointed Dining Saloons, where Meals and Refreshments can be obtained.
12 Bugle Street, Western Esplanade, Southampton.
G. W. PAYNE, T.D., General Manager.

Shirley Press Ltd., 1a Church Street, Southampton. 26-8-52

Telegrams :— "SIWEPACO,"
Telephones :— Southampton

Welcome to the Balmoral

The original Specification Book for the **Balmoral** survives to this day and is a beautiful brown leatherette-bound work complete with gold embossed cover text. The Red Funnel Group has kindly loaned the complete work to the author and they have taken a keen interest throughout the gestation period of this book about their former flagship. Interestingly, their corporate logo to this day depicts the **Balmoral's** flat-topped funnel as its central image. The contents are threaded and bound with thick silk string and even after the intervention of all these years, are still sealed with the original John I. Thornycroft & Co. Limited, Engineers and Shipbuilders, wax seal. Significantly, the book is dated 10th March 1948 and has been signed throughout by the general managers of both Thornycroft's and Red Funnel in confirmation of its contents. Various amendments have been added later and these too have been signed by both parties.

Despite the shortages straight after the War, the specification stated that the **Balmoral** was to be a fine ship in all respects. In her construction it was specified that *'All material and workmanship to be of first class description and in accordance to the best practice'*. For her machinery, the requirement was *'The whole to be of the best material and workmanship and fitted on board to the satisfaction of the Board of Trade and Lloyd's Surveyors'*.

The specification details every significant item covering the hull, machinery and electrical fittings. Plans of the ship are annexed in the back of the book. Interestingly, the ship was originally designed with a funnel very similar to that of the **Vecta** having it raked with a sloping top. At that time, officially at least, the proposed new ship had no name and the book was simply entitled *Specification of a Steel Passenger Vessel for the Southampton, Isle of Wight and South of England Royal Mail Steam Packet Company Ltd.*

The **Balmoral** was completed in 1949 and was the second proud holder of the name.

The first **Balmoral** was the superb paddle steamer built at Ayr by S. McKnight & Co. Ltd. in 1900 for the Red Funnel Company's long distance and cross-Channel excursion business. The contract for her building was with Hutson & Co., Glasgow who constructed her machinery but sub-contracted the hull to McKnight's. She was of 473 gross tons could make 20 knots with all her steam valves wide open. She gave excellent service in both World Wars. In the Company's centenary book entitled *The First Hundred Years*, its author Mr. G W O'Connor states:

'The once-proud ship was shamefully neglected whilst commandeered and when she returned to Southampton, reconditioning was found to be impossible.

She was towed round to a mud berth at Northam and for two years, remained a sight that saddened all who knew her and her brave story until she was mercifully broken up'.

However, there was indeed a powerful lobby within the Red Funnel board of directors and its management who would have preferred to see the tried and tested, albeit very elderly, **Balmoral** (and the first **Lorna Doone**) refurbished and recommissioned.

What is even more important in this context is the origin of the name **Balmoral** and for this, we can do no better than to turn to the *Southampton Times* of 21st July 1900, kindly extracted for us by Mr. T. Cooper, for the rather grandiose sounding answer:

*'Named after the Highland residence of Her Majesty, the name **Balmoral** is suggestive of loyalty, a feeling in another sense that ought to, and to a great extent does, sway the people of Southampton in their choice of an excursion steamer. The **Balmoral** fully justifies the Company, which*

*27th June 1949 and the **Balmoral** glides gently down the slipway of J. I. Thornycroft & Co. Ltd., Woolston, Southampton, moments after Mrs C.B. Pinnock had named the ship. On the right is H.M.S. **Caprice**, whilst across the River Itchen in Southampton's Outer Dock lies the cross-Channel boat **Falaise** (middle) and two fleetmates.*
Photo: National Maritime Museum.

*The exact moment when, on a glorious, sunny, Monday 27th June 1949, the bottle of champagne smashes against the **Balmoral's** knife-edge bow and Mrs. C.B. Pinnock sends the ship down the slipway to meet her element.*

Photos: Southern Evening Echo/Red Funnel Archives.

has had such a long and intimate connection with the town and port for many years'.

The piece then went on at some length in the same eloquent vein. It should be remembered that the Red Funnel Company had for many years previously displayed tremendous loyalty to the throne and patriotism in their choice of names for their ships. Names such as *Victoria*, *Duchess of York*, *Prince of Wales*, *Princess of Wales* and *Her Majesty* must all have pleased H.M. Queen Victoria greatly. Earlier, the Company had named a paddle steamer *Carisbrooke* after the Isle of Wight village with its 11th century castle. Had it been available, Osborne would have been an obvious choice of name for the *Balmoral*. This was Queen Victoria's favourite country house retreat, situated near Cowes. She died there in 1901 just one year after the old ship was built. In fact, Queen Victoria herself had a Royal Yacht named *Osborne* at the time, which meant the name could not be used by Red Funnel Steamers.

That is how the first *Balmoral* received her title back in 1900 and how, after she was finally broken up in 1948/49 following valiant war service, it became her legacy to the motorship which is the subject of this work.

The financial commitment of building a new vessel, together with any possible reduction in cost benefit to be achieved by waiting (if shipbuilding prices slumped again as they had after the First World War) were good reasons for proceeding with the utmost care. Ever-cautious though they were, in the meantime Red Funnel Steamers had to ensure that they could re-start and maintain the continuity of their services so this they did with the purchase of first one and later several second-hand ships. Mostly, they really were old but, for want of better alternatives, served (rather briefly, always expensively and sometimes unreliably) until the fleet could be re-built with new purpose-built tonnage.

After much discussion, the contract for the new ship was executed following the Red Funnel board meetings held on 27th October 1947, 2nd February and 15th March 1948 at a time when widespread rationing still existed after the War and shortages of many basic materials were profound. Red Funnel's general manager, Captain Clarke had wanted to have a long-distance, fast excursion steamer but he had to settle for a compromise.

The new *Balmoral's* previous namesake made money for just a few weeks in the high summer but in the lean times of the late 1940s, to cover the opportunity value of the investment in the new ship, she was to be capable of operating economically throughout the year. She was to be a maid of all work.

In the first week of December 1947, undoubtedly at Captain Clarke's request, J. I. Thornycroft & Co., Ltd. produced an early design plan of the vessel we now know as the *Balmoral*. The basic parameters had to include a draft of no more than 7 feet and a length not exceeding about 200 feet. The lack of water available at Cowes at low water spring tides dictated both of these dimensions when the ship was operating on the ferry run. For Captain Clarke's vainly hoped-for other purpose, the new ship had to be strong enough and fast enough to run long day excursions and to cross the Channel. The new ship was to test the design capabilities of her builders J. I. Thornycroft & Co. Ltd. whose experience in building naval ships was to prove invaluable.

The *Balmoral's* underwater design, frames, scantlings and engines were all originally proposed as being suitable for the long-haul excursion work, as well as for use on the passage to Cowes and as a tender for visiting liners. To produce a ferry with additional open-sea capability, able to make18 knots or more within a hull length of only 200 feet and on a restricted draft is a very skilled task. More power means more weight and a deeper draft therefore results and so the vicious circle goes round.

However, a ship with a displacement (not planing) hull can never overtake her own bow wave and its turbulence pattern is substantially a function of the length of the ship. It follows that for main engines of a given power output, having a greater length of vessel is the secret to her speed; but in the *Balmoral's* case her length was strictly limited to about 200 feet.

THE TWIN-SCREW PASSENGER MOTORSHIP 'BALMORAL'.
Built and Engined by Messrs. John I. Thornycroft & Co. Ltd., Southampton

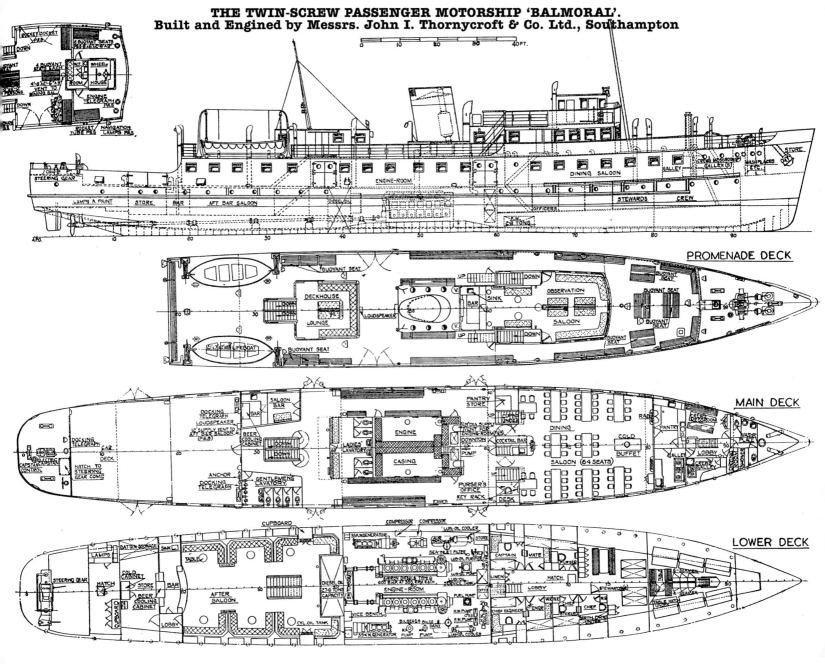

PROMENADE DECK

MAIN DECK

LOWER DECK

Opposite: The final design and shipbuilder's plans of the **Balmoral** *appeared in the various trade magazines of the day and in particular, in the February 1950 edition of The Shipbuilder and Marine Engine-Builder. The author is grateful to Mr. M. Casey, former engineering superintendent of the Isle of Man Steam Packet Co. Ltd. for obtaining a clean set of plans for this book, from the Institute of Marine Engineers.*

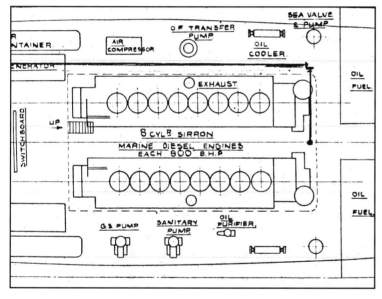

This plan section provides the evidence that in the original design for the **Balmoral**, *it had been intended by J. I. Thornycroft & Co. Ltd. and Captain Clarke, Red Funnel's general manager, to fit her with big, powerful, 8-cylinder diesels. Being heavier too, these would have given her a deeper draft consistent with a maximum speed of 18 knots and the capability for long-distance excursion work. In the final event, she was given smaller, lighter main engines. Plan: Extract from Plan T1463C reproduced with the permission of the National Maritime Museum.*

She ended up with a moulded length of 202 feet 6 inches, whilst at the waterline she measured just 196 feet 8 inches. In the beam, in order to give her the necessary fine entry lines, her moulded breadth at the waterline was 27 feet, whilst at main deck height she was fully 3 feet wider. At promenade deck height, her tumblehome had reduced the breadth to 28 feet 6 inches and this was an essential aid to coming alongside liners when tendering and piers when running excursions. Without it narrowing, the upper deck and bridge would have been permanently contacting pier piles at low water and the sides of liners she was to breast. None of these measurements included her fenders which were specified in detail to be made of fine English elm measuring 12" x 9" on either side. Her extreme length was therefore 203 feet 6 inches, extreme breadth was 32 feet, her depth to the main deck was 11 feet, and her average draft was 6 feet 8 inches.

The **Balmoral** was built to the general design shown on Plan T1463C (as later amended) copies of which are held at the National Maritime Museum at Greenwich. Whilst in overall dimensions and at first glance visibly a near-sister of the **Vecta**, the **Balmoral** was a rather more substantial vessel in every sense of the word. She was a little deeper, her foredeck was completely enclosed and she was fitted with more solid bulwarks forward, clearly all designed for open sea work. Most importantly, further evidence of Captain Clarke's long-distance cruising aspirations for the ship is confirmed with the original configuration of her machinery. The first design concept for the **Balmoral** was that she should have twin 8-cylinder Newbury Sirron diesel engines developing 1,600 horse power, which could propel her at over 18 knots, provided she was fine enough. On the early plans (a copy of which the National Maritime Museum has kindly provided to the author) the two big, 8-cylinder Newbury Sirron diesel engines, each developing 800 b.h.p. are clearly shown. Thornycroft's were well used to building warships with fine lines and clearly the **Balmoral** has inherited the underwater hull form and an almost transom-like stern, more akin to a destroyer or torpedo boat. However, warships are notoriously

*The **Balmoral's** wheelhouse.* (N.M.M., G6718)

The after saloon looking forward. (N.M.M., G6728)

The virgin teak deck planking of the vehicle deck. (N.M.M., G6470)

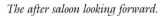

The deckhouse lounge looking aft. (N.M.M., G6720)

wet and uncomfortable in rough weather so in the **Balmoral's** design the effects of her fine lines at water level and below were partly attenuated by her spreading beam, the rather modest flare of her bow and stern all providing extra buoyancy. Even so, she is renowned for being lively in a seaway and to this day, as the author can freely attest, the **Balmoral** leads a class of her own when it comes to rolling in a beam sea.

When it was finally decided that the **Balmoral** would regularly have only Class III and IV certificates and would not (normally) be sailing very long distances or across the Channel, smaller engines were introduced into the design. These were lighter and the trim of the ship would have been adversely affected if left without attention. As it was, with new lighter twin 6-cylinder engines developing 1,200 horsepower, her propellers and rudders were often barely submerged and in the end additional ballast had to be added to help correct matters. Her main fuel bunker tank was redesigned for about 27 tons (6,000 gallons) of diesel oil and was then moved abaft the machinery in space taken rather too obviously from the lower saloon bar. Previously, two large fuel tanks were provided in her design, forward of the main engines with one on each side of the ship. As originally planned, these were to give her good operational range and help trim the ship forward with the extra weight of the big twin diesels further aft. Various other changes in the design of her saloons and accommodation were also prescribed but it appears that she kept her bulkheads and framing so as not to upset her displacement more than necessary. Her porthole and window arrangements were altered too, commensurate with her perceived duties now being restricted to calmer waters and, as it was thought she would have to provide more catering facilities on local trade, her dining saloon seating was increased from 48 to 64.

Her build quality and strength have subsequently stood her in very good stead. It takes seriously bad weather to make the **Balmoral** admit defeat and, when she does, it is usually for the sake of her passengers. It is also interesting to note that the design specifically provided for windows to be strategically positioned all round the engine room to permit passengers to watch the engineers at work and listen to the machinery. This is very much an excursion steamer detail, so common in the old paddle steamers, and serves to highlight the leisure side of the **Balmoral's** original intended work.

The **Balmoral** was built subject to Lloyd's Register classification and upon completion, she and her machinery were classed ✠Al at Lloyd's. She was of partly electric-welded construction and was quite advanced for her day. Quoting again from the Specification Book under its heading RIVETING: *'Generally all seams to be single riveted, usual spacing for watertight work. All shell butts to be welded. Special care to be taken with riveting in order that first class workmanship may be produced'*. Her Lloyd's ✠Al classification was for service Southampton to St. Helens and the Needles within the Isle of Wight and on to Langstone Harbour. Also, she could operate from Southampton to Weymouth and Newhaven during the months of April to October. Five years later however, at their meeting on 25th September 1953, the directors of Red Funnel Steamers resolved to withdraw the **Balmoral** from Lloyd's Register classification, presumably as an economy measure.

According to the specification, particular care was to be taken with the **Balmoral's** decks. The car deck was to be of teak whilst the remainder of the main deck and quarter deck was to be of Columbian pine measuring 4 x 2½ inches, all to be fastened to every beam with half-inch diameter galvanised bolts. In the specification we read: *'The deck timber to be free from knots, sap, shakes and other defects. The decks to be carefully and thoroughly caulked with best oakum and payed with marine glue'*.

Another manifestation of the requirement for her complete reliability in service (and common amongst her larger peers) was that the original specification also called for two sets of navigation lights, one set to be oil burning and the other set electrical, all in copper to Ministry of Transport requirements. If necessary, the oil burning light could be filled, lit and trimmed prior to being hauled up the mast and this was far more expedient than trying to send a seaman aloft in a gale of wind at night, to change a bulb or look for faulty wiring.

In the early plans showing the layout of the ship, the purser's office was to starboard and a mailroom to port respectively on either side of the ship just forward of the forward gangway. In later plans, the mailroom had given way to the pantry store.

On the subject of the **Balmoral's** engines, their designers, Newbury Diesel Co. Ltd., were marine engine manufacturers who had been taken over in the 1930s by Everard's, the well-known British coastal cargo shipping company. Almost the whole of the output of the Newbury engine works was given over to producing power units for Everard's cargo boats. Their experience was therefore in making engines for single screw cargo boats. The Newbury Sirron (named in reverse, after its designer Kent Norris) came in basic power designs of 50, 100 and 200 horsepower per cylinder. The early versions were made as simple as possible as there was then a world shortage of marine engineers with diesel experience, most having been trained on steam reciprocating or turbine engines.

In the **Balmoral's** case, the engines were actually built by Thornycroft's to the Newbury Sirron, O type (100 horsepower per cylinder) design. This was a new departure for Thornycroft's but over the years, they did build several more marine engine plants for Newbury Diesel. The **Balmoral's** engines were constructed but, being twin screw, this followed some discussion between Thornycroft's and Newbury Diesel Co., Ltd., over how to alter the port engine design so that, when running ahead, the two propellers were contra-rotating (outwards). This had to be done within the engine itself as she was to be direct drive with neither clutch nor gears through which reversing could otherwise have been achieved.

Being conceived during a period of considerable austerity and when the Company's resources were well stretched, the standard of specification set for the **Balmoral** and her estimated price of £154,750 were reassuringly high. Indeed, hers was virtually the same contract price as was paid by British Railways for the **Southsea** and **Brading**, which were larger and more powerful. The estimated cost of the **Balmoral** comprised the following:- hull £79,480, machinery £37,100, overheads £27,970, builder's profit £10,200. The final price paid by Red Funnel for the **Balmoral** was said to have been £150,762 and the difference is probably accounted for in design changes and the scrap value of the old paddle steamer **Balmoral**, which Thornycroft's were instructed to dispose of and to account to Red Funnel for the proceeds.

However, before the **Balmoral** was completed, Captain Clarke had bought the old paddle steamers **Queen of Kent** and **Queen of Thanet** from the New Medway Steam Packet Co. Ltd. and the other second hand ships mentioned previously. Old and somewhat unreliable though they were, he put them all to work with varying degrees of success to the point that he then was able to suggest (thankfully unsuccessfully) that the need for the new **Balmoral** no longer existed at all!

As Red Funnel had spent a lot of money in the acquisition of the shares in Cosens & Co. Ltd. and on buying all the old steamers, there were serious concerns as to how they might manage to keep up the payments due for the construction of the **Balmoral** under the building contract with Thornycroft's. Red Funnel Steamers were forced to think about selling the ship, even before she entered service.

In the Thornycroft Papers, there is correspondence between J. I. Thornycroft & Co. Ltd. and Red Funnel Steamers as to why it was seen as being so important that Red Funnel should retain the **Balmoral** and dispose of the old fleet as quickly as possible. The chairmen of both companies were involved in the discussions together with Mr. K. C. Barnaby (later author of the Thornycroft centenary book) who was the J. I. Thornycroft & Co. Ltd. naval architect and director, who also sat on the board of Red Funnel Steamers.

There were a number of compelling reasons put forward by her builders why Red Funnel should keep the **Balmoral**. These were

The main deck, port side looking aft.   *Photo: Red Funnel archives.*

The dining saloon looking forward.   *(N.M.M., G6725)*

The forward observation lounge looking forward   *(N.M.M., G6724)*

The forward observation lounge looking aft.   *(N.M.M., G6723)*

The engine room, port side looking forward. (N.M.M., G6734)

The engine room looking aft between the main engines. (N.M.M., G6732)

*The **Balmoral's** part welded, part riveted construction is very evident in this photograph taken on the slipway looking aft towards her starboard propeller, on 27th June 1949, immediately before her launching.* (N.M.M., G7106)

*The **Balmoral** under trials on 12th October 1949 in Southampton Water. Note the Thornycroft flag flying at her pole mainmast.*

(N.M.M., N12847)

*Here we see the handsome **Balmoral**, leaving Cowes well loaded. In the foreground is the landing jetty for the Island Sailing Club. The famous Royal Yacht Squadron is close by with its own rubber carpet covered jetty and 21 cannons in case of visiting Royalty.* Photo: Author's negative library.

based mainly on the need to demonstrate that they had a modern fleet, capable of running to a timetable and offering comfortable accommodation for passengers all-the-year-round. Without the **Balmoral**, only the **Vecta** and the **Princess Elizabeth** met the criteria as both the **Medina** and the **Norris Castle** were too slow and the rest of the fleet far too old. J. I Thornycroft & Co. Ltd. were also able to produce the definitive figures that proved overall, far from being the economic alternative hoped for, the purchase of the two former Medway paddlers had actually been a very expensive exercise compared with the cost of the new **Balmoral**.

No doubt partly as a result of Thornycroft's persuasive advocacy and despite the internal controversy, the **Balmoral** was completed, paid for and, as is now plain for all to see, became indispensable.

When Mrs. C. B. Pinnock, wife of the Chairman of Red Funnel Steamers, launched the new ship on a warm and sunny Monday, 27th June 1949, she and the gathered assembly would have been well pleased with the result. Within the design limits for what was principally to be an Isle of Wight ferry with excursion and tendering capability, a more handsome and pleasing looking vessel it would be difficult to imagine. However, Mrs. Pinnock would have had to be perspicacious in the extreme to know that 50 years later, we would be celebrating the half-century of the ship she sponsored.

The *Southern Evening Echo* of Monday, 27th June 1949 carried on its front and back pages the photographs of the launching ceremony of the **Balmoral** and the following headline article:

New Balmoral Takes to the Water

Today's launch at Woolston

by 'Echo' Shipping Reporter

First post-war passenger ship built for the Southampton and Isle of Wight Co. the **Balmoral** was launched this morning at the Woolston yard of John I. Thornycroft and Co. by Mrs. C. B. Pinnock, wife of the Chairman of the Red Funnel Line, from a specially constructed platform which flew the Red Funnel and Thornycroft flags. The **Balmoral** herself was dressed overall. After striking against the bows of the ship, a bottle of champagne tied in red, white, blue and green ribbon, Mrs. Pinnock said, 'I name this ship **Balmoral**. May God bless her and all who sail in her'

A few seconds after she had finished speaking, the ship began to move, almost imperceptibly at first, but gathering speed until she slid gracefully into the waters of the Itchen. Waiting tugs afterwards took her to a fitting out yard. Cheers were given as the ship began to move away and again, as she became water-borne.

On 2nd July 1949, the *Isle of Wight County Press* reported similarly and went on to say that *'after the launching, over 200 people were the guests of the Southampton and I.W. Steam Packet Co. and of Messrs Thornycroft at the lunch at the Polygon Hotel. Mrs. Pinnock was presented with an inscribed platinum wrist-watch, set with diamonds, by Sir John Thornycroft on behalf of his firm. Toasts were proposed to 'The Ship and her Sponsor', 'The Builders' and*

'The Company'. Clearly, it was a wonderful occasion.

J. I. Thornycroft & Co., Ltd. published the details of the new **Balmoral**. These were in turn printed in all the relevant trade journals such as *The Shipbuilder and Marine Engine Builder* (August 1949 and February 1950), *Lloyd's List & Shipping Gazette* (16th November 1949), *Shipbuilding and Shipping Record* (24th November 1949), *The Motorship* (December 1949) and *Engineering* (23rd December 1949).

For the technically minded, a synopsis of the primary information they all published can be condensed as follows:-

TSMV *Balmoral*

'The **Balmoral** is a twin-screw passenger motorship, length (moulded) 202' 6", beam (moulded) 30 feet, depth to main deck 11 feet, average draft 6 feet 8 inches, gross tonnage 688 tons. The new ship will also be very suitable for excursions and for acting as tender to liners visiting Southampton Water. The new **Balmoral** has three principal decks - promenade, main and lower. Above the promenade deck, abaft the wheelhouse there is also a small bridge deck area. The total passenger capacity is 800 to 900, less when carrying vehicles and in the winter.

In the **Balmoral** forward on the promenade deck, there is an observation lounge and bar. Seating is provided for 64 people in the dining saloon, also forward

*This photograph dated 11th September 1949 (ten weeks after her launching) is of the starboard main engine being lowered into the **Balmoral**. This counters the belief held by some observers that, because her funnel was fitted at the time of her launching, so too were her main engines. It is clear from this photograph that they were not.*

Photo: National Maritime Museum.

but below on the main deck, thus reducing vibration. The pantry and galley are at the forward end of the dining saloon. The dining saloon has a small cocktail bar at its after end. The rectangular windows of the dining saloon and other public areas afford excellent views. On the main deck amidships, there is a deck bar as well as toilet accommodation. The car space of which there is 1,060 square feet (for the carriage of about 12 cars) is at the after end of the main deck and is partly sheltered by the promenade deck. Cars are only to be carried when the ship is sailing on her Class IV passenger certificate. Large double doors in the bulwarks facilitate the loading and discharging of vehicles.

(Note that in *Shipbuilding and Shipping Record*, they rather optimistically stated that the vehicle payload was for 30 cars!)

The combined saloon and bar on the lower deck aft has comfortable seats in bays and is entered by a double stairway from the main deck and the lounge on the promenade deck. It has portholes, not picture windows. Accommodation for the officers and crew is arranged forward on the lower deck whilst the crew's mess, galley washroom etc are forward of the fo'c's'le bulkhead.

The propelling machinery, constructed by the shipbuilders J. I. Thornycroft & Co. Ltd. under licence, consists of twin, six cylinder and airless-injection Newbury Sirron diesel engines, each developing 600 b.h.p. at 300 r.p.m. The engines are of the direct-reversing type having neither clutch nor gearbox. They are started using compressed air held in three reservoirs totalling 73 cubic feet, and when the engines are running, the propellers are turning. These were the first such engines built at Woolston by Thornycroft's.

The diesel fuel consumption is not to exceed 0.39 pounds weight of fuel per b.h.p. per hour. The main engines drive two solid gunmetal propellers, each having four blades and a diameter of 5 feet 6 inches. *The **Balmoral** has twin rudders steered from the wheelhouse via hydro-electric steering gear and, in addition, there is an emergency wheel situated right aft on the poop.*

*The **Balmoral** is fitted with Marconi Seamew marine radio transmitting and receiving equipment. In addition, for generating electric power on board ship, there are two 35 kW Laurence Scott generators driven by two Lister diesel engines running at 1,000 r.p.m. The ship's capstan and windlass are both electric powered. A Britannia boiler rated at 165,000 b.t.u provides domestic hot water.*

Windows have been fitted around the engine room in order that passengers can view the ship's engines'.

The captions on the official photography and other reliable sources consulted show that her trials took place over a three-week period starting on 12th October 1949 and ending on 3rd November 1949. Mr. Ron Sims, one of her present shore-based engineers, has kindly provided a copy of the official sea trials data. These are date stamped 2nd November 1949 by Thornycroft's and signed by their Engineering Department and show that in her six runs up and down the Stokes Bay mile the **Balmoral** made a mean speed of 16.55 knots with her engines running at 303 r.p.m.

Main engine fuel consumption during her three-hour, full-power test was 178.8 gallons. Allowing for the fact that her machinery was all brand new and very tight and that the absolute full-power test is a very severe one, her consumption of about 60 gallons per hour was not unreasonable. In service, 14 or 15 knots on the passage to Cowes was sufficient to ensure a journey time of well under an hour and fuel consumption could be expected to be normally of the order of 45 gallons per hour in operation.

She was handed over to Red Funnel Steamers on 10th November 1949. The first master of the new ship was to be Captain A.G. Gattrell who had been with the Company for nearly 30 years.

On several occasions in mid-November 1949, the ship was put through her paces with invited guests aboard.

At first sight, she was similar in layout to the Company's previous passage vessel, the **Vecta**, except that the position of the dining saloon and the garage space had been reversed. Closer inspection revealed that considerable time and effort had gone into making her a more robust, good-looking and well proportioned ship and for this, her builders, designers and owners, deserve much credit.

When the **Balmoral** entered commercial service on 13th December 1949 it was stated by general manager, Captain W. Clarke, that her arrival would enable the very elderly **Princess Helena** to stand down but remain in reserve for the time being.

This was whilst the (even older) cargo paddle steamer **Lord Elgin** received her annual survey and overhaul.

Whilst the arrival of the **Balmoral** may well have allowed the decrepit old **Princess Helena** to sail into well-earned retirement, the local public really wanted to feel that the new **Balmoral** was to take the place of the much-missed, crack paddle steamer of the same name that had recently been scrapped.

In truth, their sense of loss could only be partly assuaged by the arrival of the new motorship, fine in all material respects though she was.

This scene dates from 10th November 1949 and depicts the brand new **Balmoral** *proudly flying her name pennant and the Red Funnel houseflag at her foremast for the first time, having just been handed over by her builders.*
Photo: National Maritime Museum (N.M.M., N12853).

Contemporary Fleetmates

Before the advent of the purpose-built car ferries, soon after the end of the War and throughout the 1950s and early 1960s, Red Funnel Steamers operated the new **Balmoral** and various other passenger-carrying vessels too. This was in addition to the second-hand ships they had purchased, that were then for the most part quickly withdrawn, and the old cargo steamers **Lord Elgin** and **Princess Helena**, whose days were also numbered.

Unlike their paddle fleetmates, some of which were quickly called up by the Admiralty, it was intended that the **Medina** and the **Vecta** would remain on the Cowes service throughout the War.

Handsome though the **Vecta** was, by the end of the War this, the newest member of the purpose-built Southampton fleet (their second diesel-powered ship) had proved to be something of a problem mechanically. The **Vecta** had been built just before the War in 1938 and, measuring almost 200 feet in length overall, had a gross tonnage of 630 tons. She was licensed to carry up to 855 passengers divided into two classes. Her dining saloon on the main deck was described as being originally for 60 first-class passengers and the forward observation lounge and bar on the promenade deck was reserved for their use too. Below the car deck was the second-

class lounge bar whilst the after deckhouse on the promenade deck was also for second-class passengers. At Red Funnel, it appears that the distinction between first and second class was permanently discontinued at the beginning of the War.

When constructed by J. I. Thornycroft & Co. Ltd. at their Woolston, Southampton shipyard, the **Vecta** had been fitted with twin 6-cylinder, 4-stroke English Electric diesels delivering a total of 1,300 b.h.p. In normal service they turned her two shafts at 325 r.p.m. which was reduced down to 135 r.p.m. through bevel gears above the vertically-mounted propulsion blades of the Voith-Schneider units. These were an early design of German Voith-Schneider cycloidal propulsion units, which both powered and steered the ship. As built, she had neither rudder nor any need to have the capability of running her main engines astern, as all this was catered for in the design of the Voith-Schneider units.

*What a truly magnificent spectacle this scene makes! Here we see the mighty Cunard liner **Queen Elizabeth**, which in her day was the world's largest passenger liner at over 83,000 gross tons, being escorted by Red Funnel Steamers' **Vecta** at just 630 gross tons.*

Photo: Christine Smith.

The late arrival of her machinery delayed her entry into service until the spring of 1939, just a few months before the outbreak of war. The Voith-Schneider system used controllable wing-shaped fins, mounted vertically on two rotating disks beneath the stern, to provide the forward or astern motion and sideways thrust. This is in contrast to the screw propeller, by which a ship is traditionally pulled along and which results in the force of water over the rudder by which the ship is steered. In the early part of the War during a bombing raid on Southampton, the store in which Red Funnel Steamers kept their spares for the Voith-Schneider units was destroyed.

Not surprisingly, during the rest of the War it proved impossible to obtain spare parts from Germany and so in the end, when the War was finally over, some fairly drastic measures were needed to correct matters. In May 1940, the **Vecta**, like so many others of our ferries and excursion steamers, answered the call and set off to help with the Dunkirk evacuation. Unfortunately, she broke down on her way to Dunkirk and finally had to limp back to Dover without having been able to help.

The only other British vessel to have this German propulsion system was the Southern Railway's car ferry **Lymington,** running from the port after which she was named, to Yarmouth. Both ships' Voith-Schneider units proved to be very troublesome and presented many problems, especially

*This rare photograph of the **Vecta** was taken immediately prior to her launch at the Woolston shipyard of J. I. Thornycroft & Co. Ltd. on 14th July 1938. Shipyard staff and other interested onlookers have gathered at vantage points around the ship, which is dressed overall for her debut. Her twin Voith-Schneider propulsion units, that were soon to give so much trouble, are clearly visible.*

Photo: Red Funnel archives.

initially. But, whilst the **Lymington** persevered with hers and finally succeeded, as we shall see, the solution chosen for the **Vecta** was quite radical.

Following a period of enforced lay-up from January 1942, because her machinery was totally unserviceable, in 1946 the **Vecta** had major reconstruction of her stern and finally emerged with conventional rudders and twin screws. However, the task was not an easy one and, in finding a satisfactory result, happily the **Vecta** was not required to surrender her individuality completely.

Because her main engines had no means of being reversed, some form of new astern gearing or reversing mechanism was needed for use in conjunction with traditional propellers. Therefore, this hurdle was overcome when it was decided to provide the ship with electric final drive to the propellers. In consequence, she remained a highly manoeuvrable ship with the ability to start, stop or reverse her electric drive motors at the master's discretion, with remote control direct from his bridge. On her original trials, the **Vecta** made a mean speed of 15.45 knots. According to *Shipbuilding and Shipping Record*, after conversion to diesel-electric machinery, her mean speed was reduced to 14.92 knots. This is accounted for mainly by her increased displacement as she now weighed 10% more and also the drag effect of her new A-brackets and rudders. Whilst the new machinery arrangement produced infinitely variable manoeuvring ability, her captains have reported that there was a very pronounced time lag between moving the telegraphs and the required response of the propellers. This was not without its disadvantages when wind and tide were conspiring together to make a difficult manoeuvre even harder. After conversion, it was possible to select one of two main engine speeds: 375 r.p.m., for fast ferry work or 325 r.p.m., for leisurely cruising.

The first diesel-powered member of the fleet was the rather slow **Medina**, which had been built at the same shipyard as the **Vecta**, but in 1931. They were not sisterships, indeed the **Medina** was noticeably smaller than the **Vecta,** measuring just 143 feet in length and having a gross tonnage of only 347 tons. She could carry 650 passengers. Unfortunately and purely cosmetically, her funnel was too small and was not visible when viewed from ahead. As the vessel was well built-up forward and with no accommodation aft to help balance the image, she gave the overall appearance of being rather dumpy and squat.

On one of several occasions when the matter was visited by the Red Funnel board at the directors' meeting held on 28th April 1950, their resolution carried an air of desperation regarding the **Medina's** slowness. On that day the directors called for an inspection of the **Medina's** engines by Gardner's representative *'with the object of considering if anything at all could be done to improve the vessel's speed'*.

Until she was re-engined with Crossley diesels in 1953 she could finally manage only about 10 knots. Thereafter her speed was 13

*The **Vecta** arriving at Cowes on a sunny, calm day in the summer of 1964. Her side doors leading straight onto the garage deck are being swung open in readiness for cars to disembark and passengers are looking on from above with interest.*
Photo: Tim Cooper.

knots. The idea of fitting new engines in her was first mooted back in 1947 but it took nearly six years to come to fruition. In the meantime, her timetable had to be rescheduled to allow 75 minutes for the crossing and Thornycroft's suggested that she might benefit from being slipped more frequently as the build-up of marine growth was proving to be too much for her ailing engines to overcome, especially against adverse weather and tide. With her new engines came a new, raked, pear shaped funnel, which was also an improvement on the original.

Nevertheless, whatever she may have originally lacked in beauty, she made up for in modest efficiency. With the amount of winter traffic then on offer, she was the ideal passage steamer mostly running from Southampton to Cowes where she berthed at the Company's floating pontoons. The **Medina** proved to be rather unsuitable for pier and excursion work due to the massive flare of her overhanging bows and, likewise, could not easily be used to tender visiting liners either. However, she was called upon for these duties from time to time when no other vessel was available. Much later in her life, having been sold for use at Gibraltar, some alterations were made to improve matters in this respect.

Designed principally for the passage journey of supposedly

This photograph of the **Medina** *shows her after the fitting of new Crossley diesel engines in the spring of 1953 after which she was good for 13 knots. At the same time, she was given a larger, self-supporting, pear-shaped funnel that was sited slightly further forward than the original. In Red Funnel service, she only ever had one mast and that was situated immediately abaft the wheelhouse. As she measured just 143 feet in length (and the 1954 lighting regulations applied to vessels exceeding 150 feet) unlike her larger consorts, she never needed to comply with this requirement.*
Photo: Andrew Munn collection.

about an hour, with dining saloon and bar, both the **Vecta** and the **Medina** were very comfortably equipped for the year-round service from Southampton to Cowes ferrying passengers, cars, light items of cargo carried on deck and the Royal Mail.

Red Funnel Steamers had a lovely name for its catering department at the time. They called it the Provedore Department, derived no doubt from the word provender, being the provision of food (but usually for animals).

The **Medina** was built with space for about 10 cars on her open car deck, aft. This was later advertised as being space for 8 vehicles. In this she was quite unlike the service paddle steamers which had been built with open foredecks for carrying vehicles and with the obvious disadvantage that the cars carried on the paddlers would be covered in salt spray when the going was rough.

However, when the **Vecta** was designed, she reverted to the traditional practice of carrying cars, of which she could carry 12 or more, forward on the main deck but in a garage (not aft and in the open as in the **Medina**) and for the first time they were reasonably well sheltered. This meant that the cars suffered less from the sea and spray being shipped over the bows although, immediately forward of the bridge structure surprisingly, the car deck was open to the elements above. Right forward in the fo'c's'le there was the rope handling area for the crew. Down below on the main deck the car space extended some way aft, below the observation lounge and bridge above. Throughout her Red Funnel days her promenade deck did not continue right forward so, for this first period of the **Vecta's** career, passengers were restricted to the area abaft the wood-covered railing surrounding the forward observation lounge.

Following the poignant loss of the **Gracie Fields** at Dunkirk in May 1940, the next most important vessel in the fleet after the motorships became the

paddle steamer **Princess Elizabeth**, named in honour and recognition of the birth of our present Queen, H.M. Queen Elizabeth II.

The **Princess Elizabeth** had been built in 1927 by Day, Summers & Co. Ltd., Northam, Southampton and an excellent job they made of her too. She was 195 feet in length and had a gross tonnage of 371 tons. The **Princess Elizabeth** was a near copy of the paddle steamer **Princess Mary** which they had built in 1911 but, sadly had been lost on war service in the First World War.

As can be read in L. A. Ritchie's book *The Shipbuilding Industry* and more fully in K. C. Barnaby's centenary book about J. I. Thornycroft & Co. Ltd. entitled *100 Years of Specialised Shipbuilding and Engineering*, straight after Day, Summers & Co. Ltd. had delivered the **Princess Elizabeth**, they went into liquidation. In 1929, J. I. Thornycroft & Co. Ltd. then acquired their main business and the shipyard and repair yards whilst the remainder was taken into Pollock, Brown's adjacent ship-breaking yard.

*In this photograph, we see the **Vecta** speeding along Southampton Water, bathed in rosy sunlight. Her hull shell doors are open but on deck there is barely a passenger to be seen.*

Photo: Richard Howarth collection.

When built, the **Princess Elizabeth** was principally used on the service route to Cowes and could operate in all weathers, summer and winter. About ten cars or vans or a small lorry (and items of light deck cargo) were carried on her open foredeck and were driven aboard from the floating pontoons at Southampton and Cowes, through side doors cut into her bulwarks just forward of the bridge. She could carry a maximum of 707 passengers. During the summer months she also ran excursions, mostly from her home port of Southampton. Later, on more than one occasion she was based at Bournemouth until the arrival of the ill-fated and short-lived paddle steamer *Gracie Fields*.

In 1936, her funnel was lengthened and had a cowl top fitted for the first time. This was an attempt to answer the complaints of passengers who kept getting sooty smuts on their clothes and in their eyes. The complaints soon stopped. Two years later, she was fitted with a wooden wheelhouse and bridge, in place of the previous white canvas railed affair, that had been wide open to all the elements.

The evergreen paddle steamer **Princess Elizabeth** *was, in her day, one of the most successful vessels Red Funnel Steamers ever owned. She could manage about 15 knots with all her steam valves right open and her engineers were known to have such a propensity occasionally. This superb photograph of her, well laden with passengers going down Southampton Water at speed, was taken after she had her mainmast fitted in 1954 and prior to her ending summer service in 1958.*

Photo: Red Funnel archives.

Right: Pure nostalgia! This photograph captures perfectly, the tranquillity of the scene at the Royal Pier, Southampton and will remind many readers of happy hours spent, like the gentleman in the foreground, whiling away the time in a deckchair, on a pier or at the seaside. Summer frocks and shirtsleeves aboard the **Bournemouth Queen** *suggest a warm summer's day, but it will no doubt feel much cooler out on the water. The very handsome but forever coal-burning* **Bournemouth Queen** *is seen here after her post war refit during which she received a wooden bridge, wheelhouse and new funnel and after the fitting of a mainmast in 1954. On her bridge the master and mate are ready, even anxious, to bring the gangway in and get underway but as always, last minute passengers are still hurrying aboard. Back in early 1952, at the same board meeting when, for economy reasons, the decision was taken not to recommission the* **Lorna Doone** *(II) they decided to try to sell the* **Bournemouth Queen***. In one of the closing acts of his reign as their general manager, Captain Clarke was instructed by the Red Funnel board to see if he could find a buyer for the 1908-built paddle steamer at a price in the region of £35,000. The troopship* **Empire Fowey** *is under tow in the background. She was formerly the* **Potsdam** *being one of several vessels required to be handed over by the enemy by way of reparations after the War and was subsequently managed by P. & O. until 1960 when she was sold for further service in Pakistan.*

Photo: Red Funnel archives.

During her exemplary war service, the **Princess Elizabeth** first became a minesweeper and played a major part in the evacuation of Dunkirk in May 1940. Later she served as an anti-aircraft vessel based at Harwich and in April 1941 she shot down one (and damaged another) enemy aircraft with her gun! Towards the end of the War she was engaged in carrying American forces personnel back to waiting troopships.

Upon her return to peacetime service after the War, she was thoroughly reconditioned. The recent happy and safe return of both the **Princess Elizabeth** and the **Calshot** was celebrated at the board meeting held on 20th May 1946. In the 'Elizabeth' her main aft saloon, which had previously been narrow with an alleyway all around it, was extended out to the full width of the ship. The opportunity was taken to convert her from burning coal (with its attendant waste products, ash, which had to be disposed of daily and soot) to oil. Thereafter, she became renowned for the cleanliness of her engine room and her polished brass and well-oiled steel on show below for all to see were legendary. Camper &

Nicholson's carried out the boiler conversion and, using that lovely (if archaic) word, she became famous for her great celerity.

So the story goes, one Christmas after the **Princess Elizabeth** had been converted to oil firing, her duty engineer who lived on the Island left the ship at Cowes and only a greaser was at the engine room controls for the return trip to Southampton. It appears that the greaser was equally keen to get home for Christmas but he lived in far-away Bournemouth and did not want to miss the last train. So, left in complete charge of the old 'Lizzie's' steam valves, the greaser opened everything right up and it is said that she almost flew up Southampton Water, taking little over 45 minutes for the scheduled one-hour trip!

As required, the **Princess Elizabeth** worked from time to time as an excursion vessel and day-trip boat serving Ryde, Southsea, Sandown, Ventnor and Shanklin and was also on stand-by for the main passage service from Southampton to Cowes.

The paddle steamer **Bournemouth Queen** was built in 1908 purely for excursion work and did little else. She was constructed in Scotland at the Troon yard of Ailsa Shipbuilding Co. Ltd. and could carry 704 passengers.

She was a very popular and handsome ship although in her final years, no doubt on account of the major alterations she had later in her career, she seemed to be very tender and took on a list for little obvious reason.

As her name implies, throughout her long and somewhat lazy career, every summer she was to be seen operating principally from Bournemouth but latterly from Southampton following the take-over of Cosens & Co. Ltd. after which the competition would have been wasted.

She was called on for war service for the second time in her long life, in 1942, rather later than some of her contemporaries. She spent

*The **Princess Elizabeth** is seen here going astern from the Royal Pier at Southampton towards the end of her career with Red Funnel. There are no cars on her foredeck which suggests she may be operating a cruise or excursion.*
Photo: John Havers collection.

The tug/tender **Calshot** *dating from 1930 served Red Funnel for 34 years before being replaced by a modern tug/tender bearing the same name. The* **Calshot** *is now undergoing rebuilding at Southampton, prior to active preservation.*

Photo: Author.

tender to liners visiting Southampton Water.

The **Calshot** and the **Paladin** were peers of the **Balmoral** and because they were tug/tenders combining towing capability with accommodation for over 600 passengers, they earn their inclusion in this book.

The **Calshot** was built in 1930 by J. I. Thornycroft & Co. Ltd. at Woolston and in addition to her main towage duties, was also used on occasions for the Company's peak summer passenger sailings between Southampton and Ryde; she also ran excursions when required. With triple-expansion, steam reciprocating engines of 1,500 i.h.p., she cannot have been the most economic vessel for such business. Of more note to readers with an engineering interest, the **Calshot** had one coal-fired boiler and one which was oil-fired. In July 1955 it was agreed that J. I. Thornycroft & Co. Ltd. would be consulted to ascertain the cost of converting the coal boiler to oil, on account of the rising cost of coal. Three months

three years serving first as an anti-aircraft ship, later in 1944 as an accommodation vessel before returning home at the end of 1945.

After the War, she had been given a major rebuilding which included plating-in her promenade deck forward of the bridge where previously there had been open railings. Her bridge was rebuilt with varnished timber brightwork and she then sported a wooden wheelhouse too. Her already good lines were improved further by the fitting of a new, larger funnel - but she was never converted to burn oil fuel. At least her big, old coal-fired boilers would have provided some weight low down, to compensate for all the extra steel and timber added when the promenade deck was plated-in and the new funnel and wheelhouse were fitted. Every winter, the **Bournemouth Queen** was laid-up and, in addition to her excursion work each summer, was occasionally used as a

The old tug/tender **Paladin** *makes an impressive sight as she steams along at speed, with plenty of rope fenders and 'bow pudding' in evidence!*

Photo: Author's collection.

later, the board was considering Thornycroft's quote, which came in at £11,700. It was resolved that in view of the age of the **Calshot**, the high cost and the length of time the ship would need to be out of service, they would not proceed.

Both the **Paladin** and the **Calshot** were better known for their bollard pull than their other facilities, some of which were fairly spartan. With a full complement aboard, passengers on many trips could spend lengthy periods queuing for the somewhat limited facilities.

The **Calshot** was described in the official Red Funnel Steamers 1953 edition booklet (price in old money 1/3d) as follows:

*'Now, what is a Tug Tender? Take the **Calshot**. External appearances indicate deck spaciousness, a big efficient-looking towing hook and the usual pudding (bow fender) and side fenders, but apart from this the vessel has two well equipped saloons, where passengers can while away the time in comfort whilst en route for their liner anchored off Cowes. In short, the **Calshot**, deceptive perhaps from outward appearances, is comfortably equipped to carry over 600 passengers between Southampton Docks and liners in Cowes Roads. With ample room on deck for motor cars, baggage, mails etc. it must not be thought, however, that on account of these amenities the **Calshot** is not a very fine tug'.*

The **Paladin** was originally built on the Clyde in 1913 for the famous Anchor Line, but falling business had forced her sale to Clyde Shipping Co. Ltd., operators of a large fleet of coasters and tugs, just before the War. She was acquired by Red Funnel in 1946 as a replacement for the **Sir Bevois** lost in the War.

On occasions, only when hard pressed, the Company used her as a tender and, at rare times, she was also known to run excursions but the paucity of her passenger comforts dictated that her use in this connection was sparing.

Then came the pioneering and successful **Norris Castle**. This ship was one of a number bought second-hand by the Company, soon after the War. Like so many ships built for the War effort, her construction had been completed using some pre-fabricated frames and sections built elsewhere. However, it was from Alexander Findlay's Clyde works at Old Kilpatrick that, as a wartime landing craft for the Admiralty, she met her element in 1942 complete with tank-landing bow ramp and diesel engines by Davey, Paxman & Co. Ltd., themselves by then part of Ruston & Hornsby Ltd. She was heavily engaged in the Normandy landings in 1944 operating from Poole, Dorset and running onto the famous invasion beaches.

Soon after she had been purchased by Red Funnel Steamers in 1947, work was taken in hand by J. I. Thornycroft & Co. Ltd. at their Northam, Southampton yard to enable her to carry cars, commercial vehicles and passengers on the service route to Cowes. Initially, from 1948 she ran to West Cowes along with the regular service passenger steamers. Later she was able to use the slipway at East Cowes on the other side of the Medina River.

It was intended that she should carry more than 30 cars and up to 250 passengers in comfortable, new accommodation built well aft. In terms of vehicle capacity, this was to be a major step forward and virtually doubled the number of cars that could be carried in total, when compared with the existing main units, **Medina**, **Vecta** and **Princess Elizabeth** combined! Put another way, with a full load of cars, her total payload was only a little less than that of the then brand new railway-owned car ferry, **Farringford**, which preceded her into service by just a few months. Ultimately replacing the patriarchal cargo paddler **Lord Elgin**, the **Norris Castle** was to pioneer the development of the whole business of Red Funnel Steamers carrying rolling freight, lorries and lift vans (the forerunner of today's containers).

The viability of the **Norris Castle** was marginal in the beginning, especially for as long as **Lord Elgin** was still in service but, thereafter, this was a business from which neither Red Funnel Steamers nor the **Norris Castle** ever looked back.

However, before she could commence in her new role, she was rebuilt and one of the main alterations was to be *'the raising of the car deck to above the waterline, thus strengthening the hull and guarding against the inrush of water in the event of the failure of the bow doors'.* The other work included overhauling her machinery and constructing comfortable new passenger accommodation aft.

Although the Company quoted her service speed as being 9½ knots, it was more generally reported that 8 knots was probably her normal maximum. This indicated a time on passage to Cowes of 1½ hours (or longer in adverse weather conditions) which must have seemed more of an endurance test than a ferry crossing! At the Red Funnel board meeting held on 27th October 1947, at which so many important and far-reaching resolutions were made, it was noted that J. I. Thornycroft & Co. Ltd. had estimated a figure of £30,000 for the adaptation of the **Norris Castle** for civilian passenger and vehicle-carrying service. In trying to obtain full benefit from this vessel, the Company was hampered by the fact that petrol for private motoring remained very hard to come by and it was not until that problem was overcome, that the family car (and therefore the **Norris Castle**) really came into its own.

What a splendid photograph this is! Neither of the two ferries was renowned for having a good turn of speed. The **Medina** *is heading out gently from Southampton, carrying passengers and cars bound for Cowes. The former Birkenhead ferry* **Upton***, bought by Red Funnel Steamers in 1946, is probably on one of her (rather too strenuous regular three, later only two) round trips from Southampton to Ryde. In her Birkenhead days like the other Birkenhead ferries of the era, she had no bridge at all and the ship was navigated from one of three boxes, mounted on the upper deck for the purpose. The* **Queen Elizabeth** *is in the Ocean Dock 46/47 berths.*
Photo: Red Funnel archives/B.V. Sexton.

This evocative close-up scene was taken at Sandown Pier on 27th June 1967. On Thursdays in the high season and also on selected Tuesdays, the **Balmoral** *would cruise right round the Isle of Wight having called at Ryde, then back across Spithead to Southsea, thence on to Sandown and Shanklin. On other days (except Saturdays and peak Fridays when she was needed on the ferry service to Cowes) she ran trips to Ryde, docks cruises and excursions that would call at most or all of those piers and then cruise gently along the coast before returning the same way. Occasionally, the tug/tenders* **Calshot** *or* **Gatcombe** *took the trip to Ryde and back.   Photo: Pat Murrell.*

*The **Balmoral** is seen to advantage in this wonderful photograph whilst passing Calshot at speed, en route from Southampton to Ryde on Sunday 11th June 1967. After Ryde, she often sailed on to Southsea, Shanklin, Sandown and then cruised along the Island coast before returning.*   *Photo: C.C.A. archives.*

The Balmoral's Red Funnel Days

After her entry into commercial service on 13th December 1949, the new **Balmoral** eventually became the pride of the Red Funnel fleet. However, this did not happen immediately, as there were other ships, more charismatic than the new motorship, yet to eclipse. Within three years, the lowly old vessels **Upton** and **Robina** and the splendid looking **Lorna Doone** and **Solent Queen**, all bought second-hand after the War, had been withdrawn.

Even though the use of these old ships by the Company was an expensive and short-term measure, the ships certainly had their admirers. If nothing else, they enabled Red Funnel Steamers to return to what remained of the excursion business. However, to those willing to see, it was clear that that side of their business was well past its heyday and would never again sustain so many ships.

The **Upton's** principal problems stemmed from the fact that she had been built for Birkenhead Corporation where she was on the 15-minute, Liverpool to Rock Ferry run. She was the smallest of the quintet built between 1925 and 1933 which also included the **Hinderton**, **Thurstaston**, **Claughton** and **Bidston**. It was hardly surprising that she had considerable difficulty in maintaining a full head of steam all the way from Southampton to Ryde. However, she plodded on until 1950 (after which she was finally relieved by the **Bournemouth Queen** in 1951) and normally, having wheezed her way across from Southampton to Ryde, soon recovered enough composure to manage the return journey, as long as she was not expected to steam too fast. She really was very slow and even when tried out as a tug later in 1951, her static bollard pull test failed to impress. Various attempts to sell her at a price of £25,000 were made but in the end she was consigned to the scrap-yard in early 1953 for the princely sum of £4,500.

Then the humble (and none too nimble) **Robina** (built 1914) had been bought. Her purchase in August 1948 was an emergency step as the boilers in the ancient **Solent Queen** (I) had failed without warning. The **Solent Queen** was towed away to Grays, Essex where Thos. Ward Ltd. broke her up that October. The **Robina** happened to be at Southampton at the time and was available for purchase but her boilers were troublesome too! For the winter of 1948/49 she was mainly operated on the Cowes route but did some tendering and special excursions too.   From 1950 onwards Red

The paddle steamer **Solent Queen** *(I) was a relic of another era. She was iron-hulled (not steel) and, with her navigating bridge abaft her two thin funnels and single short mast, she was not a very attractive looking ship when viewed from any angle other than broadside on as she is in this photograph. She was, however, very useful and could carry a few cars on her foredeck too. Her boilers gave out in 1948 and she was then scrapped, being replaced by the second-hand* **Robina**. *Interestingly, her wartime master, the very senior Captain A.G. Gattrell, went on to become the first master of the new* **Balmoral** *in 1949.*
Photo: Richard Howarth collection.

Funnel Steamers had her up for sale again but, despite a notional plan for her to see Red Funnel service in 1951, this never happened. Director, Mr. Barnaby went to the lengths of requesting that it be specifically noted in the records that he was completely against any plans for the **Upton** and the **Robina** to be returned to service in either 1951 or later. The **Robina** was finally towed away to Rotterdam in 1953 and raised the sum of £6,000 for scrap.

As we read earlier, in December 1948, with the new **Balmoral** then well under construction, somewhat surprisingly Red Funnel Steamers acquired two (of the original 32 built by the Admiralty) former 'Racecourse' class paddle minesweepers, by then owned by the New Medway Steam Packet Co. Ltd. These were their **Queen of Kent** and the **Queen of Thanet**, which in Red Funnel Steamers'

hands became the **Lorna Doone** (II) and **Solent Queen** (II) respectively. In addition to the perceived operational benefits of owning these two big excursion steamers, there was also considered to be a risk that had Red Funnel not bought them, an opponent in the form of the Poole ship-builder J. Bolson & Son Ltd. might. However, their arrival in the Red Funnel Fleet proved to be a very expensive interlude and one which would probably never have happened had it not been for Red Funnel's general manager, Captain Clarke.

In fact, it was a side of the business that was declining rapidly. Thornycroft's were very quick and forceful in their arguments that these two old ships, whilst cheap to buy at £23,500 for the pair (which in truth was not a lot more than their scrap value and less

*The **Solent Queen** (II) and her sistership, the **Lorna Doone** (II) were the two final ships bought second-hand by Red Funnel Steamers after the War, just prior to the arrival of the new **Balmoral**. They were most handsome, popular vessels and the **Solent Queen** deserved a more dignified end than catching fire on the slipway at White's Shipyard in June 1951 and having to be scrapped as a result. In these two photographs we see the **Solent Queen** arriving at the South Parade Pier, Southsea and alongside at Shanklin.*
Photos: V.C. Jones/Ian Allan library.

than the £30,000 authorised by the board previously) were phenomenally expensive when the true costs of bringing them up to Red Funnel's standards of operation were included.

Both were big, beautiful, old steamers and both had been converted to oil firing back in 1931, but it was mostly (and substantially) on the debit side of the Profit and Loss Account that they featured. Measuring 235 feet in length, negotiating Cowes at low water in bad weather was a manoeuvre that their masters and mates must have dreaded.

Not surprisingly, given his overt predisposition in favour of long distance excursions, Captain Clarke had hoped to be able to use the newly acquired **Lorna Doone** on trips across the Channel to France. At first these were to be non-landing cruises at least until proper arrangements could be made to put passengers ashore there. Unfortunately, even though in her previous ownership she had regularly sailed to Calais, Boulogne and Dunkirk, the ship was no longer fast or reliable enough, nor were her passenger facilities considered by Red Funnel Steamers to be good enough for such long trips.

In Mr. R.B. Adams' fine book entitled *Red Funnel and Before* (Kingfisher, 1986) we read that in the case of the **Lorna Doone**, Red Funnel Steamers had retained her six original lifeboats and a marine radio operator (all being necessary for her Class II certificate) in the hope of being able to re-start cross-Channel services. We know too that certainly latterly, the first **Balmoral** carried a marine radio operator for her sailings across the Channel to France. Apart from receiving weather forecasts and advising estimated times of arrival at destination ports, the radio operators must have had a fairly leisurely existence.

Then, there was the ancient paddle steamer **Lord Elgin** that had been only partly displaced by the **Norris Castle's** arrival on service in the summer of 1948. Once a passenger ship and dating from 1876, the **Lord Elgin** was converted to carrying cargo for Red Funnel Steamers from 1911 onwards. She remained in regular cargo service until the autumn of 1952 and was kept on for three

further years as relief cargo boat. Finally, the old **Princess Helena** remained moribund, having been displaced by the new **Balmoral**.

However, whilst the results of the short term use of the other second-hand vessels could be said to have been very disappointing overall, the operation of the **Norris Castle** was improved considerably in June 1950 when the Southampton Harbour Board installed a floating pontoon and vehicle loading bridge. This was known as the 'buffer pontoon' and was constructed by their Works Department from parts of the former wartime Mulberry Harbours. The whole thing had a payload of 40 tons, over which even the heaviest lorries could load, directly over the **Norris Castle's** former tank-landing, bow ramp.

The **Norris Castle** was operating mainly in the summer months only at this time, whilst the old **Lord Elgin** still had two years of operational cargo-boat service to come. However, also in 1950, the **Norris Castle** was able to begin running to East Cowes as soon as the concrete slipway on that side of the Medina River was adapted for her use. Initially she was billed to make one round trip sailing on weekdays, departing from Southampton at 11.00 hrs. and returning from East Cowes at 14.30 hrs. As the **Norris Castle** was well equipped for carrying passengers (unlike the old **Lord Elgin**, which really was not) her extra new service added noticeably to available capacity on the route to the Isle of Wight.

That same summer of 1950, the new **Balmoral** was reported in the *Isle of Wight County Press* newspaper as having joined the **Solent Queen** to operate some of the excursions to Ryde and Shanklin Piers and trips round the Island and the docks, mainly from Southampton. This important step marks the real beginning of the **Balmoral's** excursion sailings.

The profit figures for Red Funnel's 1950 operations as attributed to each vessel individually confirm how important it was for them to dispose of the old fleet as quickly as possible.

The five profitable ships were:- **Vecta** £11,000: **Medina** £9,600: **Balmoral** £9,000: **Princess Elizabeth** £4,000: and **Lorna Doone** just £198.

*Complete with red lead paint in abundant evidence, the **Balmoral** is seen here undergoing her annual overhaul at Weymouth where Cosens & Co. Ltd., majority-owned by Red Funnel Steamers since 1946, had a very useful and extensive marine workshop facility. Astern of the **Balmoral**, also laid-up, lies Cosens & Co. Ltd.'s paddle steamer **Embassy**.*

Photo: Ken Saunders/Richard Clammer collection.

*The old **Lord Elgin** can claim to be the very last paddle-propelled cargo vessel operating in U.K. waters. After she came to Red Funnel in 1908 and was converted to mainly cargo operations, she was likely to be found carrying cars for shipment to the Isle of Wight, or sheep and cattle. In addition, as in the photograph, she carried freight of all descriptions (which she could handle with her own derrick) on her deck.* Photo: Tim Cooper collection.

*The ancient **Princess Helena** is seen here alongside the Royal Pier, Southampton in 1947. In this photograph she has a small wheelhouse on which her mast-head white light now resides but no foremast which was removed to facilitate the easier stowing of cars. Earlier in the book, another photograph of the ship may be seen, taken prior to the wheelhouse and mast alterations. The service passenger steamer **Medina** is just visible above the pier superstructure.* Photo: V. C. Jones/Ian Allan library.

The losers lost money as follows:- **Robina** £4,400: **Upton** £4,100: **Solent Queen** £3,700: **Princess Helena** £1,479: **Bournemouth Queen** £1,470: **Lord Elgin** £1,200: and **Norris Castle** £48 and therefore their operation wiped out half the profit.

Until Red Funnel handed over the Bournemouth business to its new associated company Cosens & Co. Ltd. after the summer of 1951, they had previously had one or more vessels stationed there for the summer. For 1949 and 1950, the **Lorna Doone** was the main Bournemouth steamer, together with the **Bournemouth Queen** which was then relegated to serve Swanage.

Probably the **Balmoral's** least-known and rarely-mentioned fleetmate (if that is not too grand a description) was their oiling

barge named **Brownsea**, which was based at Poole for fuelling vessels on the Bournemouth station. The files of the early 1950s show that she was the subject of continuing discussion as to what should be done with her and of the amount of remedial work needed in view of her dilapidated condition.

At their meeting held on 29th January 1951, not only did the directors discuss the rusting old **Brownsea** but, far more importantly, they resolved to *'Set up a sub-committee to consider the cost of repairs to the Company's vessels and also the running of the vessels on excursion services with a view to curtailing expenses as much as possible'.* The sub-committee comprised two directors namely Mr. Redman and Mr. Barnaby, the general manager Captain Clarke and the Company's marine superintendent. The findings of that sub-committee were not individually broadcast in the minutes of subsequent meetings of the directors. However, in view of the continued disposal of the excursion fleet and new attention to maintenance costs, it must be assumed that its recommendations were quite severe.

In 1951, Red Funnel Steamers' final year at Bournemouth, the **Lorna Doone** called at Totland Pier on Sunday 17th June 1951 and again the next day with 285 passengers to land there. It was announced that it would thereafter be a regular port of call. The pier had been disused for 20 years and had had to be extensively re-built, as it was one that was deliberately breached in the War.

The 18th June 1951 was the day that the new railway-owned motorship **Shanklin** entered commercial service on the Portsmouth-Ryde route. Up until 1951, as remains the case with the trains themselves, the accommodation in their Isle of Wight ferries was also divided into two classes but this was abolished at the time of the arrival of the new **Shanklin**. We have already seen that at Red Funnel it appears they did away with the class-distinction at the beginning of the War, the **Vecta** being the last Red Funnel vessel built with two class service in mind.

In truth, it had always been a problem for shipowners everywhere trying to effectively police the separation of classes of passenger accommodation and, in this, neither the Southern Railway nor Red Funnel Steamers were exceptions. Nothing was more likely to annoy a travel-weary passenger, struggling with family and baggage after a long hot journey on an overcrowded train or motor coach, than hearing a seaman bellowing words importing the meaning (but not always saying so quite as politely) *'first class only to the left, second class down there to the right, if you please'*.

In fact, the **Shanklin** and her two older sisterships were fitted out to a very high level of specification. To achieve the separation of first and second class accommodation, in the **Southsea** and the **Brading** this was divided with first class passengers having their lounge and smoke room aft, whilst second class were accommodated forward, adjacent to the luggage compartment - all on the main deck.

Further below, the second class passengers had their saloon and refreshment area on the lower deck, whilst on the promenade deck the area aft of the bridge was first class. Forward, the second class passengers had some deck seating and also, here, was the hatch down to the luggage hold below.

Unlike many of the diesel-powered passenger vessels of the era, the **Balmoral** included, which almost seemed to make a virtue of their noisy machinery, in the **Shanklin** particular emphasis was placed on passenger comfort and reduction in engine room noise emissions. In this respect she excelled all others.

Four days after the arrival of the new **Shanklin** at Portsmouth, the former paddle minesweeper **Solent Queen** caught fire whilst on the slipway at White's Shipyard, following which disaster she never sailed again. On 20th July 1951, the directors of Red Funnel Steamers resolved that 'a Notice of Abandonment' of the **Solent Queen** be served on the Underwriters as the cost to repair the fire damage amounted to £25,000, which was the insured value of the ship. She was finally scrapped at Dover in October 1951. The **Lorna Doone** was recalled from Bournemouth to cover for the **Solent Queen's** 1951 season.

On 5th November 1951, after a long period of ill-health, Captain Clarke resigned as general manager of Red Funnel Steamers, and this was to be effective from 31st March 1952 or some later mutually acceptable date, if his successor were not by then incumbent. His time with Red Funnel was at a very difficult period, straight after the War and with no spare money in the reserves. Paradoxically, it has been said that, single-handed, he alone did more than anyone for the preservation of old paddle steamers and ferries in the 1940s and 1950s; but at what price?

At this time in 1952, Red Funnel Steamers took on as a shorthand typist Miss Hazel Nicholson and she worked for the

Company for 46 years before taking well earned retirement in 1998. Miss Hazel Nicholson M.B.E., as she is now, recalls that at the time, the **Balmoral** was just three years old. *'When the **Balmoral** was running on excursions, her car deck aft was a haven for the trippers for whose pleasure large numbers of deck chairs were set out. Unfortunately, the view from there was none too good and it could be quite smutty too, with emissions from the funnel raining down'.*

As the years went by, Miss Nicholson rose through the ranks of secretary, assistant to the company secretary, assistant secretary and finally company secretary in 1990. With aspects of corporate governance so important these days, Europe has recognised the definition of company secretary as being the chief administrative officer of a company. Clearly Red Funnel Steamers rightly recognised Miss Nicholson's vast experience of their affairs as being of inestimable value too. The metaphoric 'glass ceiling' (said to bar the way for female staff to reach the top positions in British companies) rightly opened to let her through. She was and, even in retirement, remains an excellent ambassador for the Red Funnel Group.

Originally, it was intended that the **Lorna Doone** should be recommissioned for the 1952 season but in January work on her stopped. It is thought likely that this was following receipt of the reports from the recently appointed sub-committee looking into the whole business of running the old excursion steamers. One of Captain Clarke's final acts was to try to sell the **Lorna Doone**. In February, the offer of the sum of £5,800 was accepted following some negotiation with breakers British Iron & Steel Corporation, and a further month later in March 1952, she too was towed away from her mud berth at Northam to Dover for scrapping.

Following Captain Clarke's retirement from Red Funnel Steamers, he remained a director of its Weymouth subsidiary Cosens & Co. Ltd. for a while. His successor as general manager

Opposite: When the author found this never-to-be-repeated photograph amongst the precious Red Funnel archives in the vaults at Bugle Street, it was immediately obvious that the scene was something very special. In this wonderful action photograph, the converted landing craft **Norris Castle** *is seen at the slipway at East Cowes. At first glance it appears that the* **Norris Castle** *is about to unload her cargo of coaches but this is not the case. What we see here is probably the last of nine coaches being backed onto the* **Norris Castle** *for the voyage to Southampton and all the coach passengers are already aboard. The photograph was taken during the railway strike of 1955. The Brambles Chine Holiday Camp (whose name can be clearly read on the coach) had, in the absence of any mainland trains, hired a fleet of coaches from West Wight Motor Bus Company to return their 'campers' to Victoria Coach Station in London. The author appreciates the help of Miss Hazel Nicholson in locating this and other photographs and of Mr. Tim Cooper and Mr. Pat Hall for their help in ascertaining the details of the event. Even by modern-day standards, nine full-size coaches are a good payload for such a relatively small (180 feet long) vessel.*
Photo: Red Funnel archives/T.G. Savage.

Seen here off Fawley (home of the famous oil refinery) the **Vecta** *heads down Southampton Water in her final month as a Red Funnel, Isle of Wight passage steamer.*
Photo: Tim Cooper.

was announced as the sagacious and go-ahead Mr. C. Warren Payne. Whilst back in 1952, 'head-hunting' was a phrase yet to reach the dictionary, it is thought that Warren Payne had been plucked from the ranks of management elsewhere and he quickly became renowned for his business acumen and not for his love of his predecessor's old excursion steamers.

The appointment of Mr. C. Warren Payne as general manager was confirmed at the meeting of directors held on 25th February 1952. Mr. Payne was to take up his new duties on 28th April 1952 and his arrival was to be felt immediately, throughout the corridors of 12 Bugle Street, Southampton.

For the first time, in 1952 Red Funnel Steamers began to use the **Balmoral** logo/motif on their handbills and sailing announcements. That followed the withdrawal from service of the last of the old second-hand tonnage, leaving the **Balmoral**, as undisputed team leader.

The 69 year-old paddler **Princess Helena** that had gone on to the reserve list when the **Balmoral** came into service three years previously was towed from Chapel Wharf round to Pollock, Brown & Co. Ltd. Northam, to be scrapped in July 1952. Before the work had started in earnest she managed to capsize after getting caught on the dock wall on a falling tide and, before she could be broken up, she had first to be pumped out and refloated!

Once the old boats had been dispatched to the breakers' yards, the remaining fleet of passenger vessels then comprised the following vessels: the diesel-engined motorships **Balmoral** and **Medina**, the diesel-electric **Vecta**, the now oil-fired evergreen paddle steamer **Princess Elizabeth** and the old coal-fired paddle steamer **Bournemouth Queen**. In addition, they had the converted naval landing craft **Norris Castle** which, whilst able to carry up to 32 cars, 254 passengers, or all the freight, lorries and heavy loads destined for Cowes, was not yet fully geared-up to do so. The **Lord Elgin** was still operating the cargo service and occasionally the two tug/tenders **Calshot** and **Paladin** were to be found helping out too.

In September 1952, fully five years after the idea was first mooted, Lloyd's List carried the announcement that the **Medina** was to be re-engined during her annual overhaul, the following spring. J. I. Thornycroft & Co. Ltd. were awarded the contract to remove her ageing Gardner diesels and replace them with more powerful engines by Crossley's of Manchester. These would enable her to sail at speeds of 13 knots or more in future.

As we have already seen, when it came to rolling in a heavy sea the new **Balmoral** excelled and when combined with a tight turn, the result could be quite dramatic. However, in just this one respect, the **Medina** had the edge on her as she could roll quite alarmingly in even the slightest swell but whether her new engines, when finally installed, improved this propensity to be boisterous is debatable.

As was often the case, 13th August 1952 found both British Railways and the Red Funnel Fleet vying for business. The local press advertisements for this occasion were to witness the arrival of the then brand-new Blue Riband liner **United States** and the departure of Cunard Line's flagship **Queen Elizabeth** to New York.

Before the days of radar being universally available, fog was one of the worst nightmares for all mariners, especially in confined busy waterways such as at Southampton. Ocean liners, particularly the two famous Cunard 'Queens' on the Atlantic ferry, could not afford to be held up, even for a few hours. Red Funnel vessels are on record as having occasionally provided navigational assistance to the big liners during extended periods of dense fog in Southampton Water.

With their expert local knowledge and being relatively low down sometimes beneath the worst of the fog, they have been able to give enough knowledge as to the extent of the fog, to enable the liners to creep on into port and thereby make the tide before it ebbed. These services were greatly appreciated by the liner captains who invariably rewarded the ferry with several throaty blasts on their mighty sirens, giving them something to yarn about well into the future.

But, the big event of 1953 had been the Coronation of Queen Elizabeth II and on 15th June 1953 the Coronation Naval Review took place at Spithead in the presence of tens of thousands of spectators. Her Majesty the Queen reviewed the proceedings from H.M.S. **Surprise**, as the Royal Yacht **Britannia** was not commissioned until 1954. Readers may recall that late in 1953 and 1954, the young Queen sailed round her Pacific Dominions in the Shaw Savill liner **Gothic**, which had been fitted out as a Royal Yacht for the purpose. The old **Gothic** (irreverently known as the 'Got Sick') suffered several breakdowns and so repairs had to be made surreptitiously (behind the headland or over the horizon) to ensure that the public was not aware of the difficulties.

Red Funnel had all of their passenger-carrying vessels at the Coronation Naval Review; namely, the new **Balmoral**, **Bournemouth Queen**, **Princess Elizabeth**, **Vecta**, **Medina** and the tug/tenders **Calshot** and **Paladin**. Many ships, including those of Red Funnel Steamers were chartered for the day by major corporate entities. The **Balmoral** was on charter to Pirelli. That evening, the converted tank landing craft **Norris Castle** was billed to run a cruise from Cowes to see the illuminations and this is probably the only excursion she ever ran!

British Railways had many cross-Channel boats drafted in for the occasion of the Review in addition to their Portsmouth and Lymington-based ferries and excursion steamers. General Steam Navigation Co. Ltd. and its associated company, New Medway Steam Packet Co. Ltd. were present with the **Royal Sovereign**, **Royal Daffodil** and the smaller excursion paddler **Medway Queen**. P. & A. Campbell Ltd. had their paddle steamers **Glen Gower**, **Cardiff Queen** and **Bristol Queen** and Cosens & Co. Ltd. had four ships, **Consul**, **Embassy**, **Monarch** and **Emperor of India,** all watching the Review. What a wonderful sight it must have been!

*Cosens & Co. Ltd. bought the paddle steamer **Shanklin** from British Railways in 1951 and renamed her **Monarch**. She remained coal-fired throughout her career. It is interesting to see the 'SOLD OUT' stamp on the adjacent Red Funnel Steamers' handbill, which is promoting a Coronation Fleet Review sailing by the **Monarch** belonging to Cosens & Co. Ltd., their subsidiary. Photo: Author's negative library.*

RED FUNNEL STEAMERS
SOUTHAMPTON

ADDITIONAL SAILINGS

Monday, June 15th

REVIEW OF THE FLEET

BY

H.M. THE QUEEN

SOLD OUT

S.S. "Monarch" will leave South Parade Pier, Southsea, at 12.30 p.m., and cruise through the lines of the Fleet to an allotted anchorage to witness the Review of the Fleet by H.M. the Queen, arriving back at about 6.30 p.m.

Fare £2 0s. 0d.
(NO REDUCTION FOR CHILDREN)

ILLUMINATION OF THE FLEET

The S.S. "Monarch" will leave South Parade Pier, Southsea, at 7.30 p.m. and cruise through the lines of the Fleet to an allotted anchorage to witness the Illumination of the Fleet and Fireworks, arriving back at about midnight.

Fare £1 10s. 0d.
(NO REDUCTION FOR CHILDREN)

ADVANCE BOOKING — see back.

The problem of bestowing local names on vessels becomes very noticeable when the ship moves into different areas of operation. The name of the **Glen Gower** *(seen here at Bristol with the* **Britannia** *just visible on the inside berth) was hardly suitable for her work on Campbell's Sussex station when she was based at Brighton from time to time until 1956. She ran her final South Coast and cross-Channel sailings in that year.* Photo: Bristol Evening Post.

The Annual General Meeting of Red Funnel shareholders was held on 18th May 1953 aboard the **Balmoral** (and for a number of years thereafter) moored at the Royal Pier. In later years it was held at the Polygon Hotel, Southampton.

Following the fitting of her new engines, once again the question of the **Medina's** speed and build-up of marine growth on her hull came up for discussion and, in November 1953, it was agreed that she should be slipped three times a year to try to keep the problem under control. A year later, director Mr. Barnaby reported to his colleagues that he had visited the ship on the slipway at Northam and that in his opinion, the state of the ship's hull fully justified the third annual hull cleaning.

April 1954 saw Sandown Pier re-opened for the first time since the beginning of the War. The **Balmoral** was chosen to represent the Red Funnel Company for the trip and 300 people boarded at the newly re-built pier.

That same season saw the cross-Channel sailing restrictions lifted for the first time since the War. Campbell's **Glen Gower** made the first such trips that year to Calais and Boulogne for which she could carry 562 passengers on her Class II certificate. She did the same again for the following two years only.

To comply with new lighting regulations affecting vessels exceeding 150 feet in length, those ships that did not already have one received a full height mainmast in 1954, together with the forward facing white light, set at the regulation height above the one on the foremast. The **Balmoral's** previous stubby pole mast was removed at that time and a new mainmast was fitted.

It was during one of the **Princess Elizabeth's** periods of service on the Southampton-Cowes passage on 27th July 1954 that the author, then aged 7, first sailed in her and, later, the **Balmoral**. Some older readers may remember that at that time, despite it supposedly being high summer, the country was being lashed by severe storms. The blustery walk down from the Dolphin Hotel, past the ruins of the Holyrood Sailors Church, blitzed in November 1940 but now preserved as a monument to the men of the Merchant Navy, gave some indication of the journey ahead. The deserted and windswept pavements of High Street, Southampton, told only part of the story. Nevertheless, the paddle steamer **Princess Elizabeth** was scheduled to take a sailing from Southampton to Cowes that grey morning and not even the weatherman's threat of further gales was going to be allowed to upset the timetable, at least not more than was unavoidable.

With her whistle blowing its steamy chime, pennants flying and black smoke billowing from her tall, red and black-topped funnel, it was with a light load of a few hardy passengers (including the author and his father) two or three cars and some cycles, that she let go from her berth at Southampton's Royal Pier. As the **Princess Elizabeth** paddled past the famous Ocean Terminal (completed in

Above: Cosens & Co. Ltd.'s paddle steamer **Consul** *was well suited to running her owner's excursions right into Lulworth Cove. There, she would gently rest her bows on the sloping beach from where her passengers could walk ashore down her long, rather wobbly bow gangplank. Several of Cosens' smaller, old paddlers made quite a feature of this manoeuvre, which was simple to them.*

Photo: John Edgington.

Left: The **Embassy** *belonging to Cosens & Co. Ltd. looks splendid, dressed overall in this view of her alongside Bournemouth Pier in July 1964.*

Photo: John Edgington.

71

1950 but since demolished) and docks to port, the sea was already getting noticeably rougher and it was becoming clear that it was to be a very boisterous crossing.

Passing Hythe then Fawley well to starboard and Netley and its famous castle to port the little steamer ploughed on slowly, doing the best she could, and throwing up spray and soaking the cars and cyclists huddled on her open foredeck. Ominous dark troughs were appearing in the sea ahead and the breaking waves were beginning to roll in. The **Princess Elizabeth** shuddered uneasily as she began to battle her way down Southampton Water.

The author, his father and a newspaper photographer had

taken up station behind the canvas dodgers at the top of the two companionways beneath the wheelhouse, from which vantage point the worsening conditions could be surveyed.

At the far end of Southampton Water, passing Calshot and its castle, the ship altered course to starboard and headed down the deep Thorn Channel towards the Isle of Wight. By this time, green seas were running and the **Princess Elizabeth** was plunging along under the full force of the oncoming waves as she wallowed from peak to trough, pitching and rolling very uncomfortably. Solid water was thundering by and roaring up under the vessel's sponsons surrounding the paddles on either side. Gale blown spume and spray were in the air everywhere as she ploughed along. All the while could be heard the mechanical groan of her old steel plates as she laboured on against the heavy sea.

After each angry wave struck her she staggered back uncertainly on to an even keel, only to be hit by another coming crashing in, throwing the **Princess Elizabeth** over once again. Looking ahead and ducking under the canvas dodger as the waves broke over the bow, all that could be seen was that the foredeck was now completely awash. Undaunted, the **Princess Elizabeth** shouldered the onslaught, streaming tons of seawater each time she rallied to the oncoming seas.

Finally she made the lee of the Island and safely reached the mouth of the Medina River, which opened before her. The **Princess Elizabeth** had brought her passengers and cars safely through the gale, to the Fountain Pier at West Cowes, just as she had done thousands of times previously over the years. To her it was simply another crossing, just a bit rougher than usual.

The author wrote home of his great adventure that day back in 1954 and this marks the clear starting point of his love of and writing about excursion ships and ferries. Amazingly, two days later, the actual photograph *(see opposite)* taken by the photographer who was sheltering behind the canvas dodger, next to the author aboard the **Princess Elizabeth**, appeared in the national press.

THE MANCHESTER GUARDIAN THURSDAY JULY 29 1954

...day weather.—Two cyclists take cover under their capes as waves break over the bows of the ferry steamer Princess Elizabeth, on her way from Southampton to Cowes during Tuesday's gales

Later that visit, several trips were accomplished in the **Balmoral**, the **Vecta** and the **Medina** but it was upon another occasion that the **Princess Elizabeth** was to take the author and his father on a docks cruise to view the liners. A good crowd was aboard as the steamer paddled away to give her passengers a ringside view of the **Mauretania** at 46 Berth, a lilac-hulled Union Castle liner at 47 Berth and the peerless **Queen Mary** at the Ocean Terminal, all in the Ocean Dock. As the paddler neared the head of the dock, most of her passengers surged across to the starboard side of the ship. This caused her to list violently and for her port side paddle to lift clear of the water. With that, the ship sheered unexpectedly and sharply round to port. Amidst much urgent ringing on the ship's telegraph, the **Princess Elizabeth** finally came to rest uncomfortably close, right under the bows of the **Mauretania**. Officers' faces appeared as if by magic on the bridge wing of the liner, peering down haughtily at the diminutive **Princess Elizabeth** as she struggled to get out of her predicament. Clearly they were not enamoured of the prospect of the smoky, little paddler denting their pristine newly painted steel plates. Facing in the wrong direction, the **Princess Elizabeth** was still listing heavily under the weight of her human payload and not answering her helm at all.

Most harbours have a classic view and in this photograph we see Weymouth to maximum advantage. The magnificent Town Bridge separating the main harbour from the inner harbour and backwater has raised its substantial iron bascules to allow the **Princess Elizabeth** *to be towed through towards the main harbour and out to open sea. The paddle steamer already has a good head of steam up and looks to be absolutely pristine and ready for a busy summer season's work.*

Photo: Dorset Evening Echo.

*In the spring of 1955 both the **Balmoral** and the **Vecta** had an improvement carried out that these days would certainly be called 'eco-friendly' or 'green'. Their banks of emergency lead-acid batteries, originally fitted under the seating on the upper deck (so that they would be the last things to get wet and fail in the event of a calamity overwhelming the ship) were replaced with a Russell-Newbury auto-diesel emergency electric generating set. This scene depicts the manoeuvrable, diesel-electric **Vecta**, barely disturbing the water at all, going gently astern out of Southampton with passengers and cars bound for the Isle of Wight.*

Photo: John Edgington.

The ship's Tannoy system crackled into life with the firm request from the Captain *'would all passengers kindly move away from the starboard rail as it is making navigation of the ship in the confined waters of the dock very difficult'*. Obligingly, everyone then moved to the port side with the inevitable result of the paddle steamer taking on a severe list, but this time the other way, bringing her mast even closer to the overhanging hull of the **Mauretania**. A further request over the public address system brought about the necessary movement of passengers amidships and enabled the **Princess Elizabeth** to back off, going very gingerly astern until well clear of the liners. The author can personally confirm that not one scratch was put on any vessel - but it was a close call!

26th March 1954 found the Red Funnel directors considering the ancient **Lord Elgin**, which was still running the cargo service only and very much overshadowed by the **Norris Castle**. As they were not yet quite ready to abandon their antiquated paddler, they agreed with charming frankness *'that the* **Lord Elgin's** *hull should be patched-up to enable her to run until the end of the year'*.

On 11th May 1955, with the **Norris Castle** ready for service following her two week overhaul, her relief ship, the old **Lord Elgin,** made her final round trip to the Island. For this she was given a civic send-off and was dressed overall. There was much whistle-blowing and hooting of sirens as the 80-year-old ship left the pontoon at Southampton with cargo for the last time. Two days later she sailed herself to her own funeral, for breaking-up at Northam. The **Lord Elgin** was notable for being the very last British-registered cargo paddle steamer.

Cosens & Co. Ltd., since 1946 a majority owned subsidiary of Red Funnel, were finding it necessary to reduce their fleet - to downsize, using the present day vernacular. They had already

scrapped their very old **Monarch** in 1950 and then the old **Victoria's** time was up. She was scrapped at Northam in 1953. Two years later the **Empress** suffered the same fate and she too was broken up at Pollock, Brown & Co. Ltd. after making her last sailing on 9th September 1955.

1956 was notable for the withdrawal of another favourite old excursion steamer. This was Cosens' beautiful old paddle steamer the **Emperor of India**, originally built in 1906 as the **Princess**

Every winter, the **Embassy** *(the last of Cosens & Co. Ltd.'s paddlers) would lay-up at Weymouth. Eventually, she was withdrawn from service at the end of September 1966 and was put up for sale at the asking price of £7,000. In the end, she was broken up in Belgium the following May.*

Photo: Ken Saunders/Richard Clammer collection.

The paddle steamer **Princess Elizabeth** *is seen here going astern from Weymouth towards the end of her working life. In 1959 Red Funnel Steamers sold her to Torbay Steamers Ltd. for just £4,000.*

Photo: John Edgington.

This fascinating photograph is of the **Medina** *on the slipway at Northam. Its inclusion serves to highlight the problem of her lack of tumblehome. That is to say, in the* **Medina's** *case the higher up the ship, the wider she was. For pier work and coming alongside other ships, some progressive narrowing of the ship above the belting would have saved much potential damage to the vulnerable upper hull.*

Photo: Red Funnel archives.

Royal for Red Funnel Steamers. She finished her 1956 season and was towed away from Weymouth in January 1957 for breaking-up in Belgium.

In April 1957, Red Funnel Steamers received a polite letter from P. & A. Campbell Ltd. asking if they had any objection to Campbell's running short 1½ hour cruises on Fridays during the summer when their *Crested Eagle* would be running to Shanklin from Brighton. The *Crested Eagle* is the same ship which, as the *New Royal Lady*, Red Funnel Steamers had considered buying themselves ten years previously. After considerable discussion '*it was agreed that although not in favour of same, to raise no objection to these particular cruises on the firm understanding that there would be no application for any further trips of this nature*'. It all sounds very gentlemanly.

In fact P. & A. Campbell Ltd. ceased South Coast operations after the 1957 season except for a brief return twelve years later but they did carry on in the excursion ship business until 1980, mainly in the Bristol Channel and, until the end of the 1969 season, in North Wales.

One of the benefits of having acquired Cosens & Co. Ltd. proved to be that they provided a source of cash funds with which, on occasion, Red Funnel Steamers could help to finance the whole operation. For example, in September 1957 with the bank rate at 7% and deposit rate only 5%, it was agreed that it made good business sense for Cosens to lend Red Funnel £25,000, rather than take an overdraft from the bank.

Then, Red Funnel's grand old lady, the fine paddler *Bournemouth Queen* ran only a short summer season, which ended on 29th August 1957. Mr. E.C.B. Thornton, in his book *South Coast Pleasure Steamers* (T. Stephenson & Sons Ltd. 1962) rightly described it as '*spent pottering around the Solent*'. During the previous season, on 17th June 1956, the *Bournemouth Queen* had hit the headlines when she struck and sank a Naval sailing dinghy off Fawley. After the collision, she had hove-to and safely rescued the three servicemen who had been in the dinghy and no action was taken against Red Funnel Steamers.

Despite the decision that she should be withdrawn at the end of August 1957, the directors did reconsider the **Bournemouth Queen's** future once more when the matter was placed before them at their meeting held on 28th October 1957. Sadly for the old ship and her followers the 'Statement of earnings and running costs' indicated that she was utterly uneconomic and confirmed the decision that she should be permanently taken out of service. However, it was agreed that *'all useful articles such as flotation seats suitable for use on other vessels be removed before offering the vessel for sale'*.

In December 1957, she was towed away for breaking-up by Van Heyghen Frères, at Ghent, the graveyard of so many other fine excursion ships and ferries over the years.

This just left Red Funnel Steamers with one paddle steamer, the **Princess Elizabeth** and she tended to share the summer excursion business with the **Balmoral** and the **Vecta**.

The bigger problem for the Red Funnel Company was trying to accommodate the growing numbers of private cars needing to be conveyed to and from the Island. The converted tank landing craft **Norris Castle** could carry over 30 at a time but she was very slow. The four other vessels though much faster could in practice carry only about ten cars each. Therefore, Red Funnel Steamers had a new car ferry designed, the order for which they placed with Thornycroft's in 1957. She was to be able to carry 1,200 passengers, or about half that number plus 45 cars or a mix of cars and lorries. The expected cost being £310,000 was approved by the directors who authorised the placing of the order at their meeting on 29th April 1957.

Here we see the **Vecta** *on 11th January 1956 on the slipway at Southampton undergoing annual overhaul and survey. This view shows that her vehicle garage was open, forward of the bridge area, and was not plated in until she was sold to Campbell's nine years later.*

Photo: Red Funnel archives/R G Lock.

Southampton at its best! This photograph shows the first purpose-built Red Funnel car ferry **Carisbrooke Castle** *outward bound for Cowes and one of the Hythe ferries arriving back at Southampton. In the background is the P. & O. liner* **Chusan***. Note that the car ferry and the liner both have the patent Thornycroft smoke-dispelling funnel but unlike the car ferry, in the* **Chusan's** *case, it was added after she was built during a refit in the 1950s.* Photo: Author's collection.

The new car ferry was named **Carisbrooke Castle** when she was launched on 27th November 1958. Her gross tonnage was 672 and she was powered by 8-cylinder Crossley diesels developing a total horsepower of 1,800 b.h.p. giving her a speed of 14.7 knots on trials. She was designed to be able to serve both East and West Cowes and could make the crossing in about 45 minutes. Her passengers were accommodated in a large observation lounge and saloon on the promenade deck with a buffet and bar, toilets and ladies' rest room. She introduced the cafeteria system of serving meals to passengers. The accommodation was described as being

bright, airy and with large windows affording excellent views of the waterway whilst passengers remained seated. In addition there was outside deck space for them too, when the weather was good enough to enjoy it!

In the author's discussions with Red Funnel's erstwhile company secretary, Miss Hazel Nicholson, the other thing she particularly recalled was the **Balmoral's** silver-service dining room. Sadly, that had to give way to a cafeteria following the advent of the car ferry, **Carisbrooke Castle** in 1959 with its self-service catering facilities. In any event, by then it was simply no longer

A busy scene with ocean liners ahead sees the **Balmoral** *coming up Southampton Water at speed whilst working the passenger and car ferry service from Cowes. By this time, with the advent of the Red Funnel car ferries, the* **Balmoral** *normally only worked the ferry service at peak weekends whilst for the rest of her season she ran excursions and docks cruises.* *Photo: Tim Cooper.*

possible to provide waiter service for everyone in the time available on passage.

Interestingly, four years earlier in September 1955, the directors had met to give the matter of the **Balmoral's** dining room their consideration and had resolved that *'Various alterations be made in the dining saloon of the* **Balmoral** *to improve catering facilities and also increase the seating accommodation to 94, also that the small bar on the main deck be converted into a buffet for serving teas and snacks. The works to be carried out by Red Funnel staff at the repair facility at Chapel Wharf'*.

Four years later, following the arrival into service of the **Carisbrooke Castle**, the directors received the quote amounting to £1,125 by Thornycroft's for the conversion of the **Balmoral's** restaurant to self-service. So ended the silver-service era which had prevailed for almost a century.

The arrival of the new **Carisbrooke Castle** into service in May 1959 brought about the disposal of the last remaining Red Funnel paddle steamer, the **Princess Elizabeth**. The possibility of transferring the paddle steamer to the fleet of Cosens & Co. Ltd. was seriously considered but, according to the minutes of the

On 19th May 1958 the **Balmoral** *sailed east from Southampton to Shoreham, Sussex, for special duties to be carried out the next day, in connection with the official 'Opening of the New Harbour Works at Shoreham Harbour'. The harbour works included the new lock gates on the Aldrington Basin. H.R.H. Prince Philip, the Duke of Edinburgh, flew in by helicopter from Buckingham Palace on the morning of 20th May and went aboard the* **Balmoral** *and up on to her bridge for the ceremony. This involved the* **Balmoral** *sailing into the lock and her bows actually breaking the silk ribbon stretched across the lock entrance. From there, the* **Balmoral** *was escorted by the Sussex-based, coastal minesweeper H.M.S.* **Curzon** *beyond the new lock and along the Canal into Aldrington Basin. The Trinity House flag is flying at the* **Balmoral's** *foremast, as His Royal Highness is Master of the Corporation of Trinity House.*

Photo: Red Funnel archives.

directors' meeting held on 23rd May 1958, this was found to be impracticable owing to the requirements of the Ministry of Transport to restore a Steam 3 Passenger Certificate. Whether hers had lapsed by then or whether the difficulties stemmed from the tightening of the rules that might be applied to any new owners is not clear from the records. The paddler had a useful season in 1958 running mainly local excursions, which she finished off with a final trip from the Isle of Wight back to Southampton on 12th September 1958. She remained on standby throughout the

remainder of the autumn and winter. According to *Sea Breezes* magazine, which ran a long article about the Company by D.K. Jones in February 1966, the ***Princess Elizabeth*** made one last sailing to Cowes on 23rd February 1959.

Later that year, on 6th July 1959, the sale of the ***Princess Elizabeth*** to Torbay Steamers Ltd. for £4,000 *'as she lies at the Royal Pier'* was approved by the directors of Red Funnel Steamers. Her new owners had her refitted by J. I. Thornycroft & Co. Ltd. in the winter of 1959/60, following which she did regain her former

Steam 3 Passenger Certificate. In the late spring of 1960 she began running for them at Torquay where she remained, rather uncomfortably, for the next two years. Her sale out of Southampton service was an emotive affair for local people who, like the author, had built up a tremendous affection for the old ship. To them, after over thirty years' service, she was often simply called the 'Elizabeth', or the 'Princess Lizzie' and occasionally even the 'Old Tin Lizzie'.

The same meeting of directors held on 6th July 1959 heard of the trim problems being experienced by the brand-new **Carisbrooke Castle** when carrying loads of 25 tons or more on her foredeck. Before a permanent remedy could be devised by Thornycroft's, it was found that by carrying 10 tons of dry ballast well aft, the matter was at least temporarily solved, enabling loads of up to 40 tons to be carried forward thereafter.

1959 was the year that British Railways took delivery of another vehicle ferry for the Lymington-Yarmouth, Isle of Wight service. Launched on 24th June 1959, she was named **Freshwater** after the earlier paddler of the same name had had the suffix II added to hers. The new ship began service on 21st September 1959. The old ship was withdrawn and sold for further service under the names **Sussex Queen**, later **Swanage Queen,** before finally being scrapped in Belgium in May 1962.

In their own historic biography, J. Samuel White & Co. Ltd., the old **Freshwater's** builders, make a lovely comparison between the little paddler (built 1927, 264 gross tons, 11 knots) and the original (not the motorship) **Crested Eagle** (built 1925, 1,110 gross tons, 20 knots) which was the crack cross-Channel paddle

After the **Princess Elizabeth** *was bought by Torbay Steamers Ltd. in July 1959, they took her round to Thornycroft's at Northam for a refit where she is seen in this photograph dated 23rd March 1960. Note the canvas covering the top of her funnel. The old Red Funnel steam tug* **Neptune** *is thought to lie to the left.*
Photo: Southern Daily Echo.

In 1959, when the paddler **Freshwater** *was replaced by a modern car ferry of the same name, the old* **Freshwater** *(by then with the suffix II added to her name) was sold. She operated, not very satisfactorily, for three more seasons known first as the* **Sussex Queen** *and then in 1961 as the* **Swanage Queen** *as she is seen here, before being scrapped in 1962. Photo: Author's collection.*

Red Funnel's impressive looking tug/tender the **Gatcombe**, *is seen here at the lay-by berth on the Royal Pier at Southampton in 1964 whilst, astern of her, the* **Vecta** *maintains the ferry service.* Photo: David Parsons.

steamer they built for the General Steam Navigation Co. Ltd. With considerable understatement they simply say '*a few years after (the* **Crested Eagle**), *the Southern Railway placed an order for another paddler, less ambitious in design but a very pleasing little ship, the* **Freshwater**'. She was certainly less ambitious but a great little ship, all the same.

Almost 40 years after it was first written, the author found the following press cutting from the *Southern Evening Echo* dated 16th October 1959. They ran a piece by Mr. A. M. C. McGinnity under the headline: **NO MORE PADDLE STEAMERS IN SOUTHAMPTON**. It went on to say:

'*With autumn drawing to its close and the majority of holidaymakers back at home, a familiar sight usually to be seen at the Royal Pier is missing. Craft known to generations of Southamptonians have gone: there are no more paddle steamers - symbols of the summer and balmy breezes, of joy brought to thousands who held them in great affection, awaiting their final trip up the River Itchen to the lay-up berth on the mud at Northam or to lie hidden at Chapel Wharf*'.

What is significant about the press cutting is that the same Mr. Tony McGinnity who, years later went on to become a director of P. & A. Campbell Limited, wrote it. He became involved in ship operations and brokerage and amongst other things, handled the final sale of the **Balmoral** to Craig Inns and the purchase and sale of the **Scillonian** (II) by Campbell's. Finally, he stayed with P. & A. Campbell Ltd. right until their corporate demise.

The author, too, loves to recall the scene from the carriage window when arriving or leaving Southampton by train, first running parallel to the Itchen wharves and quays, then crossing the River. During winter visits in the 1950s it was possible to see all the old steamers, funnels and masts in profusion, laid-up at rest enjoying their winter slumbers and awaiting springtime refits.

The cost of major replating work needing to be done on the hull of the former tank landing craft **Norris Castle** was found to be £20,000. The expenditure was approved on 23rd October 1959 and, as it was going to take several weeks, this caused the first overhaul of the **Carisbrooke Castle** to have to be deferred until the **Norris Castle** could return to service.

Mr. Keith Adams tells that whilst at Southampton, for many years the **Balmoral's** regular engineer was a Mr. McCloud. He was a former deep-sea engineer with Union Castle and had come home to be with his family. Apparently, he kept the engine-room in the **Balmoral** absolutely spotless, just as it is today.

No doubt by mutual consent, Red Funnel Steamers' associated company Cosens & Co. Ltd. managed to keep some of their old paddlers running for several years after the final departure of the **Princess Elizabeth** from the Red Funnel fleet.

In June 1960, their **Monarch**, the former Portsmouth-based, railway-owned paddle steamer **Shanklin**, ran a special trip from Bournemouth to Portsmouth to witness the return of H.M.Y. **Britannia** with H.R.H. Princess Margaret and her new husband Anthony Armstrong-Jones aboard, back from their honeymoon. In fact, the **Monarch** only lasted for the rest of that season and whilst she was newer than Cosens' other Bournemouth ship, the **Embassy**, the **Monarch** was never converted to burn oil and was rather more spartan in her accommodation.

The elderly steam

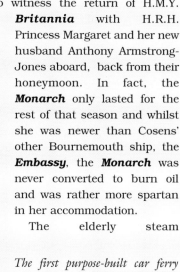

The first purpose-built car ferry ordered by Red Funnel Steamers was named **Carisbrooke Castle** *and was delivered by J. I. Thornycroft & Co. Ltd. in 1959. Her expected arrival on service rendered the last of the Company's paddle steamers, the* **Princess Elizabeth**, *redundant.*

Photo: Red Funnel archives.

reciprocating Red Funnel tug/tender **Paladin** was superseded by the new purpose-built **Gatcombe** in July 1960, whereupon the old ship was sold through brokers H.E. Moss & Co. Ltd. for £5,500. This was exactly the same price as Red Funnel Steamers had paid for her 14 years previously and she was towed away on 5th July

This interesting scene (believed to have been photographed on 31st January 1961) is of the inner harbour or backwater at Weymouth and shows the **Monarch** *(II) being towed out by the harbour tug. On the right, the* **Consul** *and the* **Embassy** *being all that then remained of the fleet of Cosens & Co. Ltd. are in winter hibernation. Whilst the original photograph itself is physically undated, its detail compares very closely with another which appeared on the front page of the* Dorset Evening Echo *on 31st January 1961. In fact what happened was that she had been boarded up ready and towed by the local harbour tug as shown in the photograph, down the backwater and through the Town Bridge. Unfortunately, the weather was then too rough for the long tow to Cork to be contemplated. So the* **Monarch** *waited a whole month until 1st March 1961, when the weather moderated sufficiently for her to be towed away by the deep-sea tug* **Salvonia**, *to Eire for scrapping.*

Photo: Dorset Evening Echo.

1960 to Rotterdam for breaking-up.

In March 1961, the **Monarch** was towed away for breaking-up in Cork. This left Cosens & Co. Ltd. with the 1911-built **Embassy** based at Bournemouth and the ageing 1896-built **Consul** at Weymouth.

Meanwhile, at the end of the previous season, the **Balmoral** whilst on a charter cruise on 26th September 1960 called at the old Victoria Pier at Cowes and in so doing became the last substantial vessel to moor there. Until 1939 the Pier had been in regular use.

To replace their original vehicle ferries **Fishbourne**, **Wootton** and **Hilsea** (which were then to be withdrawn) on the Portsmouth to Fishbourne route, British Railways took delivery of two new ships from Philip & Son Ltd. at Dartmouth. The two ships named **Fishbourne** and **Camber Queen** entered service in July and August respectively in 1961. Both had Voith-Schneider propulsion units, as had the old **Lymington** and the new **Freshwater** both based on the Lymington-Yarmouth run.

The Southern Railway operated a service for vehicles (and passengers) from Portsmouth to Fishbourne (deepwater Wootton Creek near Ryde) using three newly built double-ended ferries, starting in 1927. The first was the **Fishbourne**, *seen here in Portsmouth Harbour near the end of her life, having had the suffix II added to her name, in readiness for her successor's arrival in the summer of 1961.*

Photo: Author's negative library.

As may be seen from this topical press photograph, the **Balmoral** *did quite a lot of damage to herself when she collided with the Sitmar Liner* **Fairsky** *on 21st November 1961 and managed to get her rigging entwined with the liner's anchors.*

Photo: Southern Daily Echo.

That same year saw Cosens & Co. Ltd. celebrate the golden jubilee of their paddle steamer **Embassy**. There was a champagne party organised by the Paddle Steamer Preservation Society (P.S.P.S.) held aboard the vessel at Totland on 25th August, being the 50th anniversary of her launching on the Clyde. On her return sailing to Bournemouth, she flew the special P.S.P.S. flag at her masthead.

Red Funnel Steamers, the Southampton, Isle of Wight and South of England Royal Mail Steam Packet Co. Ltd., celebrated its formal centenary on 10th September 1961, one hundred years after its original board had registered the Company. They produced a now rare, centenary book entitled *The First Hundred Years*, by G.W. O'Connor, a copy of which takes pride of place in the author's collection.

Unjustly, the **Princess Elizabeth** was in trouble at Torquay on more than one occasion. The local harbour authority there, seemingly working to some hidden agenda, decided that they would refuse to allow the bunkering of the **Princess Elizabeth** at Torquay. The reason given was that the ship persistently ignored the weather warning flags put up by their harbour master for the benefit of yachts and small pleasure craft. That was hardly surprising as the local town councillors and their harbour master had no right to interfere with the operations of a steamship as large and seaworthy as the **Princess Elizabeth**.

The matter came to a head with Torquay's deputy town clerk reported in the *Daily Telegraph* of 16th September 1961 as saying 'The **Princess Elizabeth** is not legally bound to obey the weather warnings and the Corporation is not legally bound to provide bunkering facilities'. Unilaterally, they brought about the end of the service and the **Princess Elizabeth** had to be withdrawn for want of fuel oil. Later she operated out of Bournemouth and Weymouth, where, quite rightly, she was made more welcome. Thankfully, the *Daily Telegraph* particularly and a number of other broad sheet newspapers took the plight of the **Princess Elizabeth** seriously and always found room in their columns for serious stories and some lovely photographs of the ship.

The **Balmoral** has, for the most part of her long and splendid career, been reasonably free from breakdowns and accidents. That is not to say she has not had the occasional engine failure, minor groundings and bumps with intransigent piers and the like but, as far as is known, in all her fifty years, once at sea she has never failed to complete any passage through mechanical breakdown.

However on 21st November 1961 something quite serious occurred. The event was well reported in the *Southampton Evening Echo* of the same day and the *County Press* on 25th. It transpires that the **Balmoral**, with no passengers aboard, moved out of Cowes to permit the **Medina** in to take the 15.45 hrs. service to Southampton. The **Balmoral** had been scheduled to take the next sailing an hour later. Caught in the strong tidal current off Cowes,

This is a classic photograph of the Royal Pier at Southampton in about 1960. The **Medina** *and the converted tank landing craft* **Norris Castle** *are alongside but, despite the gathered crowds enjoying the weather, neither vessel seems to be on service. In the centre background lie the New (or Western) Docks and the Union Castle Line's* **Pendennis Castle***, dating from 1958. Also, there is another of their intermediate class ships to the left, whilst the troopship* **Devonshire***, managed by Bibby Line, can just be seen behind the pier pavilion.*
Photo Author's negative library.

the **Balmoral** collided with the Sitmar liner **Fairsky**, anchored in Cowes Roads with 400 passengers from Australia. Greaser Mr. Tom Toleman said to the *Southern Evening Echo* reporter at the time that *'the collision put us all on our backs in the engine room. Just before it happened we were stationary. Then suddenly the skipper rang 'Full Astern', three times. We were just going astern again when suddenly there was a terrific crash'.*

The triple ring for 'Full Astern' which has its equivalent around the globe known as the double or triple rap, would have been the only way Captain Larkin in the wheelhouse of the **Balmoral** could tell his engine room of the impending danger to the ship.

Captain Jorge Petrescu of the **Fairsky** reported that *'his ship was waiting off Cowes and the **Balmoral** was manoeuvring, apparently to go round the liner's bows to reach her anchorage. Suddenly, the ferry was caught in a strong current, which thrust her against my bows'* he said. *'We were locked together for a matter of minutes, chiefly because my anchor hooks caught on the stay of the **Balmoral's** mast'.*

The **Balmoral** suffered significant damage to her starboard side, which was torn open in the incident and where her clinker-built lifeboat was completely smashed. Later that day, the **Balmoral** sailed under her own power to Northam where J. I. Thornycroft & Co. Ltd. were to repair the damage. They also took the opportunity of accelerating the normal January timing of the **Balmoral's** survey and overhaul and the whole task was completed all at once.

The accident had occurred whilst the **Carisbrooke Castle** was herself off-service for annual overhaul. Whilst the **Balmoral** was under repair, the winter service to Cowes was maintained by the **Vecta**, **Medina** and **Norris Castle**.

Thereafter, to aid navigation astern, the **Balmoral** had a periscope fitted into her rather cramped wheelhouse.

The second purpose-built car ferry arrived in March 1962. She was named **Osborne Castle** and had been launched by J. I. Thornycroft & Co. Ltd. on 23rd November 1961, two days after the **Balmoral's** assault on the **Fairsky**. The **Osborne Castle** had clearly evolved from the design of the **Carisbrooke Castle** with improvements made in the light of operational experience gained with the earlier vessel. Indeed, some of these improvements, including extending the boat deck right aft, were then effected on the **Carisbrooke Castle**. Whilst the earlier car ferry was adorned with the then typical Thornycroft patent smoke-dispelling funnel with its prominent flutes and slats, the new ship had an altogether more shapely, oval one. Also, the new ship was of deeper draft so that she could carry more commercial vehicles.

During March 1962, having the two purpose-built car ferries installed on service, the Company was able to announce publicly the withdrawal of both the **Medina** and the **Norris Castle**. In fact, well prior to this, two things had happened. First, the previous July, brokers H.E. Moss & Co. Ltd. had been instructed to find a buyer for both ships with delivery in April or May 1962. While they were trying to do this, on 29th September 1961, the directors then considered the possibility of transferring the **Medina** to Cosens & Co. Ltd. but, despite agreeing to consider the matter again in full detail, nothing came of the proposal.

The **Medina** was sold to M.H. Bland & Co. Ltd. for tender work at Gibraltar. She had a brief underwater survey at Husband's shipyard, across the other side of Southampton Water at Marchwood and then, complete with a noisy whistle-blowing send-off from her fleetmates and with her new Spanish crew, she set sail for The Rock on 28th April 1962. Bland's renamed her **Mons Abyla** and according to *Sea Breezes*, February 1966, she arrived at Gibraltar on 7th May 1962.

After 15 successful years with Red Funnel, the former tank landing craft, **Norris Castle** also made her last trips for the Company in March 1962. The *Southern Evening Echo* dated 14th March reported that she was in service the previous day when she was passed by the new **Osborne Castle**, out on a demonstration run. Given that the pioneering old **Norris Castle** was about the slowest ship afloat in Southampton Water, overtaking her was no great achievement! The **Osborne Castle** entered service on 16th March 1962 due to the **Balmoral** having broken down.

The railway-owned paddle steamer **Ryde** *laid-up at Newhaven undergoing winter refit and overhaul. Red lead paint is being liberally applied to her Sealink blue hull. She had only until the summer of 1969 in operational service before finally becoming redundant.* Photo: Author's collection.

This Weymouth scene dates from July 1964 when the former Red Funnel paddle steamer **Princess Elizabeth** *was getting established after her debut at Torquay where she was made very unwelcome. Astern of her lies the former Cosens paddler* **Consul**, *which tried, not very commercially and certainly unprofitably, to compete with the 'Elizabeth'.* Photo: John Edgington.

The **Norris Castle** found a buyer quite quickly and on 27th May 1962, set sail for the warm waters of the Mediterranean where she was to operate between the Greek Islands under the name **Nereis**. Shortly thereafter she became the **Aghios Dionisios** and had a number of subsequent owners, all with very Greek, unpronounceable names.

The dear old 'Elizabeth' was back in the area for a short while that June. Torbay Steamers had transferred her to new owners named Coastal Steamer and Marine Services Ltd. and she was out of the water on White's slipway prior to starting her new duties. She had been expected to begin sailings from Brighton, Hastings and Eastbourne but in the event she turned up at Bournemouth. The following year in July 1963, she was reported as running a trip from Weymouth to Yarmouth carrying 440 passengers.

After the 1962 season, Cosens & Co. Ltd. found that the

The Southern Railway's stately paddle steamer **Whippingham**, *seen here earlier in her career, and her sister the* **Southsea** *(which was mined in the War) came from Fairfield Shipbuilding & Engineering Co. Ltd. in 1930. She remained coal-fired throughout her life and whilst capable of 16 knots when new, she could barely manage 10 knots when she was withdrawn from service at Portsmouth in December 1962.* Photo: Tim Cooper.

economics of running two elderly paddle steamers were too much and the **Consul**, dating from 1896, was withdrawn and later sold to South Coast and Continental Steamers Ltd. There can have been little hope of the ancient **Consul** ever fulfilling any 'continental' sailings for them and for two unhappy seasons thereafter, she was plagued with mechanical breakdowns. Finally she was sold again and reverted to her old name, the **Duke of Devonshire**, for use as a yacht club headquarters on the Dart until 1967 and was finally broken up at Southampton in 1968. As a result of the sale of the **Consul**, the paddle steamer **Embassy** was the last ship operating for Cosens & Co. Ltd.

That same year saw the end of the lovely but slow and ponderous old railway steamer, the **Whippingham**. Her last trips were on 1st September 1962 and she was towed away from Portsmouth for scrapping at Ghent on 17th May 1963.

After the advent of the car ferries, the **Balmoral** and the **Vecta** had relatively leisurely existences mainly running relief sailings and the Red Funnel Company's excursions and docks cruises. However, on 28th December 1963 the **Carisbrooke Castle**, which was inbound from the Island in thick fog, was in collision with the tanker **Esso Argentina**, which had strayed into the path of the innocent ferry. The result was inevitable as the tanker, more than thirty times the size of the ferry, presented a target that could not be avoided. In the ensuing process of repairing the damage, the **Carisbrooke Castle** needed a new bow ramp and ramp lifting gear. The interruption meant that the Company's proposed introduction of sailings calling at both East and West Cowes had to be postponed.

At the time of the collision, the **Balmoral** was about to sail down to Weymouth where Cosens & Co. Ltd. were to have carried out her annual overhaul at their marine engineering works. Having these facilities within the Red Funnel Group was one reason for their acquiring the majority of the Cosens & Co. Ltd. shares back in 1946. In the event, the **Balmoral** and the **Vecta** were pressed into service in place of the damaged car ferry.

A month later, the **Balmoral** was in the news again, this time in her own right. It seems surprising to us, having now reached the Millennium, that even as late as January 1964, the **Balmoral** still did not have radar fitted. If she had enjoyed this facility, there is little doubt that the next incident would not have occurred. On the afternoon of 21st January 1964, on her 14.45 hrs. sailing to the Island, in thick fog, the **Balmoral** ran aground off Princes Green, Cowes, not 20 feet from the walkway. So close, in fact, that local resident John Plummer had heard the vibrations of the **Balmoral's** engines and had seen the **Balmoral** approaching in the gloom. He had been able to shout to the ship *'Go Hard Ahead'*; sadly all to no avail and at that moment the **Balmoral** struck hard.

Local launches belonging to Mr. M. Luter and Mr. H. Spencer were summoned and they took off all the 45 passengers from the stranded ship which remained fast on the rocks with its cargo of eight vehicles on board. Passengers were landed at Cowes pontoon together with the delayed copies of the *Southern Evening Echo*. Meantime the **Balmoral's** plight had become a local spectacle with hundreds of people watching the floodlit efforts to refloat her *(see opposite)*.

With the aid of the next high tide and a heave from the Company's tug **Thorness**, the **Balmoral** came cleanly off the rocks at 04.10 hrs. the next morning and was towed back to Southampton where her propellers were found to have taken the main force of the accident. She was hauled out onto Thornycroft's slipway where new propellers were fitted, after which she was able to proceed to Weymouth for her anticipated overhaul.

After that little incident and with both car ferries back in action, Red Funnel Steamers were finally able to announce from 27th January 1964 the start of its new service calling (Mondays to Saturdays only) at both East and West Cowes. On Sundays, the car ferries only ran to West Cowes. Southern Vectis buses connected with the ships at both East and West Cowes for taking passengers on to Newport, Ryde and elsewhere.

At the Annual General Meeting of the Company held at the Polygon Hotel in Southampton on 29th May 1964, Company chairman Mr. F. S. Thatcher announced that they were placing an order with J. I. Thornycroft & Co. Ltd. for another new car ferry, this one to replace the **Vecta**. The new ship was expected to be ready for the 1966 season.

The old steam-reciprocating tug/tender **Calshot** was withdrawn from service in 1964, her place having been taken by a new diesel-engined vessel of the same name. Happily, the old **Calshot** found new owners in Eire, where she was given diesel engines and renamed **Galway Bay**. After several years of uncertainty, she has now come back to Southampton, been renamed **Calshot** again and is in the process of being renovated by a small band of dedicated engineers and enthusiasts.

Lights blaze aboard the Balmoral and silhouette some of the hundreds who last night went to Princes Green, Cowes, where, in thick fog, the steamer was aground almost broadside to the promenade, her stern only 20ft. away from the pavement.—Photo: Owen, Newport.

FERRY IS STUCK ALL NIGHT

"Echo" Staff Reporters

THE Red Funnel's Southampton—Isle of Wight steamer Balmoral was refloated on the early morning tide today after

Following her unfortunate grounding at the beginning of the year, in July 1964 the **Balmoral** finally had radar fitted. It speaks volumes for the seamanship of the Red Funnel officers and crews that they had maintained the service to and from the Isle of Wight for over a hundred years in one of the world's busiest waterways with so few mishaps. Hopefully radar would make it an even safer route.

At the end of 1964, British Railways, in their absolute wisdom, decided to dispense with the traditional look of all their ships, the Isle of Wight ferries included, by the introduction of their (hideous) new fleet livery. Blue hulls, grey superstructure (later white), red funnels with an ultra narrow black top band and the new double arrow device were all now part of the new image and would shortly be applied to their fleets.

In May 1965, the Portsmouth Harbour Ferry Co. ordered two new ships of revolutionary, double-ended design. Just like the **Balmoral** back in 1947/48 and many Red Funnel ships before her, the order went to the Woolston shipyard of J. I. Thornycroft & Co. Ltd. The new ferries were built in tandem and launched virtually simultaneously on 5th April 1966, being named the **Portsmouth Queen** and **Gosport Queen**.

The paddle steamer **Princess Elizabeth** *was withdrawn from Red Funnel service early in 1959 and was then sold. Following refit at Thornycroft's she found useful work based at Torquay and later Bournemouth then Weymouth. She was finally withdrawn after her 1965 season and, as seen in this photograph, was laid-up at Weymouth where she was offered for sale.*

Photo: Ken Saunders/Richard Clammer collection.

This photograph was taken in the summer of 1968, the **Balmoral's** *last season working for Red Funnel Steamers. In glorious afternoon sunshine, she looks to be just arriving at the Royal Pier from the Isle of Wight. Her skipper has just kicked the engines astern to take the way off her as she comes gently alongside.*
Photo: Tim Cooper.

At the end of the 1968 season, the **Balmoral** *was ultimately displaced from the Red Funnel Fleet to make room for their latest purpose-built, drive-on commercial vehicle, car and passenger ferry. Here we see the new* **Norris Castle** *and the older* **Carisbrooke Castle** *at Southampton's Royal Pier in June 1970.*
Photo: John Edgington.

At the end of the 1965 season, the paddle steamer **Sandown** ran her final sailings on 19th September and then sailed to Newhaven for final lay-up. She was towed away to Ghent for scrapping the following February.

By that time, the author was well into his career in banking with the Midland Bank (now part of HSBC) at Newhaven where he had been posted since 1963. The Portsmouth-based Isle of Wight ferries were all regular visitors there to the marine workshops owned by British Railways, so too were their cross-Channel boats from near and far.

Throughout the 1960s, Blue Funnel Cruises and the Portsmouth Harbour Ferry Company's Green Funnel fleet were also busy with cruising, the latter in addition to their cross-harbour duties. They, and many smaller outfits too, cruised across to the Island at Cowes, Yarmouth and elsewhere, up

Southampton Water to view the liners and also up the beautiful Beaulieu River.

Following the announcement at the Red Funnel Company Annual General Meeting in May the previous year, that the **Vecta** was to be replaced by a new car ferry, it came as no surprise when the time for her to be withdrawn finally came.

After the initial problems with her temperamental Voith-Schneider propulsion units, which were removed altogether and replaced with diesel-electric drive after the War, the **Vecta** had proved herself to be a popular and reliable member of the fleet. Whilst she had been a regular vessel on the main Cowes passage, she was also a very useful excursion ship and was often used for tender work, especially for the Cie. Générale Transatlantique (French Line) ship, the **Liberté**.

The *Southern Evening Echo* dated 15th September 1965, in

This scene is of the Royal Pier at Southampton on 19th September 1965. Here we see the **Osborne Castle** *and the* **Vecta,** *the latter having been inspected and bought for use by P. & A. Campbell Ltd. on the Bristol Channel. Still in Red Funnel colours and (for now) retaining the name* **Vecta,** *she set sail the next day bound for Land's End and Cardiff.* Photo: Tim Cooper.

The **Balmoral** *is seen here at Cowes on 7th September 1968 and this was her final visit to Cowes as a Red Funnel ferry before moving on to operate for Campbell's in the Bristol Channel from 1969 onwards.*

Photo: Edwin Wilmshurst.

announcing her imminent withdrawal, reported that the ship was to be sold for use in the Bristol Channel by P. & A. Campbell Ltd. She would finish service at Southampton on 18th September and be handed over two days later. For the tax purposes of Campbell's owners, she would be registered in the name of Townsend Car Ferries Ltd., another of their subsidiaries.

Complete with a Red Funnel captain and engineers, but with a crew provided by Campbell's, the **Vecta** set sail around Land's End and up to Cardiff where her new owners planned to evaluate her for use on their wide variety of Bristol Channel routes. This they did and, still named **Vecta**, she remained in Red Funnel colours for the remainder of the season running in the Bristol Channel until 11th October 1965. On 12th October 1965 she then came back round to Weymouth for mechanical attention at Cosens & Co. Ltd. where she stayed until the following February.

The new Red Funnel Steamers car ferry, named **Cowes Castle**

was launched at J. I. Thornycroft & Co. Ltd. on 11th October 1965 and entered service two months later.

Meanwhile, the paddle steamer **Princess Elizabeth**, much missed on the Southampton scene following her withdrawal in 1959, had spent three years at Weymouth following Cosens & Co. Ltd.'s sale of the **Consul**.

By 1965, the **Princess Elizabeth** had changed hands again, this time to Coastal Steamers (Weymouth) Ltd. For 1965 she was advertised as running trips from the Pleasure Pier at Weymouth to the Isle of Wight on Wednesdays and Fridays, price 25/- (£1.25). She was billed to leave Weymouth at 09.30 hrs. and to return at 20.00 hrs., allowing 3 hours ashore, which must have made the voyage quite an extended one, especially when it was rough! When she ended her service there, she was laid-up at Weymouth after which there was an abortive plan a year later for her to become a floating casino but nothing became of this.

The following season turned out to be the last for the **Embassy** and, axiomatically, the end of pleasure steamer operations for Cosens & Co. Ltd. (but they continued with their marine engineering business for many years thereafter). At 18.00 hrs. on 28th July 1966, whilst on one of her regular passages from Totland to Bournemouth, the **Embassy** broke down in the North Channel near Hurst Castle. She had 350 passengers aboard when a fractured driving arm caused part of her port paddle wheel to drop into the sea. There she anchored whilst a tug was sent to assist but not before the wind had risen to near gale force. The tow home to Poole by the tug **Wendy Ann II** was a long and uncomfortable trip, finally ending at 01.30 hrs. the next day when her exhausted but very relieved passengers were able to go ashore at Poole and be taken home by bus.

She was repaired and operated until 22nd September 1966 when her career permanently ended. Put up for sale at an asking price of £7,000, she found no buyers other than the shipbreakers, Van Heyghen Frères at Ghent, to whose yard she was towed from Weymouth on 25th May 1967.

All three Red Funnel car ferries went off service in turn for their overhauls at the beginning of 1967 during which one of the two older vessels, the 'Osborne', was to have her passenger accommodation considerably improved and enlarged. The **Balmoral** was called on for extra duty during this period after which she was to go to Weymouth in March for her annual overhaul at Cosens'. However, Red Funnel was now fully geared up for the transport of cars, vans, lorries and trailers, as well as passengers, so the **Balmoral** was those days normally only needed on the passage service to Cowes on peak weekend sailings. The rest of the time she was either running excursions or was lying tantalisingly, but idle, at the lay-by berth at Southampton's Royal Pier.

It says much for the affection in which the **Princess Elizabeth** was held nationally, no doubt partly because of her valiant wartime service, that her fortunes should have been followed so closely by the national heavyweight press, especially by the *Daily Telegraph*. On 9th October 1967 they faithfully recorded the passing of the old ship into the hands of breakers at Woolston.

Conveniently indeed, whilst the author was on a training course which took him from the Midland Bank at Newhaven, to the bank's training school at Marland House, Southampton, the 'Elizabeth' was towed up from Weymouth on 24th October 1967. She had been sold for scrapping to Metrex Ltd. of Newhaven but they sold her on to Ferry Services and Supplies Ltd. Woolston, Southampton.

Crossing back and forth to Woolston on the chain ferry each day, for the rest of his course the author had to witness the prospect of what seemed to him to be the heartless butchering of his lovely ship, the **Princess Elizabeth,** and the removal of her beautiful machinery. Beside her on the quay, were heaped the scrapped remains of the last Princess flying boats too.

In Mr. Tim Cooper's **Balmoral** reminiscences, written for inclusion in this book, he recounts the arrival of the famous Cunard liner **Queen Mary** following her final Atlantic crossing from New York. He says:

*'My own particular celebration came on 27th September 1967 on the occasion of the Queen Mary's final arrival in Southampton from New York. The trip to meet and accompany the liner was fully subscribed and the **Balmoral**, **Cowes Castle**, **Gatcombe** and **Calshot** (other commentators mention the **Osborne Castle**) were scheduled for the excursion. The vessels turned and left Southampton's Royal Pier at 13.00 hrs that day, in line ahead but only the **Balmoral** had a Class III certificate and left the others by the Forts off Southsea and sailed on alone to The Nab. Shortly after our arrival there, the **Queen Mary** was observed coming up past Dunnose. Soon she turned to port at The Nab, still making over 20 knots, and swept past us without acknowledging the greeting sounded on our whistle. In the **Balmoral** the skipper had clearly told his chief engineer that when he rang down for 'Full Ahead' he meant just that! I had*

*May and June 1966 was the period of the economically devastating seamen's strike and this view must have been photographed fairly early during the strike, as later many more ships had to be crowded into dock. This magnificent photograph shows the **Balmoral** lying, under-worked and idle at the Royal Pier but, as far as is known, not strikebound. In the background, at Southampton's New (or Western) Docks we see the strikebound **Reina Del Mar**, once belonging to Pacific Steam Navigation Co. Ltd. but then more recently owned by Union Castle Mail Steamship Co. Ltd. Moored inside her is her fleetmate, the **Edinburgh Castle** and astern of them the **S.A. Vaal** (ex-**Transvaal Castle**).*

Photo: C.C.A. archives.

RED FUNNEL STEAMERS

TUESDAY, 31st OCTOBER, 1967

CRUISE TO SEE THE DEPARTURE OF THE R.M.S.

'QUEEN MARY'

AND ESCORT HER TOWARDS COWES ROADS

THE FINAL DEPARTURE OF THIS WORLD FAMOUS LINER
FROM THE PORT OF SOUTHAMPTON TO LONG BEACH, CALIFORNIA, U.S.A.

Depart Southampton (Royal Pier) 09.30 hrs.   Back about 11.30 hrs.

FARE 10/-
Children Three and Under Fourteen years, Half Fare

REFRESHMENTS OBTAINABLE ON BOARD   FULLY LICENSED BARS
OBTAINED IN ADVANCE FROM THE RED FUNNEL STEAMERS
OFFICE, ROYAL PIER.

...Packet Company, Charterers.

RED FUNNEL STEAMERS

PASSENGER AND VEHICLE SERVICE

BETWEEN

SOUTHAMPTON AND WEST AND EAST COWES

UNTIL 22nd SEPTEMBER, 1968

AND

EXCURSION PROGRAMME

1st SEPTEMBER to 15th SEPTEMBER, 1968

REFRESHMENT FACILITIES AVAILABLE ABOARD ALL VESSELS

THE ABOVE SERVICES AND EXCURSIONS ARE LIABLE TO ALTERATION AT SHORT NOTICE AND THE TIME OF ARRIVAL MAY VARY, BEING SUBJECT TO WEATHER AND/OR OTHER CONDITIONS OUTSIDE THE CONTROL OF THE COMPANY

EXCURSIONS by M.V. 'BALMORAL' or other vessel

SUNS.	SEPTEMBER 1st, 8th, 15th	At 10 45	To RYDE, SOUTHSEA, SHANKLIN, SANDOWN and CRUISE ALONG ISLAND CO... RETURN TIMES—From SHANKLIN 15 50, SANDOWN 16 10, SOUTHSEA (South... (Clarence Pier) 17 20, RYDE 18 20.
MON.	SEPTEMBER 2nd	At 10 45	To RYDE, SOUTHSEA, SHANKLIN, SANDOWN, and CRUISE ALONG ISLAND... RETURN TIMES—From SHANKLIN 15 50, SANDOWN 16 10, SOUTHSEA (South... (Clarence Pier) 17 20, RYDE 18 20.
TUES.	SEPTEMBER 3rd	At 09 00	TO RYDE, SOUTHSEA, SANDOWN, SHANKLIN and ROUND THE ISLAND RETURN TIMES—From SANDOWN 17 40, SHANKLIN 18 00, SOUTHSEA (Sou... RYDE 19 40
	SEPTEMBER 10th	At 09 00	To RYDE, SOUTHSEA, SANDOWN, SHANKLIN RETURN TIMES—From SANDOWN 17 00, SHANKLIN 17 20, SOUTHSEA (Sou... (Clarence Pier) 18 50, RYDE 19 20.
WEDS.	SEPTEMBER 4th, 11th	At 10 45	To RYDE RETURN TIME from RYDE 17 45
THURS.	SEPTEMBER 5th, 12th	At 09 00	TO RYDE, SOUTHSEA, SANDOWN, SHANKLIN, and ROUND THE ISLAND RETURN TIMES—From SANDOWN 17 40, SHANKLIN 18 00, SOUTHSEA (Sou... RYDE 19 40

DAILY — COMBINED STEAMER and COACH TOUR
ROUND THE ISLAND by Southern Vectis Coaches from COWES.
Leaving SOUTHAMPTON by 09 15 Steamer.   Inclusive fare 25/-.

FARES			Day return	Single
To Sandown or Shanklin	..	..	16s. 0d.	9s. 0d.
„ Southsea or Ryde	..	..	11s. 0d.	7s. 6d.
Round the Island	..	..	22s. 6d.	—
Cruise along the Island Coast	..	..	17s. 6d.	—

DAILY — CIRCULAR STEAMER and C...
Steamer to RYDE, Southern Vectis Omnibu...
COWES to SOUTHAMPTON.

SEASON TICKETS AVAILABLE FO...
Between Southampton and Cowes, 40/- per...
excepted), obtainable at the Company's Ticket...

The regulations of the Board of Trade, limiting the number of passengers the vessel is entitled to carry, are strictly observed.

*certainly never sailed so fast on the **Balmoral** before and do not think I have done so since. We made a thrilling dash up Spithead and the North Channel, vibrating every rivet, a thin trail of black smoke stretching out astern, overhauling every other craft on the water as we did so'.*

As a sequel, on the last day of October 1967, Red Funnel Steamers (and most of the other operators of the area) ran trips in connection with the last ever departure of the three-funnelled **Queen Mary**. She was to sail to Long Beach, California, U.S.A. where she had been bought for static use as a hotel and convention centre. The **Balmoral**, the car ferry **Osborne Castle** and the tug/tender **Gatcombe** all went out loaded with passengers to witness the sad event - which many saw as a closing chapter in the story of the British passenger liner. The tug/tender **Calshot** was assisting the **Queen Mary's** departure and had Cunard officials on board for a private party to witness the occasion.

That same month Red Funnel Steamers ordered their fourth car ferry from Thornycroft's. To be named **Norris Castle**, after her pioneer namesake, the new ship was due for delivery late in1968. In fact there had been two previous **Norris Castles**. One was the well-known former tank landing craft and the other, a less well-known launch of 24 tons, which had operated the Company's subordinate service between East and West Cowes until war broke out in 1939.

During the 1967/68 winter refit of the **Carisbrooke Castle**, she received the same improvements to her saloon, buffet bar and other passenger accommodation that had been given to the 'Osborne' the previous year. That brought the standards on the three current car ferries reasonably up-to-date.

In May 1968 came the amazing announcement that the 41-year-old **Princess Elizabeth** had once again evaded the nautical Grim Reaper. Only her machinery had been removed at Woolston so now without engines, the ship was towed to a mud berth on Hayling Island where, at Northney, she was to become the centrepiece of their proposed new marina. Another year later nothing had become

of this plan, save for the author and other like-minded people visiting the ship from time to time. Access was possible over a rather frail gangplank, for those who did not mind getting wet and muddy in the process. She changed hands again before eventually being towed to London where she enjoyed yet another career, this one lasting almost 18 years, in static roles for several different owners. From first-hand experience, the author can attest she was quite successful as a floating nightclub and restaurant and an evening aboard was nostalgic and pleasant. She is now berthed in Paris.

The summer season of 1968 found the **Balmoral**, now Red Funnel Steamers' last remaining excursion ship, still billed to take many day-trips and excursions, just as she had done since soon after she was built. That June she was sailing to Ryde, Southsea, Shanklin and Sandown and, on Thursdays only, she sailed right round the Island. The price for the whole trip was 22/6 (£1.13).

Sunday 16th June was a special day when the **Balmoral** ran a Coastal Cruising Association charter from Southampton to Southsea, Littlehampton (where landing and boarding was by tender) Worthing Pier and thereafter cruised past Brighton. On the return journey, the **Balmoral** also called at Portsmouth Harbour to make it easier for passengers travelling by train to make their connections.

September 1968 found the last railway-owned paddle steamer from Portsmouth, the **Ryde**, on charter to the famous gin family of Gilbeys. The records show that it took just 15 tons of best Welsh coal to steam round to London's Tower Pier where she arrived on 12th September to undertake some promotional work and cruises for Gilbeys. Thereafter, she sailed back to Newhaven for lay-up and an uncertain future. She was recommissioned again for 1969, which was to prove to be not only her last season in service, but also the final year that Portsmouth was to be regularly served by that once so popular class of vessel, the paddle steamer. Early in 1970, she was sold for static use in the Isle of Wight, where, in a muddy berth she remains forlornly to this day.

Sadly, for Southampton and the Isle of Wight, the immediate future of the **Balmoral** was an unpleasant certainty. With the Company's fourth car ferry, the new **Norris Castle**, due in service by December, the **Balmoral** was to run a few final excursions before being taken out of service and placed on the sale list.

The *Isle of Wight County Press* newspaper carried a large advertisement for various trips, billed as *'Final Excursions by m.v. Balmoral'*. She ran her final sailing to Cowes on Saturday 7th September 1968.

She then made four more excursion sailings including her last which was 'Round the Isle of Wight' on 12th, but no more to Cowes. The *Southern Evening Echo* ran a similar advertisement for what should have been her very last sailing for Red Funnel Steamers, planned for Sunday 15th September 1968. In the event, the country was lashed with torrential rain and flooding and the entire final day's sailing was cancelled. No substitute trip was ever offered and the almost twenty-year-old **Balmoral** was denied what should have been her benefit.

The **Balmoral** had originally entered service at a time when those lucky enough to have a family car at all probably had one that would be a classic car today. By 1968, the number of passengers wishing to go on excursions by sea was falling away rapidly and the tremendous growth in the carriage of cars and other vehicles by sea (for which the **Balmoral** was really not well equipped) had now to be catered for more or less exclusively. For the first time in her career the **Balmoral** faced redundancy and was put up for sale.

She was placed into the hands of Cory Brothers Shipping Ltd., brokers, and the asking price was £65,000.

This photograph dates from 16th April 1969 and is very significant. On the left, the original **Shearwater** *hydrofoil has newly arrived at the Royal Pier from Sicily and will soon take up the high-speed service to Cowes which began commercially in May 1969, under the name Red Funnel Seaflight. Seen on the right, the* **Balmoral** *had that day, just returned from Thornycroft's with a freshly painted red and black funnel and cream upperworks. Only the funnel will be repainted again at Cosens' Weymouth yard, the following week (this time all-white) prior to the vessel going on her first season's charter to P. & A. Campbell Ltd. at Bristol.*

Photo: Keith Adams.

Setting the Scene for the White Funnel Era

During the same hopeful period that Red Funnel Steamers were busily struggling to throw off the ravages of the War by rebuilding their profitable business and their fleet (having also acquired the majority of Cosens & Co. Ltd.) there were two distressing situations developing simultaneously in North and South Wales. In the end, the one that was to prove terminal in many ways became a life-giving donor for the other.

All the while, there was a plethora of smaller boat operators whose overheads were much lower, offering trips on both sides of the Bristol Channel, the Avon, the River Severn and at various points round the coast of West and North Wales too.

By the late 1950s, it was becoming all too apparent that several of Britain's coastal passenger and excursion shipping companies, especially those placing undue reliance on summer-only trade, were beginning to lose the financial struggle. Those that had failed to keep up with the times or, through other circumstances, found themselves with larger, obsolete vessels and insufficient business to help finance their replacements, were in the most trouble.

The subsequent destinies of two such companies have a significant bearing on our story.

The first of these was P. & A. Campbell Ltd. established in Bristol in 1888 (but not incorporated until 1893). Traditionally their Bristol Channel based excursion ships ran a vast network of services linking South Wales ports with their opposite numbers on the English side. They served Welsh ports and harbours including Newport, Cardiff, Penarth, Barry, Porthcawl, Swansea, Mumbles and Tenby. On the English side, they operated to and from Bristol, Portishead, Clevedon, Weston-super-Mare, Minehead, Lynmouth, Ilfracombe and Clovelly. Lundy Island (21 miles west of Ilfracombe) was a popular destination too. In addition they ran some special trips farther afield and some to remoter harbours and piers, which were much appreciated. As we read earlier, they had vessels operating to and from various resorts on the South Coast of England too.

The second operator to feel the cold economic wind was the Liverpool & North Wales Steamship Co. Ltd., established in Liverpool in 1891 and subsequently reconstituted shortly before we take up their story. Throughout the summer months, they ran excursions and cruises from Liverpool, Llandudno and Menai Bridge along the North Welsh Coast, occasional trips up the Manchester Ship Canal and also around Anglesey. In addition they used to run a service once or twice a week to the Isle of Man (54 miles north-west of Llandudno).

By the early 1950s P. & A. Campbell Ltd., whilst having a superficially fine fleet of excursion paddle steamers, had to face the fact that its fleet was already fast becoming obsolete and owed its origins to an era which, lamentably, was long gone and never likely to return. That must have been a bitter disappointment to management and passengers alike, as their two newest vessels had been built brand new, straight after the War. Sadly, the business for which they were specifically constructed never re-materialised. Pride, hope, faith and optimism were the forces that drove the building of the ***Bristol Queen*** and the ***Cardiff Queen***, spurred-on by Campbell's natural desire to offer the fullest possible service as soon as they could after the War ended.

P. & A. Campbell Ltd. had lost no less than five ships during the War, and two more were unfit for further service, so something had to be done quickly.

With the benefit of hindsight that makes all decision-making seem simple, P. & A. Campbell Ltd. had already unwittingly sown

the seeds of its ultimate destruction having rather boldly contracted with Ailsa Shipbuilding Co. Ltd. at Troon for the building of a new steamship just before the War.

This was not just any new steamer but the truly splendid **Empress Queen**!

No sooner had she been built than she was called-up by the Admiralty, renamed **Queen Eagle** and went off to war from which she returned over six years later to an economic climate that had totally changed.

A twin screw, 20 knot, turbine steamer of 1,781 gross tons, the **Empress Queen** was too large, too fast and too expensive for the limited business that was available on her return to her owners after the hostilities. She had been tried for four seasons at Brighton and then at Torquay. When, despite Campbell's superhuman efforts to find a solution, the long distance and cross-Channel work for which she was originally designed failed to re-materialise and could not be found sufficiently elsewhere, she was put up for sale in 1952.

Finally, after an indecently long lay-up, in 1955 she was disposed of to the Greeks, with as much dignity as

Left: This powerful view of the **Cardiff Queen** *was taken towards the very end of the 1965 season where she is seen at Cardiff Pier Head on 26th September 1965. Two days previously she had gone aground at the notorious Horseshoe Bend in the Avon and had been hastily patched up for the final few sailings. Here we see her, very rusty, deckrails buckled and looking thoroughly neglected. Perhaps she understood the full implications of the former Red Funnel ferry* **Vecta**, *having been acquired by Campbell's a week earlier? Sadly, the* **Cardiff Queen** *sailed for only one more season before being withdrawn and scrapped. At the time she was not even twenty years old.* Photo: Malcolm McRonald.

possible. Following this, her new owners, Kavounides Bros. renamed her **Philippos** and her almost new turbines were replaced with economic diesel engines. She served them very successfully in the Mediterranean for many years thereafter, before finally catching fire.

Sadly, this book about the **Balmoral** is not the place for a fitting epitaph for the **Empress Queen**; arguably the finest pleasure steamer ever. To go further in the way of adulation, laudable though that would be, would take our story too far off-course.

However, despite this major disappointment, the directors of P. & A. Campbell Ltd. were not disposed to taking fright easily.

Their remaining pre-war vessels, the **Ravenswood** (built 1891), **Britannia** (built 1896), **Glen Usk** (built 1914) and **Glen Gower** (built 1922), were all reaching dowager status and could not reasonably be expected to last a lot longer. However, each was destined to be nurtured along for the foreseeable future.

Towards the end of the War, but long before it became known to them that the

Empress Queen was to become a commercial failure, P. & A. Campbell Ltd. made further major decisions that would turn out to be crucial. Believing and hoping that business would take off after the War, they set in motion plans for the conception of more new paddle steamers as soon as government post-war ship-building regulations permitted them to have the steel.

Only two were ever built. The first was delivered in 1946 by Charles Hill & Sons Ltd. at Bristol and was named **Bristol Queen**. As Hill's were too busy to do the second, named **Cardiff Queen**, she came a year later from the well-known Govan yard of Fairfield Shipbuilding & Engineering Co. Ltd. on the Clyde.

*The **Empress Queen**, always a good looking vessel, looks absolutely superb with her French grey paint having been brought a strake lower as she is seen here at Southampton in 1948.*

Photo: Tim Cooper collection.

Like the **Empress Queen** which was in a class of her own, the new **Bristol Queen** and **Cardiff Queen** were amongst the finest British paddle steamers ever built. However, even their quintessence could not ultimately save them either and for P. & A. Campbell Ltd. the capital investment in the two new paddle steamers was to prove crippling.

These superb vessels were large, sleek, fast and extremely handsome two-funnellers but like all the other 'summer butterflies' around our coasts, were designed only to make a living for their owners for a few months in the summer each year. From October, through the winter and until the following Easter, not only did they earn nothing but even when laid-up they were a drain on already stretched resources.

This was a particularly bad period for Campbell's who by now, were haemorrhaging seemingly fatally. In fact, despite some ominously worrying symptoms, they were not just about to die.

However, in his letter from his home at Walton, near Clevedon, to the author, chartered accountant Mr. Clifton Smith-Cox wrote as follows: '*In 1952, after a couple of very bad years, the then Chairman, Mr A. Roy Boucher, invited me to become a member of the Board. I did and in 1954, I became joint managing director and in 1955, sole managing director. It was a condition of the Westminster Bank's willingness to help support the Company that I took on this office*'. Another requirement was that sailings on the South Coast should be significantly curtailed if not stopped and

*P. & A. Campbell Ltd.'s ancient paddler **Ravenswood**, having had several major facelifts throughout her life, is seen here in the Avon towards the end of her 65-year career, following which, in 1955, she was scrapped. She was originally built in 1891 and then had two funnels, conventional ornately decorated paddle boxes, large saloon windows along the whole length of the ship and a completely open bridge.*

Photo: Bristol Evening Post.

that the best units of the fleet should be concentrated on the Bristol Channel.

So, in his own modest words, that is how Mr. Smith-Cox took control of Campbell's and finally brought about a change in their fortunes that sustained them against all the odds for almost the next thirty years.

However, this success, limited though it was, was not attained without considerable pain and the inference contained in the offer of support from the Bank was that the poorer units of the fleet and the loss-making routes had no future at all.

Therefore, the old **Ravenswood** did not operate during the 1955 season and was sold for scrap that October having failed her survey the previous May. The **Britannia** was the next to go and she, like the **Ravenswood**, was broken up at Newport at the end of 1956. Shiplovers on the Bristol Channel were united in their sadness at the withdrawal and demolition of these two grand old ladies aged 65 and 60 years, respectively.

For the 1957 season, P. & A. Campbell Ltd. then chartered the **Crested Eagle**, the same vessel that old Captain Clarke at Red Funnel Steamers had considered buying back in 1947. She was the former **New Royal Lady** (later briefly the **Royal Lady**) built at Scarborough in 1938. A small 248 gross ton motorship, now owned by the General Steam Navigation Co. Ltd., Campbell's used her to try to keep alive their Sussex and South Coast sailings now that the **Glen Gower** was back on the Bristol Channel.

The operation was not a success and when it was withdrawn at the end of September 1957, so too ended regular sailings by the ships of P. & A. Campbell Ltd. on the South Coast, save for odd trips later and sorties by the **Queen of the Isles** on charter at the end of 1968 and for the summer of 1969.

The **Crested Eagle** was then sold to Malta where, as the **Imperial Eagle**, she sailed on (and on) mainly between Malta and Gozo. When the author visited Malta in 1996, there he found the former **Crested Eagle** where, having lain derelict for years and now barely afloat in a backwater at Valletta, she was reportedly waiting

Campbell's paddle steamer **Britannia** *dated from 1896 and lasted just one more year after the old* **Ravenswood**. *She too had been heavily rebuilt on more than one occasion throughout her long and popular life.   Photo: Bristol Evening Post.*

to be scuttled with a number of other ancient vehicle ferries, to start a new artificial reef for divers.

For P. & A. Campbell Ltd., 1958 was yet another bad year and the hoped-for surge of business in July and August, upon which excursion ship companies all rely so heavily for the material part of their revenue, failed them. The weather was appalling and any conceivable improvement would have come too late to alter the sequence of events that followed.

When the much-missed Liverpool & North Wales Steamship Co. Ltd. went out of business following the 1962 season, their motorship, the **St. Trillo** *was bought from their liquidator for use by P. & A. Campbell Ltd. Here we see her on 16th September 1962 on her final sailing for L & NWS, flying her farewell pennants. Little did they know that from 1963 onwards, she would be back, sailing for P. & A. Campbell Ltd.* Photo: Malcolm McRonald.

In August 1958, the directors of P. & A. Campbell Ltd. reluctantly concluded that it would be in the best interests of the Debenture Holder to appoint a Receiver.

Nevertheless, Mr. Smith-Cox felt able to ask another chartered accountant contact of his, Mr. Roland Wickenden, for help. Mr. Wickenden ran George Nott Industries Ltd., which had recently taken over the fast expanding Townsend Bros. Ferries Ltd. and operation of their then lone car ferry **Halladale**, running from Dover to Calais.

Mr. Smith-Cox was able to demonstrate that there were clear advantages to Mr. Wickenden's venture, then still in an embryonic state, if it owned the ailing P. & A. Campbell Ltd. and was able to claim group tax relief on its past loss-making operations. A deal was therefore struck under which P. & A. Campbell Ltd. was transferred to Mr. Wickenden's empire and a new symbiotic relationship thereby began that was to last many years.

Mr. Clifton Smith-Cox kept a fairly free hand and seemed able to run the business as only he knew best but, as we shall see throughout, there was never any spare money to spend on the ships.

The 30th August 1959 was the unhappy time that the **Glen Usk**, outward bound for Clevedon, earned notoriety by grounding on the Horseshoe Bend in the Avon with 600 passengers aboard. She was refloated on the later tide with the aid of two local tugs but not until her passengers had all been led ashore, knee deep in the noxious, glutinous, Avon sludge!

One season into their new parentage and Campbell's two-funnelled paddle steamer, the **Glen Gower** that had by then been laid-up for two years, was sold for scrap to Belgian shipbreakers in April 1960.

That only left them with the pre-war, coal-fired **Glen Usk** and the two post-war paddle steamers. At the time, fine though she was, the **Bristol Queen** was also without work and lay in Penarth Dock whilst Campbell's management were actively looking for other work for her outside the Bristol Channel.

Under their new ownership within the George Nott Industries Group, it became possible for Campbell's to re-commission the two 'Queens' but with that, the inevitable price to pay was that the old **Glen Usk** would remain laid-up, never be converted to oil-firing and ultimately be broken up.

However, the **Glen Usk** was still rusting away forlornly, in dock at Cardiff when the other key event alluded to previously, happened.

This stems from the fate of the old Liverpool & North Wales Steamship Co. Limited. The whole story is told in Mr. F.C. Thornley's lovely little book entitled *Past and Present Steamers of North Wales* (T. Stephenson & Son Ltd., Prescot)

Their fleet had grown old gracefully and whilst they were still much loved, their revenue earning capacity was at the mercy of the northern summer climate and dwindling numbers of passengers, who by then preferred to take the family car for a run rather than go on a steamer trip in the Irish Sea.

Their demise was a particularly emotive business, softened only by these facts. Their supporters were gradually becoming inured to the idea that all was not well with their beloved company, whose offices at 40 Chapel Street, Liverpool assumed the qualities of a shrine towards the end. The Company's gradual death was a prolonged affair which really began with its reorganisation ten years previously and was seriously gathering pace by January 1962 when it was announced publicly that the **St. Seiriol** was to be withdrawn, for what was described as an 'economy measure'.

For the previous quarter century, the Liverpool & North Wales Steamship Co. Ltd. had operated three ships. All were built at Fairfield Shipbuilding & Engineering Co. Ltd., Govan, which shipyard later also built Campbell's **Cardiff Queen**. The oldest and largest was the turbine-powered **St. Tudno** which was indeed an impressive vessel. She was built in 1926, carried up to 2,493 passengers at about 19 knots and was of 2,326 gross tons.

Next, in 1931, the same shipyard built another steam turbine vessel, the **St. Seiriol,** which at 1,586 gross tons and carrying

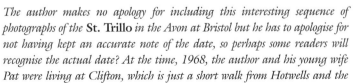

The author makes no apology for including this interesting sequence of photographs of the **St. Trillo** *in the Avon at Bristol but he has to apologise for not having kept an accurate note of the date, so perhaps some readers will recognise the actual date? At the time, 1968, the author and his young wife Pat were living at Clifton, which is just a short walk from Hotwells and the Cumberland Basin. In this sequence, the* **St. Trillo** *had a very good load of passengers as she came up the river to Hotwells prior to hurrying back down on a fast ebbing tide. It was probably Sunday 21st July 1968 when she was due to sail from Cardiff at 12.55 hrs. to Penarth, Weston, Clevedon and up the Avon to Bristol, before retracing her steps all the way back to Cardiff. As can be seen, the* **St. Trillo** *has already been fitted with the radar installation from the* **Bristol Queen**. *Photos: Author.*

1,556 passengers was a smaller and somewhat slower version of her elder sister, the **St. Tudno**.

Lastly, in 1936 came the diminutive motorship **St. Trillo**. Until the War, she was named **St. Silio** and she was very different from the two larger ships. She was just 314 gross tons, powered by Crossley diesels, surprisingly had two funnels (the forward one of which was a dummy) and carried 568 passengers on mainly short, local trips.

The most striking thing about the tall, yellow-funnelled **St. Tudno** was the generous amount of uncluttered deck space available for her passengers. All the more so when, as was sadly often the case towards the end, she had only a few passengers on board. The shelter deck and the promenade boat deck were literally vast. One particularly leisurely trip the author then

aged 10, made in her during in the summer of 1957 from Llandudno to Menai Bridge seemed positively pastoral and contrasted sharply with the trip he had made the previous day in the **St Trillo**.

This was billed as the two-hour afternoon cruise to Puffin Island and on towards Red Wharf Bay leaving Llandudno at 14.45 hrs. On this occasion, the wind blew up strongly and white-capped seas were clearly running just beyond the Great Orme. The two-hour trip was violently rough with the buoyant two-funnelled little **St. Trillo** pitching, rolling, lurching and slamming into the seas with that suddenness that can, to all but the fully initiated, quickly

This is a fascinating picture of an old ship and a new ship together at Barry pontoon. But, contrary to expectation, it is the modern looking diesel-engined St. Trillo with her two short funnels dating from 1936 that is the old ship! Perhaps surprisingly, the new ship with her quaint, lofty funnels and open bridge is the 1947-built, steam-powered paddler Cardiff Queen. Sadly, the Cardiff Queen quickly became obsolete. The photograph dates from 1963 when the St. Trillo first joined the White Funnel Fleet.

Photo: Author's collection

The good news at the end of the 1965 season was that P. & A. Campbell Ltd. had, through their parent company, acquired the use of the former Red Funnel ferry **Vecta**. *She came to the Bristol Channel still named* **Vecta** *and wearing her old colours for the last three weeks of the season before going back to Weymouth for thorough overhaul. As the* **Vecta**, *she is seen here at Hotwells, Bristol on 25th September 1965.* Photo: Malcolm McRonald.

cause distress and sap the energy after a very short while. No description of a trip in the *St. Trillo* would be complete without reference to her tea-room; seemingly always closed but with a hastily scrawled note saying 'back in five minutes' prominently posted. And was it really tea? At least it was served in a china cup and saucer.

In wintertime, the author and his father always used to comb the Birkenhead Docks in search of interesting ships and ferries and invariably the *St. Tudno*, the *St. Seiriol* and the *St. Trillo* were to be found together, tucked away in the corner of the Morpeth Branch Dock. On the other side of the dock wall, there were always plenty of wintering Isle of Man boats and the old ferryboats of Wallasey and Birkenhead Corporations too.

The *St. Trillo* was usually berthed alongside one of the two larger North Wales boats, which had their openings and funnel tops well battened down with canvas for the winter. Many of the men working on the three ships' overhauls lived in the crew cabins down below in the *St. Trillo*, which was a more convenient boat on which to generate electric power (and perhaps a little warmth).

The *St. Seiriol* remained laid-up throughout the 1962 season leaving the *St. Tudno* and the *St. Trillo* to try to earn enough money to maintain the company's precarious financial balance. The *St. Seiriol* was sold for breaking-up in October 1962 and was towed away to Ghent the following month.

Sadly, there was to be no recovery for this old organisation, which then went into Voluntary Liquidation and was wound-up.

Whilst many mourned the passing of that fine old name, the Liverpool & North Wales Steamship Co. Ltd., one ray of hope emerged in February 1963 with the news that the little *St. Trillo* had been sold by the Liquidators for use by P. & A. Campbell Ltd.

Through the author's earlier researches, he became aware that the directors of the Isle of Man Steam Packet Company Ltd. had, in November 1962 met with Mr. Alexander of the Liverpool & North Wales Steamship Company. The purpose of the meeting was to enable the Steam Packet Company properly to consider buying the

St. Trillo with a view to operating her in conjunction with the new services they were in future, to provide with their own **King Orry** class, classic passenger steamers. Unfortunately, the details showed that the **St. Trillo** was no longer in her prime, breakdowns were not infrequent and the figures proved that there was a general shortage of fare-paying business to be had there anyway. Nevertheless, it is nice to think what she might have looked like with her two neat little funnels, had she adopted the then famous Steam Packet livery.

By then Campbell's had themselves only quite recently been saved from Receivership and likely winding-up, by being bought by George Nott Industries Ltd. who owned the fast-growing Townsend Bros. Ferries Ltd. It was therefore their name that appeared on the Bill of Sale and ownership of the **St. Trillo** was registered accordingly, thus bringing capital allowances for tax purposes into the company that was actually making the profits! To complete the

18th June 1966 found the **Westward Ho** *making her first call at Minehead.*
Photo: Chris Collard.

story, the **St. Tudno** was also towed away for scrapping in Ghent where she arrived in April 1963, five months after the **St. Seiriol**.

By then the **St. Trillo** had already left the Mersey for her delivery voyage down to Cardiff where she arrived on 13th March, having been stormbound along the way. The plans P. & A. Campbell Ltd. had for her made complete sense. At the beginning and end of each season, she would operate in the Bristol Channel when it would otherwise be uneconomic to run one of the big paddle steamers whilst, in the main season, she would return to North Wales to operate around her old haunts.

Excellent news though that was for lovers of the motorship **St. Trillo**, sadly it sealed the fate of Campbell's paddle steamer **Glen Usk**, which was still gently disintegrating at Cardiff. Near the end of April 1963 she was sold for scrap and became destined for the shipbreaker's yard at Passage West, Cork in Eire where she was broken-up.

Mr. Chris Collard has produced two excellent books about the ships and services of P. & A. Campbell Ltd. and in the tome entitled *White Funnels*, we read that the old **Glen Usk** and the **St. Trillo**, her successor, had briefly shared the dock wall at Cardiff's East Dock. During this time the **St. Trillo** was repainted in Campbell's colours, having received underwater overhaul in dry-dock at Merseyside before she left for Cardiff.

The Campbell's line-up was now, at least for a short while, rationalised with the motorship **St. Trillo** and the still magnificent paddle steamers **Bristol Queen** and **Cardiff Queen** available for service.

1965 was a particularly bad year especially for Campbell's two paddle steamers. The weather for the most part was inclement and both the **Bristol Queen** and the **Cardiff Queen** seemed to be plagued with paddle wheel trouble and minor mishaps.

Meanwhile, the **St. Trillo** soldiered on, mainly in North Wales but Chris Collard tells a story about a trip he made on her down to Watchet, Somerset on 2nd May 1965. Perhaps understandably when compared with some of the majestic paddlers of the past, he says he rather disliked the **St. Trillo** and having completed the outward journey, instead of doing the return, he decided to go ashore and take a bus back to Weston. From there he intended to pick up the **Bristol Queen's** last crossing on the ferry to Cardiff, leaving Weston at 22.15 hrs. What he had not reckoned on was that, because it was a Sunday, the bus service was very sparse and he had only managed to get as far as the promenade an hour after the **Bristol Queen's** sailing time. He eventually made Bristol at 01.00 hrs. the next morning, from where he caught the milk train back home to Cardiff!

As we saw from the previous chapter, the next big event benefited both Southampton's Red Funnel Steamers and P. & A. Campbell Ltd. equally. This was the sale of the **Vecta** by Red Funnel, again to George Nott's profitable fast-expanding subsidiary Townsend Car Ferries Ltd., for use by P. & A. Campbell Ltd. She made her final Red Funnel trips to Cowes on 18th September and in exchange for the reported sale price of £40,000 was handed over at Southampton on 20th September 1965.

The **Vecta** sailed from Southampton, around Land's End and on up to Cardiff. Here she was put through her paces and clearly managed to dispel any doubts as to her suitability that may have been in the mind of P. & A. Campbell Ltd. Still in her Southampton colours and with the weather quite kind for the first time that season, the **Vecta** sailed on a number of trips and proved herself to be economic, never fast but of acceptable speed and really surprisingly manoeuvrable.

She then closed the season for P. & A. Campbell Ltd. and on 12th October 1965 sailed from Cardiff back down-Channel and on to Weymouth where Cosens & Co. Ltd. gave her machinery a thorough overhaul, seemingly as part of the purchase arrangements.

1966 was to be something of a deciding year for the two paddle steamers.

In February 1966 the **Vecta** finally came back round from her engine overhaul at Weymouth and went into dry-dock at Cardiff. She was renamed **Westward Ho** in the tradition of Campbell's

1894 built paddle steamer that had come back to Campbell's from the Second World War but, being too dilapidated, was broken up at Newport in 1946.

There, the newly renamed **Vecta** received the livery of P. & A. Campbell Ltd., a cowl top to her funnel and, most importantly, her car deck was plated over and fitted out as a comfortable passenger saloon. As a result, her tonnage was thereby increased to 739 tons. It was then the practice (only for a short while as things turned out) for the **Westward Ho** to operate the main services in the upper Channel including the Weston-Cardiff ferry whilst the two paddle steamers were scheduled to operate the Swansea, Ilfracombe, Lundy, and the other down-Channel routes.

In January 1967, lovers of the two remaining Bristol Channel paddle steamers were dismayed to find that one of their worst fears

*The **Westward Ho's** 1966 season was just ten days old and beginning to get under way when this photograph was taken. The scene is Cardiff's famous Pier Head waterfront at low tide, on 17th April 1966. In the Bristol Channel, the tidal range could be as much as 40 feet on occasions.   Photo: Chris Collard.*

*Here we see what a lovely job P. & A. Campbell Ltd. had made of the alterations to the **Vecta** when she became their **Westward Ho**. By now registered in Cardiff she is seen here at Barry in September 1966 having almost completed her first full season for Campbell's.* Photo: Tim Cooper.

*This photograph shows the **Westward Ho** off Pill in the Bristol Avon on 29th May 1967. When he lived in Bristol, Pill was always a favourite spot for the author to sit on a summer evening if shipping was expected in the river.* Photo: Pat Murrell.

was about to become a reality. It was announced that the **Cardiff Queen**, then barely 20 years old, was now permanently withdrawn and to be offered for sale. She had run her last trips in September 1966.

In 1967 and during the following two seasons as well as her normal routine, the **St. Trillo** made some interesting sorties to such exotic destinations as New Brighton and Holyhead. She was also to act as tender for the visiting cruise ship **Kungsholm** at Llandudno and Douglas, Isle of Man. In carrying out these duties, she crossed to the Isle of Man in the month of May in 1967, and again in 1969. The latter occasion was more noteworthy than the other because the **St. Trillo** actually still had on board a large number of people from Llandudno who were unable to get ashore there because a gale had unexpectedly blown up!

As her normal Class III passenger certificate would not permit a trip that far from land, it is not clear quite upon what basis she managed the uncomfortable trip across the Irish Sea. Perhaps no one had considered the possibility that the destination port for her tender trip might not be the same one from which she departed!

The 1967 season was to prove terminal for the **Bristol Queen** too. With more and more paddle-trouble causing disruption to schedules, her permanent withdrawal came that August, well before the planned end of that season. If followers of the Bristol Channel paddle steamer scene had a worst nightmare, this was certainly it. After that awful day on 26th August 1967, when she struck a submerged object with her starboard paddle, lost a blade and damaged several more, the **Bristol Queen** never put to sea again. The **St. Trillo** was brought back to Cardiff from Llandudno

*The **Queen of the Isles**, belonging to the Isles of Scilly Steamship Co. Ltd. is seen here approaching Llandudno on 9th June 1968. She was chartered by Campbell's and based at North Wales for the main summer season of 1968. As can be seen from the photograph, she was not a natural excursion ship having little in the way of open deck space.* Photo: Malcolm McRonald.

*20th September 1964 and the empty-looking **Cardiff Queen** is seen here going astern off Weston-super-Mare. All her passengers must have been on the **St. Trillo** that day, as she was re-visiting Chepstow, the first such occasion by an excursion vessel for fifty years.* Photo: Malcolm McRonald.

to enable the **Westward Ho** to cover for the remainder of the **Bristol Queen's** 1967 season in the lower reaches of the Bristol Channel.

In place of the **St. Trillo** at Llandudno, Campbell's hastily arranged a month's charter of the **Queen of the Isles**, from the Isles of Scilly Steamship Co. Ltd. Following the decline in house building in the Scillies for which demand she was originally built just three years earlier, the **Queen of the Isles** had been laid-up at Hayle in Cornwall for part of the previous season. Since then, she had run trips out of Plymouth and other places when not running to the Scilly Isles in partnership with the **Scillonian** at busy weekends. She left St. Mary's in Scilly at 19.00 hrs. on 2nd September 1967, arriving at Menai Bridge at 15.00 hrs. the next

day. She stayed until 29th September by which time the **St. Trillo** had returned safely from the Bristol Channel.

So, from the end of August 1967, until they finally ceased to trade on 31st December 1981, P. & A. Campbell Ltd. never again operated a steam-powered vessel.

By August 1967, the **Cardiff Queen** had still not found a buyer so now both ships were offered for sale.

The author arrived at Bristol in the spring of 1968 where he and his wife-to-be, Patricia, were both posted by the Midland Bank. There they lived firstly at Clifton, a short walk from Hotwells landing stage and the Cumberland Basin, and later beneath the famous Cabot Tower on Queen's Parade, Brandon Hill, from where they could see the City Docks and all its visiting shipping.

Historically, it was a very sad but interesting time to witness what was going on at P. & A. Campbell Ltd. By then the choice of vessels was very restricted, but there was still a choice. Whilst *prima facie*, the motorships were a poor substitute for the majestic paddlers, **Bristol Queen** and **Cardiff Queen,** in fact both the **St. Trillo** and the **Westward Ho** were older and their different pedigrees made them potentially quite interesting. The real problem was the speed in which regular travellers had to try to overcome their prejudices and to some it was not easy. The Company, its crews and the fare-paying passengers were all having to learn afresh but it took a while to come to terms with what had happened. Provided the traveller did not object too much to the din of internal combustion engines and the attendant vibrations, fumes, smells and great yellow-painted 45-gallon drums of oil littering the already cluttered decks (all of which contrasted sharply with the silent spaciousness of the old paddlers), things could have been worse. In the end they did get rather better as, slowly, almost everyone (not just the passengers) adapted to the change.

But fate had more agony in store for the laid-up **Bristol Queen.** As if things were not bad enough already for the once proud ship, she suffered the final ignominy of being rammed and damaged by a Liberian tanker in Queens Dock, Cardiff. Her foremast collapsed over the side and her forward rails on the starboard side were wrecked. It was in this sorry state on 21st March 1968, that she was towed away to Belgium for breaking-up.

Left: The 1946-built **Bristol Queen** *is seen here from the vantage point of Brunel's Clifton Suspension Bridge, steaming down the Avon at Bristol. She and her 1947-built near sister, the* **Cardiff Queen** *were truly magnificent coastal paddle steamers and represented the absolute pinnacle of design and construction within their class. Splendid though they undoubtedly were, their whole basis was ill-conceived and they were quickly to become a life-threatening drain on their owner's slender resources.*

Photo: Bristol Evening Post.

At about the same time, the **Cardiff Queen** was also sold initially for use as a floating nightclub but, when those plans fell through, she was sold on for scrapping at Newport where she was quickly demolished during April and May 1968.

On 6th May 1968, whilst the **St. Trillo** was at Llandudno on tender duties for the **Kungsholm** on one of her Round Britain cruises, her port propeller became entangled with a hawser, which disabled her completely for several hours. The inevitable gale had blown up making things very uncomfortable and lifeboats from Llandudno, Rhyl and Beaumaris stood by. Eventually, she was towed into Llandudno by the Conway fishing boat **Kilravock** and her 322 cruise ship passengers, many of whom were American tourists and by then seasick, and 88 crew, were housed on dry land for the night. Next day, they were reunited with the **Kungsholm** at Liverpool where she diverted instead of the Isle of Man.

The fleet for Campbell's 1968 sailings comprised the **Westward Ho** and the **St. Trillo** on the Bristol Channel and the chartered **Queen of the Isles** which ran the Scilly Isles trip in May and then went north to Llandudno instead of the **St. Trillo**. For this the **Queen of the Isles** had been given a traditional Campbell's white funnel but there was no escaping the fact that she had been built for the often rough-weather cargo and passenger service from Penzance to St. Mary's. As an excursion ship her accommodation and deck space were rather cramped and it was not possible to see ahead past all her enclosed superstructure. During her pre-season overhaul the **St. Trillo** had received the radar installation that had been removed from the **Bristol Queen** prior to her being scrapped.

It was reported that business in the Bristol Channel that season was better than it had been for several years but in North Wales, using the chartered **Queen of the Isles** on the 16 week charter, the position was very marginal and the service was expected to be completely withdrawn imminently.

One benefit of using such a ship, unsuitable though she was in many ways, was that her normal sailings to the Scilly Isles required a Class IIA certificate (rather than a Class III which carries obligatory range, time of day and seasonal sailing restrictions). Therefore the **Queen of the Isles** was able to carry passengers on her positioning voyages (not that they were often advertised) to and from North Wales (and elsewhere), which was a luxury never afforded by the **St. Trillo**.

Mr. Malcolm McRonald has provided the following nice story about this particular trip in the **Queen of the Isles**:

> '*On 29th May 1968, the **Queen of the Isles** left Cardiff for Menai Bridge, calling at Mumbles, in readiness for the start of the North Wales season, which she was to operate. It was, I believe, the only time that a Campbell sailing between South and North Wales was advertised to the public. Her captain was Captain Davies of the Isles of Scilly Company, but she also carried Captain Williams, formerly of the **St. Trillo,** for his knowledge of local waters. It was an excellent trip and the section north from Bardsey Island along the Lleyn Peninsula was particularly interesting, but it was almost dark by the time we reached the entrance to the Menai Straits at the Caernarfon Bar. The channel from there to Menai Bridge is buoyed but unlit. The only way we could navigate was by having a member of the crew standing in the bow, shining a searchlight ahead, to pick out the buoys*'.

From 1968 onwards, the **Westward Ho** also had a small tea bar fitted in her forward lounge and full meals were offered in her dining saloon.

On the Bristol Channel, where trade was good, the **Westward Ho** and the **St. Trillo** worked miracles and, against all the odds, started to claw back some of the business lost when the two paddle steamers ended service.

But as we have seen, the chartered **Queen of the Isles** was by no means a natural excursion steamer, having mainly enclosed saloon accommodation and too much space for cargo, which was not available for passengers. The thirty-year-old **Westward Ho** had a good layout and size but her quirky diesel-electric engines could be troublesome.

In the little **St. Trillo**, it was not only her catering arrangements that were likely to be quickly overwhelmed on the longer trips such as those down to Ilfracombe and Lundy. However, back on 24th March 1936 when Miss Barbara Dodd launched the **St. Trillo** into the Clyde, it was clear that Fairfield Shipbuilding & Engineering Co. Ltd. had produced a hardy little vessel and one to which the author subsequently became very attached. With her relatively deep draft, flared bow and broad beam she had plenty of reserve buoyancy and usually acquitted herself well, even if she did give her passengers a rather boisterous ride in the process. At less than 150 feet in length, her overall dimensions were small but for a little ship, she was very big-hearted. Under the stewardship of P. & A. Campbell Ltd., she had to be!

The big problem was her speed or, more precisely, her lack of it. By 1968, her twin Crossley diesels once rated at 300 b.h.p. each, were becoming unreliable and several trips ended with one or other main engine doing all the work. Certainly, it was not always that the full 12 knots were available and it was unkindly said by some, that when planning a trip in the **St. Trillo** one did not so much need a timetable as a calendar!

Usually most of the longer trips in the **St. Trillo** called for a certain amount of patience but, rather in the way that a parent loves even the most difficult child, it was easy to overlook her shortcomings. Even when both her engines were running well, as her forward funnel was a dummy and blanked off, her engines and generators all exhausted into the after funnel, which added to the rather unconventional spectacle.

At the end of her 1968 North Wales season, on 14th September 1968 Campbell's sent the **Queen of the Isles** on a publicly advertised initiation trip. She sailed from South Wales via Ilfracombe, Penzance, Weymouth, Bournemouth, through the Solent (where they passed the P. & O. liner **Iberia** at very close range) Eastbourne and Hastings to Dover. This was to enable her to establish timings for the season then contemplated for 1969. She then went on up the Thames to Tower Pier and (according to

With the chartered **Queen of the Isles** *covering her traditional North Wales sailings, the* **St. Trillo** *was able to partner the* **Westward Ho** *on sailings throughout the Bristol Channel during the 1968 summer season. These photographs show the smoky little* **St. Trillo** *leaving the Birnbeck Pier, Weston in June 1968 with the author and family aboard for the round trip from Weston to Barry and Cardiff.*

Photos: George Danielson.

Mr. Malcolm McRonald's reminiscences) with her sailed one coastal cruising stalwart, the well-known Mr. Raymond Brandreth, who had made the entire trip coastwise from North Wales, all the way to London.

Without being more pejorative than is necessary or fair, the two somewhat unlikely motorships *Westward Ho* and *St. Trillo*, unevenly matched though they were, achieved economically a reasonable proportion of that which had previously been done using a mighty fleet of very costly, majestic paddle steamers. That gave some grounds for optimism, but could the Company and the two elderly motorships last out?

The loyal followers of the P. & A. Campbell Ltd. scene were a splendid band of folk, especially where their beloved company's salvation was concerned. If people-power alone could have brought about the necessary miracle, they would have performed it.

From Hotwells to Clevedon and from Cardiff to Tenby, the talk at the end of that 1968 season was no longer if, but *when*, would Campbell's make an offer for the displaced Red Funnel fleet excursion ship, *Balmoral*.

Delicate though the situation was, at last things were looking up.

The Balmoral's White Funnel Days

The ever-faithful excursionists on the Bristol Channel were beginning to feel hopeful again and happily they were not to be disappointed. Their fervent prayers for the safe delivery of the **Balmoral** into their hands were answered in the Spring of 1969 at which time P. & A. Campbell Ltd. chartered her, initially for one season only. This expired at the end of September 1969. The bareboat charter fee for the first season was £10,000.

The **Balmoral** was hauled-out on the slipway at J. I. Thornycroft & Co. Ltd., Northam for two weeks at the beginning of April 1969 and, during that time, her funnel was repainted red and black! From Northam she sailed to Cosens & Co. Ltd. Weymouth for mechanical attention, where the opportunity was taken to repaint her funnel, this time all-white. For 1969, she had no cowl top to her funnel and her superstructure was still painted Red Funnel bright cream. This was not at all unpleasant but was altogether more colourful than the traditional Campbell's pinky-grey shade that (for some reason) they, but few others, had always called French grey.

From Weymouth, the **Balmoral** then sailed round to Barry, where she arrived on 17th May and then on to Cardiff the next day. She made her first sailings for Campbell's commencing with the Cardiff-Weston ferry service on 23rd May. Although on charter to Campbell's, initially her passenger certificates were issued in the name of Red Funnel Steamers, her owners. For all her years at Campbell's the **Balmoral** rarely carried anything but passengers, deck chairs and the occasional bicycle on her vehicle deck aft. The exception was that in 1969, on her arrival for service on the Bristol Channel, she had large weights placed on her car deck in an attempt to trim her by the stern and keep her propellers and rudders lower in the water, more of the time. At the next annual overhaul the weights were replaced with ballast tanks placed below

decks, aft. The vehicle deck remained open to the elements (or the sun if it was obliging) and became a popular spot for enthusiasts at which to gather, discuss the day in prospect and generally enjoy their favourite recreation and pastime.

From the author's experience, on hot summers' afternoons when the water level in the Avon at Bristol was as low as permitted safe navigation in the River, her former car deck was a place to experience some of the less delightful aspects of life on the river too! Nevertheless, as part of her original dual role both as a ferry and excursion ship, the vehicle deck was there for use by passengers for whose benefit the lovely old wooden deck chairs (in stark contrast to today's clinical but practical, white polypropylene version) would be laid out. Sailing down-Channel with a good sea running there was nowhere better (or worse depending on the perspective of the viewer) to be, than aft in the **Balmoral**. From this vantage point, low down on the main deck, passengers could very quickly acquaint themselves with the ship's lively movement, the shuddering of her propellers as they pitched out of the water and the sight of waves towering high above and roaring past on either side. Understandably, for poor sailors and the faint-hearted, nothing was more likely to bring about an enquiry at the Purser's office as to the possibility of returning from Ilfracombe by train!

While the **Balmoral** was at Cosens & Co. Ltd. Weymouth receiving her white funnel and an engine overhaul in April 1969 the **Westward Ho** made her one and only international voyage (other than her abortive attempt to reach Dunkirk in 1940, during which she broke down). On 29th April she sailed from Cardiff to Cobh (in the Republic of Ireland, once a famous stopping-off point for Atlantic liners) to act as tender for the P & O-Orient liner **Orsova** and then for a publicity trip at the oil terminal at Bantry Bay. She

This Cardiff Pier Head scene is dated 20th September 1969 and the **Balmoral's** *first season running for Campbell's was coming to a successful end. Note that the* **Balmoral** *does not have a cowl top to her funnel and the* **Westward Ho** *is berthed on the other side of the pontoon.*

Photo: Chris Collard.

was away just over a week and returned safely home on 8th May 1969.

P. & A. Campbell Ltd. again had the **Queen of the Isles** on charter, firstly over the Easter period in 1969 for the traditional sailings from Bristol Channel ports to the Isles of Scilly. Then Campbell's chartered her from mid-May for that summer but this time they had her revisiting their old south of England haunts, previously all but abandoned following the 1957 season using the **Crested Eagle**. With the benefit of her end-of-season trip the previous September, on 19th May the **Queen of the Isles** set sail from Cardiff bound for Weston, Ilfracombe, Penzance, Bournemouth and Hastings in readiness for her season's sailings in the South. Because of her Class IIA certificate, it was perfectly possible to buy a ticket for all (or part) of the trip and the really

dedicated coastal cruisers looked forward to these positioning voyages with relish.

Soon after the **Balmoral** had come to the Bristol Channel, the **Westward Ho** collided heavily with the Birnbeck Pier at Weston on 2nd June, requiring repairs taking ten days to complete, to be carried out at Roath Dock, Cardiff. A number of her 100 passengers received cuts and bruises, so sharp was the collision impact. The recall was sounded for the **St. Trillo**, then at Menai Bridge, and she set off as fast as her rather feeble Crossley diesels could go, bound for the Bristol Channel. It was a trip she had done many times before and (weather and breakdowns permitting) usually took all day and all night to achieve. The faithful little ship finally arrived in time to take over from the **Westward Ho** on 6th June and she stayed until 12th June 1969 before going back to North Wales.

According to Mr. Peter Southcombe, Campbell's former manager, following the end of her North Wales season on 16th

M. V. Balmoral   5th July 1970

Menu

LUNCHEON   12/6

Vegetable Soup

Ham and Tongue Salad
Boiled New Potatoes

Fruit Salad and Ice Cream
or
Cheese and Biscuits

****

HIGH TEA   9/6

Fried Fillet Plaice & Chipped Potatoes
or
Cold Ham & Chipped Potatoes
or
Cold Ham Salad

Bread and Butter

Preserves

Tea

September 1969, the **St. Trillo** came south once more for a few extra sailings on the Bristol Channel, arriving at Cardiff on 18th. After a major pageant at Lundy at the end of September, the **Westward Ho** and the **St. Trillo** then retired to Barry Dock where the **St. Trillo** paid-off at 11.00 hrs. on 30th September 1969 and the **Westward Ho** did the same later that day. As things turned out, the **St. Trillo** would never sail under her own power again and she was placed in the hands of brokers with the optimistic price tag of £17,000.

Following the **Balmoral's** first season's charter, P. & A.

Campbell Ltd. then took her on a demise charter for 10 years from 29th September 1969, which involved a single cash payment to Red Funnel Steamers of £30,000. There was nothing more to pay for the next decade and Campbell's had the right to purchase her at any time before the end of the charter, for the nominal sum of just £1. Some sources refer to the payment of an additional £1 p.a. fee.

Former Campbell's director, later joint managing director, Mr. A.M.C. (Tony) McGinnity mentioned earlier in the book, has kindly outlined the reasons for handling the acquisition of the **Balmoral** in this way. The thinking behind the setting up of the demise

*This lovely but undated photograph is almost certainly one of the very earliest taken of the **Balmoral** soon after she had arrived at Cardiff on 18th May 1969 to begin service for P. & A. Campbell Ltd. The tide is right out and the **Balmoral** is making full use of the normally floating pontoons, now on the mud at Cardiff Pier Head. Looking at her draft marks (reading less than 4 feet forward) and her exposed Plimsoll line, the **Balmoral's** bow is probably well aground too. Although her funnel was finally painted all-white for her first season's charter on the Bristol Channel, her superstructure paint work (cream and brown on the deckhouses) remains unchanged from her Red Funnel days. She has yet to have a cowl added to her funnel and this was not done until the following year's refit. Photo: C.C.A. archives.*

charter was that at the time, the Department of Transport (later Trade and Industry) who were then responsible for ship safety, would have invoked all the up-to-date safety rules under their 'Change of ownership of vessels' policy. The **Balmoral** did not comply with the latest Safety of Life at Sea requirements so through the demise charter being set up, she never changed hands and the new rules remained conveniently irrelevant. The £30,000 was a far cry from the original asking price of £65,000, but Mr. McGinnity confirms that was all they paid and the deal for the **Balmoral** was therefore consummated at that figure.

The **Balmoral** closed her first Bristol Channel season on 5th October and a week later, set sail for Weymouth where Cosens & Co. Ltd. were to carry out her annual overhaul and her repainting in full Campbell's livery. On 3rd April 1970, she arrived at Husband's at Marchwood for underwater work. Whilst in the South, she ran a special P.S.P.S. charter from Weymouth round the Isle of Wight on 2nd May 1970. Later that year, in his annual statement to shareholders, Mr. Clifton Smith-Cox, Campbell's chairman and managing director, was pleased to report very good results for their Bristol Channel services in 1969 and that he looked forward to increasing prosperity in future on those services. However, the lack of success in both North Wales and on the South Coast, meant they would not operate there again in future years.

Another name that was to become synonymous with Campbell's alongside that of

This is another historic but undated photograph taken at Cardiff Pier Head by the same photographer as the previous view. By process of a posteriori deduction, it was almost certainly taken later on 18th or on the next morning when the **Queen of the Isles** *began her South Coast summer season's charter, commencing with a positioning voyage from Cardiff, where she is seen with the* **Balmoral**, *on 19th May 1969.*

Photo: C.C.A. archives.

By now sporting the first cowl top to her funnel which was added in her pre-1970 refit, the **Balmoral** *is seen coming up the Avon in the summer of 1971 and in the City Docks. She was on a rare trip taking her through the Cumberland Basin lock gates (necessitating the main A38 trunk road to be closed) right up into the City Docks. From Princes Wharf she sailed on a special charter cruise, dressed overall for the occasion.* Photos: Author.

its managing director was Commander Foden. Tom Foden, formerly in the Royal Navy, was a close friend of Clifton Smith-Cox and lived nearby. Many years ago, he became Campbell's Agent and was involved in all manner of interesting trips and charters of the ships. When Campbell's ceased operations, he offered his services wholeheartedly to the **Waverley** organisation and happily, he remains Agent for both the **Balmoral** and the **Waverley**, even to this day.

The **Queen of the Isles** had by then been returned to the Isles of Scilly Steamship Co. Ltd. at the end of Campbell's 1969 charters, and both she and the **Scillonian** were then employed on running the service from Penzance to St. Mary's in the early part of 1970. This is the Island's all-important flower season and it is quite something to be able to have Scilly Islands' daffodils and new potatoes on the table on Christmas Day.

In May 1970, the **Queen of the Isles** went on charter to the Mersey Docks & Harbour Board at Liverpool followed, for a few days, by running for Norwest Hovercraft Ltd. at Fleetwood for what was to be their troublesome service to the Isle of Man. This was whilst they awaited the arrival of their ship **Norwest Laird** (the former **Lochiel** of David MacBrayne Ltd.).

The **Queen of the Isles** then became reasonably busy with summer excursions from Penzance and St. Ives too. Later that year, she was sold for £150,000 to the Tonga Shipping Agency for whom she was to run between Tonga and the other Friendly Islands in the middle of the Pacific Ocean. She was handed over on 10th November 1970 and on 2nd December she set sail there under her own power, across the Atlantic and through the Panama Canal. For the voyage, she had massive extra fuel tanks welded onto her fo'c's'le. In this condition the author looked over the **Queen of the Isles** for the final time at Penzance whilst she was being made ready for the long delivery voyage. For a ship of just 515 (later 529) gross tons, designed for the 3-hour trip to the Scillies, the **Queen of the Isles'** voyage half way round the world must rank as a major achievement. For her new operations she

During the winter of 1970/71 the **St. Trillo**, *the* **Westward Ho** *and the* **Balmoral** *were laid-up together at Barry. The* **St. Trillo** *was still there at the extreme inside end of the dock, having being withdrawn at the end of the 1969 season, and was by then suffering a slow but inexorable demise. In the middle was the* **Westward Ho** *with her delicate diesel-electric machinery that would, as things turned out, only struggle on for one more season. At the outer end of the dock was the* **Balmoral***, being made ready for the 1971 season.* Photo: Author.

Throughout this book, printed archive material from the collections of the author and various other long-term collectors has been reproduced. By mutual consent, as much of the material is common to several of the collections and it would therefore be inappropriate to credit reproduction to any one alone, it has been agreed to make one blanket acknowledgement to the collections of the author and the following persons: Keith Adams, Tim Cooper, Joe McKendrick, Nigel Coombes, David Parsons and Malcolm McRonald.

*The **Balmoral's** first season sailing for P. & A. Campbell Ltd. included some very attractive excursions. In this photograph taken on 24th August 1969 the ship is seen at Tenby which is a difficult harbour to manoeuvre in, being full of small boats. Next day she had an early start when she left Swansea at 07.45 hrs. for Mumbles, Ilfracombe and Padstow, a favourite haunt of the author on the North Cornwall coast.* Photo: Pat Murrell.

*This 6th September 1970 view of the **Balmoral** shows her with a good complement of passengers off Portishead. The famous power station is in the background and there must be a competition going on as to which can make the most smoke, the **Balmoral** or the power station. Certainly, any of the **Balmoral's** passengers wearing light coloured clothing would find themselves covered in smuts and be faced with a dry-cleaning bill after this trip!* Photo: C.C.A. archives.

was christened with a traditional Polynesian name **Olovaha**, seemingly derived from part of their native leaders' traditional outrigger canoes.

Throughout the 1970 season, the **Balmoral** and the **Westward Ho** sailed the usual mixture of sailings in the Bristol Channel. In May 1970, the **Balmoral** made her first pilgrimage to the Isles of Scilly, following in the footsteps of the **Bristol Queen**, which had last sailed there in May 1967 and the **Queen of the Isles** that last ran the traditional Campbell's three-day Scilly Islands trip from Bristol Channel ports over Easter 1969. The **Balmoral** also went to Llandudno as tender to the Swedish-America Line's cruise ship **Kungsholm** in May 1970 and on to the Isle of Man where she met

up with the **Queen of the Isles**, then on charter to Norwest Hovercraft Ltd. Research shows this to be the only time that two such Campbell's-connected ships ever met in Douglas Harbour.

Sadly, as a salutary precursor of events yet to become even more frequent, the **Westward Ho** broke down on several occasions towards the end of the 1970 season.

Her season ended abruptly when, on 18th September, she failed again but managed to sail home on one engine to Barry, where she joined the **St. Trillo**, still laid-up and for sale since the previous year. It should be remembered that the **Westward Ho** was diesel-electric powered so she could get along passably well on just one engine. Here it will help some readers interested in the technical aspects to quote from the 28th February 1946 edition of *Shipbuilding and Shipping Record* kindly loaned by Mr. Alan Brown:

'The use of separate exciters for the two propulsion motors allows the propellers to be controlled independently, while the total power is shared equally between the two generators at all loads. Full and independent control of the propellers is still maintained even if only one generator is in service'.

With no other serviceable ship, the **Balmoral** carried on alone until the end of the season and on 13th October 1970 joined the other two ships for lay-up at Barry. Although P. & A. Campbell Ltd. had been 'rescued' some twelve years earlier, they were now part of the major Townsend Ferries and European Ferries empire which expected results from all its operating entities. Despite the apparent anomaly, there was still no money available for preventive maintenance. Trying to juggle Campbell's limited resources to keep its fast-dwindling fleet of elderly diesel vessels operating, especially following the inevitable onset of their decrepitude, was really quite a task and not one destined to result in victory. Mr. A.M.C. McGinnity tells of the year when, in order to save money, they employed a firm of house painters to paint the **Balmoral**, as their quote was cheaper than the shipyard. Another year, rather than replace rotting boards in her wheelhouse, they simply floated a concrete floor over everything.

Campbell's declining position was exacerbated because, disappointingly, this had become a period of missed opportunities. Whilst P. & A. Campbell Ltd.'s parent company eventually grew into the massive European Ferries group (the P & O Ferries empire as we know it today) very little was actually made of the business that could have been sent Campbell's way. The local directors and management of P. & A. Campbell Ltd. had fervently hoped that things might turn out differently. All the ticket offices and kiosks that once serviced the Thames and coastal pleasure ships, now part of the same family, could all have helped to promote the vast group's last-remaining, now ailing excursion vessels. Sadly, this did not happen save for Campbell's being credited with sundry

items and odd receipts - scraps from the parent company table.

Whilst under test for insurance purposes, two sections of Clevedon Pier collapsed on 17th October 1970 giving the area a notorious tourist attraction for years to come but depriving it of life-giving steamer visits in the process. The **Balmoral** had last called there on 11th October 1970.

Later that winter, when the author paid his last respects to the trio laid-up at Barry, the **St. Trillo's** engines were partly dismantled and pieces of machinery were scattered in her engine room alleyways. Her wooden decks were no longer weatherproof or in any fit state for passengers either, although outwardly she still presented that neat, trim appearance that was so very endearing. Seemingly, work on her stopped as soon as it was realised that the North Wales service had finished, this time for good.

The highlight of the 1971 season was when the Coastal Cruising Association chartered the **Balmoral**. On 15th May (having sailed north from Bristol, arriving on Merseyside the previous day) she ran a very successful commemorative voyage from Liverpool to Llandudno and Menai Bridge and onwards towards Puffin Island. Following in the wake of the much-missed **St. Tudno** (the final sailing of which had been nine years previously on 16th September 1962) 500 passengers partook of the sailings, at various points of the trip.

The **Balmoral** then stayed on in order to act as tender to the **Kungsholm** (which followed her up from the Bristol Channel two days later) both at Llandudno and the Isle of Man. Whilst the **Kungsholm** was in the Bristol Channel on that occasion, the **Westward Ho** acted as tender for the cruise ship there, running trips between the ship, Avonmouth and Weston.

Elsewhere around the coast, liner voyages called for the services of tenders (often purpose-built) at known regular destination ports. However, the visits of nomadic cruise ships, on their Round Britain cruises, called for considerable flexibility on the part of tender operators and when it came to being flexible, no one had developed the art to a greater degree than Campbell's. For many years, providing tenders was a staple part of their business. Some very enjoyable public trips were also on offer to view the **Kungsholm** and the **Gripsholm** at anchor in Walton Roads, off Clevedon. Coincidentally, the railway-owned **Shanklin** (later to become the **Prince Ivanhoe**) provided the same service for the **Kungsholm** in the Portsmouth and Southampton area.

The obvious benefit of Campbell's being able to roster two ships, similar in all material respects, should have been a real bonus as it ought not (in theory at least) to have mattered which vessel took any particular sailing. Sadly, the **Westward Ho's** engines were beginning to be troublesome again, which was not a good sign so early in the 1971 season, but she struggled on manfully in a rather unbalanced sort of partnership, with the **Balmoral** scheduled to do a lot of the hard work.

The timetable was adapted and amended as and when required and it speaks volumes for Campbell's skills that obvious disruption was kept to a minimum. Sadly, money was still scarce and for the recalcitrant **Westward Ho**, little was done other than some engineering first aid on each occasion that she failed.

Understandably, the **Balmoral's** crew seemed unhappy at all the extra work thrust upon them as a result of the other ship's breakdowns. It was clear that Campbell's would have had to do something quickly if they were not to have serious strife on their hands. Comments such as *'we are having to do all the work and look at him sitting there doing nothing'* were not unexpected when approaching Cardiff pontoon in the **Balmoral**, with the **Westward Ho** lying lamely alongside. By now her delicate machinery was often in pieces whilst worried-looking engineers with grease-streaked faces could only look on helplessly at the sad spectacle.

However, disaster was finally to strike on the afternoon of 2nd September 1971 whilst the **Westward Ho** was at Hotwells, Bristol. She had come up the Avon prior to making her turn outside the Cumberland Basin lock gates in a manoeuvre she had done successfully on many previous occasions. With her diesel-electric drive she could turn almost in her own length without ropes and

with none of the attendant difficulty that the manoeuvre historically had caused the paddle steamers.

Unexpectedly and explosively, her port engine, recently the more reliable of the two, snapped two connecting rods and blew up, causing irreparable damage not only to the engine but also to the deck and area above. With her remaining serviceable engine called upon to provide all the power, including the tricky passage of the tortuous River Avon, she sailed with

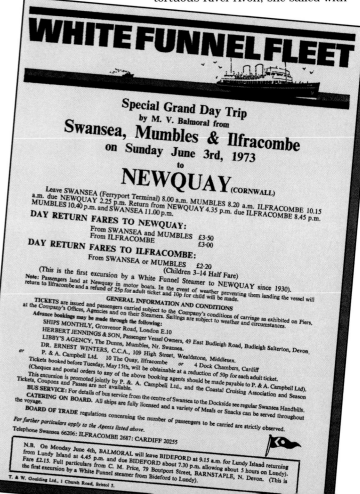

WHITE FUNNEL FLEET

Special Grand Day Trip
by M. V. Balmoral from
Swansea, Mumbles & Ilfracombe
on Sunday June 3rd, 1973
to
NEWQUAY (CORNWALL)

Leave SWANSEA (Ferryport Terminal) 8.00 a.m. MUMBLES 8.20 a.m. ILFRACOMBE 10.15 a.m. due NEWQUAY 2.25 p.m. Return from NEWQUAY 4.35 p.m. due ILFRACOMBE 8.45 p.m. MUMBLES 10.40 p.m. and SWANSEA 11.00 p.m.

DAY RETURN FARES TO NEWQUAY:
From SWANSEA and MUMBLES £3·50
From ILFRACOMBE £3·00

DAY RETURN FARES TO ILFRACOMBE:
From SWANSEA or MUMBLES £2·20
(Children 3-14 Half Fare)

(This is the first excursion by a White Funnel Steamer to NEWQUAY since 1930).
Note: Passengers land at Newquay in motor boats. In the event of weather preventing them landing the vessel will return to Ilfracombe and a refund of 25p for adult ticket and 10p for child will be made.

GENERAL INFORMATION AND CONDITIONS
TICKETS are issued and passengers carried subject to the Company's conditions of carriage as exhibited on Piers, at the Company's Offices, Agencies and on their Steamers. Sailings are subject to weather and circumstances.
Advance bookings may be made through the following:
SHIPS MONTHLY, Grosvenor Road, London E.10
HERBERT JENNINGS & SON, Passenger Vessel Owners, 49 East Budleigh Road, Budleigh Salterton, Devon.
LIBBY'S AGENCY, The Dunns, Mumbles, Nr. Swansea.
DR. ERNEST WINTERS, C.C.A., 109 High Street, Wealdstone, Middlesex.
P. & A. Campbell Ltd.   10 The Quay, Ilfracombe   or   4 Dock Chambers, Cardiff
or
Tickets booked before Tuesday, May 15th, will be obtainable at a reduction of 50p for each adult ticket.
(Cheques and postal orders to any of the above booking agents should be made payable to P. & A. Campbell Ltd).
This excursion is promoted jointly by P. & A. Campbell Ltd., and the Coastal Cruising Association and Season Tickets, Coupons and Passes are not available.
BUS SERVICE: For details of bus service from the centre of Swansea to the Dockside see regular Swansea Handbills.
CATERING ON BOARD. All ships are fully licensed and a variety of Meals or Snacks can be served throughout the voyage.
BOARD OF TRADE regulations concerning the number of passengers to be carried are strictly observed.
For further particulars apply to the Agents listed above.
Telephone Swansea 66206: ILFRACOMBE 2687: CARDIFF 20255

N.B. On Monday June 4th, BALMORAL will leave BIDEFORD at 9.15 a.m. for Lundy Island returning from Lundy Island at 4.45 p.m. and due BIDEFORD about 7.30 p.m. allowing about 5 hours on Lundy. Fare £2.15. Full particulars from C. M. Price, 79 Bouport Street, BARNSTAPLE, N. Devon. (This is the first excursion by a White Funnel steamer from Bideford to Lundy).

T. & W. Goulding Ltd., 1 Church Road, Bristol 5.

her passengers back to Cardiff where she lay at the pontoon. Worn down, enervated and looking very sorry for herself, in the following days there emerged a dreadful air of gloom that the **Westward Ho** had finally reached the end of her eventful career with P. & A. Campbell Ltd.

However there must have been at least some hope that her condition could be retrieved as it was not until 14th September 1971 that an announcement was made that she was to be withdrawn from service permanently. She then laid-up for a month

at Barry where she was berthed together with the **St. Trillo**. The **St. Trillo** was still for sale after yet another attempt to dispose of her had proved to be abortive and, all the while, the depreciatory effects of rust and rot were becoming daily all too evident.

The pontoons at Cardiff and at Barry were soon to be condemned. At forty feet, the Bristol Channel claims to have the second largest tidal range in the world (after the Bay of Fundy) and without the loading pontoons, and their ability to float up and down with the tides, there could be no sailings.

As Campbell's then had only one ship, the **Balmoral**, fit for service, they immediately announced that, from 1972 onwards, there would be virtually no sailings up-Channel (thus avoiding Cardiff and Barry) and that Swansea to Ilfracombe would be their main route in future with trips to Lundy and excursions from Ilfracombe also. In fact, its

On 15th May 1971, the **Balmoral** *ran a Coastal Cruising Association charter from Liverpool to Llandudno and Menai Bridge, to commemorate the final voyage of the old* **St. Tudno** *on 16th September 1962. Seen here at Llandudno, the* **Balmoral** *is flying the Liverpool & North Wales Steamship Co. Ltd. house flag at her masthead; she retained her clinker-built lifeboats until she was rebuilt in 1986.*

Photo: David Parsons.

*During her time with P. & A. Campbell Ltd., the **Balmoral** acted as tender for the cruise liners **Kungsholm** and **Gripsholm** on various occasions between 1970 and 1975. She often managed to combine this work with public or private sailings, briefly reminding passengers of the once more prolific North Wales services. When both the cruise ships were withdrawn by Swedish America Line in 1975, the services of the **Balmoral** as tender ceased. Here we see her in Douglas Bay with the **Kungsholm** in the distance in 1973.*   Photo: Author.

*The **Balmoral's** 1971 season was extended until 18th October following the **Westward Ho's** explosive and permanent engine failure the previous month. This lovely photograph taken on 10th October reveals the **Balmoral** lying in Lundy Roads, her passengers mostly ashore leaving their classic wood and canvas ship's deckchairs empty on the old car deck, which became known as the sun deck, aft. Some of those remaining aboard have brought out their fishing rods to do some angling, on this seemingly sunny autumnal afternoon.   Photo: C.C.A. archives.*

owners, the British Transport Docks Board, refitted part of Barry pontoon, but that in isolation was not to help a great deal. By then, Campbell's who owned the old pier at Weston were trying to sell it anyway, which they did the following year. Also, the opening of the new Severn Bridge a few years earlier had reduced traffic on the Cardiff to Weston ferry by almost half and it seems that this decimation of the ferry business had not been properly anticipated.

The final 1971 season's sailings by the **Balmoral** (which were extended by a week beyond the dates previously advertised) contained the usual scenes of merriment. The author and his wife were aboard for the **Balmoral's** final Cardiff to Weston ferry run

and the end-of-pier firework display on the night of 18th October 1971.

Towards the end of October 1971, the **Westward Ho** moved under her own power from Barry, to lay-up in the north Cornish harbour of Hayle, awaiting a buyer. With just her starboard main engine capable of being started, power from its electrical generator was well below par for such a long trip.

However, with no choice in the matter, it was with just that engine and generator running (providing electricity for both port and starboard electric drive motors) that she left Barry for Cornwall, sailing via Cardiff and Ilfracombe, making a steady 10 knots. Sadly, the **St. Trillo** could not be moved under her own power and, in any event, Campbell's thought they had a firm buyer for her, otherwise, she too might have been moved to lay-up at Hayle.

The floating pontoon at Hotwells, scene of the **Westward Ho's** sad demise, was then removed and demolished so that any future sailings of the **Balmoral** up the Avon to Bristol would terminate at the dock wall, by the entrance to the Cumberland Basin.

For the next five seasons the **Balmoral** remained the sole survivor of the once proud fleet of P. & A. Campbell Ltd. In those days, she usually went to Penzance for annual overhaul and dry-docking (also for lay-up when not wintering on the Dart as she did on one or two occasions) at N. Holman & Sons Ltd.'s shipyard where she was often in the company of lightships and buoys, as Penzance was an important district port for Trinity House. A lot could be learned about a ship by visiting her in winter lay-up when she was stripped down and receiving overhaul and barely an overhaul went by without her receiving a visit from the author and his Cornish father-in-law, Donald.

These visits down to Penzance were highly cherished and were not regarded as complete without a visit to the nearby Dolphin Hotel, for lunch. There the landlord, full of character and seemingly always glowing and red-faced would stand, swaying gracefully at the bar and bid a welcome with his booming Cornish greeting - 'ow aarre eeee, me ansums, yu'm cum ter zee tha ol bote of yorn again, av eee?' He and Donald, of course, spoke the same language! To be fair, he was always very happy and a great advertisement for his establishment.

Until quite recently, small passenger vessels had to have an 'out of water' inspection every year. Hiring a dry-dock or slipway is expensive and takes a certain amount of planning by all concerned. On occasions, in order to cut costs, two vessels have entered dry-dock at the same time but if one then requires extra or long-term work, the other remains landlocked until both are fit to refloat. For the last few years, this requirement has been relaxed for Class III ships and is now legally necessary only every second year. To get

*When the **Westward Ho's** port engine blew-up on 2nd September 1971 she retired first to Barry and then she struggled down on one engine (and its associated generator) via Cardiff and Ilfracombe to Hayle in Cornwall where she lay for a year. In October 1972 Compass Catering Ltd. bought the ship and, having painted her yellow, had her towed to Manchester. This photograph taken in the spring 1972, shows her open for business as a floating restaurant and public house in the heart of Manchester's salubrious docklands.*

Photo: Tim Cooper.

the **Balmoral** into what was then N. Holman & Sons Ltd.'s small dry-dock required the main road to be closed and the then antiquated-looking, wood and tar-covered road-bridge, swung open. The vital mechanical work aboard the **Balmoral** was done on a continuing or rotational basis. One year the port main engine might be partly or fully opened up and the next year it would be the turn of her starboard one to receive attention; likewise, her generators and other duplicated machinery. However, anything that was not vital was simply left, as there was still no money in reserve. After dry-docking and engine overhaul, she would be taken out into Mount's Bay for trials before setting off back up the Channel. Holman's men took a great pride in their work on the

Balmoral and would speak lovingly to the author of how they had
'*wound her up to maximum speed*', faster than almost any other
ship they ever worked on.

The *Balmoral's* mini-cruise to the Isles of Scilly in October 1972
was described as being 'all-in' with Campbell's offering to organise
the whole trip including accommodation, coach transfers and all if
required. Its date coincided with the final departure of the
Westward Ho from lay-up at Hayle in Cornwall and it was to be
many years before the two ships (and other former Red Funnel
vessels) were in such close proximity again.

The *Westward Ho* had been laid-up at Hayle for almost exactly
a year before being painted yellow, and leaving under tow for
Manchester on 7th October 1972 (some observers say it was a day
or two later). Campbell's had sold her for the reported figure of
£23,000 to Compass Caterers Ltd. for conversion to a floating
disco, public house, nightclub and restaurant. She arrived at
Eastham, at the entrance to the Manchester Ship Canal a week
later, from where she was then moved to Manchester South Dock
2. She was subsequently advertised as the *North Westward Ho*,
berthed at Pomona Dock, Manchester.

An editorial piece in the July 1973 edition of *Cruising Monthly*
caused more than a few ripples. Its editor of the day wrote:

'*A good meal, cup of coffee or glass of beer can add to the
pleasure of travelling on a ship. No other form of transport
has the space to provide comparable catering facilities and
there are some excellent examples of what can be achieved*'.

Whilst he resisted naming those he regarded as excellent, no
such reticence was evident when it came to the worst example - the
only one named. He went on with his attack on her catering
arrangements thus:

'*The catering on some vessels, on the other hand, is more
of an ordeal than a pleasure. On that notorious example,
Campbell's Balmoral, the tea-bar offers cardboard cups of
drinks prepared from instant tea, a powder derived from tea
and milk and the similar instant white coffee. No one can*

*imagine that such standards will encourage passengers and
all excursion operators could suffer if such conditions
continue*'.

He was, of course, quite correct in his criticism although, in the
author's experience, the *Balmoral* was not a lot worse than some
others were. Plastic or paper cups and plates, disposable cutlery,
warmish water, powdered or concentrated drink flavourings and
food with only marginally more flavour than the cardboard plate it
was served up on, were often the norm.

In 1973, four years after her withdrawal from service, during
which she had remained moribund at Barry, the decaying *St.
Trillo*, finally found a buyer. In another later letter to the author,
Mr. Clifton Smith-Cox, by then retired, was able to say that
Campbell's had sold the *St. Trillo* to a Mr. Nigel Wait for £9,000
(although some sources say £7,500 was the figure). However, after
his idea to moor her on the Thames failed, whatever other plans he
had for the rusty old boat we shall probably never know. A further
twelve months later, he sold her on to the Oldham brothers, who
wished to cannibalise her Crossley diesel engines for spare parts,
in which business they were specialists. It seems that with very
careful selection, even the old *St. Trillo's* frail engines were
capable of offering some useful donor parts. Readers may recall
that Frederick Oldham Ltd. did the same when the Mersey ferry
Egremont was sold for static use at Salcombe in 1976. Oldham's
sold the *St. Trillo* on to Hamond Lane Foundry and, from Barry,
she was towed direct to Dublin where she was beached on the
banks of the River Liffey, her timber parts were burnt out and then
she was scrapped in the summer of 1975.

From an operational point of view, lovers of the dwindling White
Funnel Fleet now had to face the fact that both the *St. Trillo* and
the *Westward Ho*, erstwhile saviours of their beloved company,
were gone; this time for ever.

Meanwhile, down south at Lymington during early 1974, both of
the railway-owned vehicle ferries, *Farringford* and *Lymington,*
were surplus, having been replaced by the new and larger ferries.

*The **Balmoral** had a lovely day off North Devon on 11th August 1973. The trip up the River Torridge to Bideford where the **Balmoral** is shown here is always very attractive.* Photo: C.C.A. archives.

*This September 1974 photograph shows the **Balmoral** having come up the Avon to the Cumberland Basin at Bristol for an evening charter cruise.* Photo: Richard Winfield.

The old ships were withdrawn within 24 hours of each other on 8th and 9th November 1973. The **Farringford** was then required to operate on the Hull to New Holland ferry service (also operated by the railways) pending the completion of the new Humber Road Bridge. She was later sold to Western Ferries (Clyde) Ltd. but never actually sailed for them and was broken up on the Humber 10 years later. By coincidence, in March 1974, the **Lymington** went direct to Western Ferries (Clyde) Ltd. as their **Sound of Sanda**. Alan Brown's lovely book entitled *Lymington, The Sound of Success*, tells the whole story beautifully. They too were eventually followed by the **Freshwater** after she was finally made redundant years later and she became their **Sound of Seil**.

Also in 1974, Red Funnel Steamers took delivery of its next car-ferry, the **Netley Castle**. Unlike every other Red Funnel vessel since the 1931-built **Medina**, which had all come from J. I. Thornycroft & Co. Ltd. at Woolston, the **Netley Castle** was built at Wallsend-on-Tyne, by the financially troubled Ryton Marine. In her day at almost 1,200 gross tons, she was the largest of all the Isle of Wight ferries until she was eclipsed by the then huge Sealink 'Saint' series of Portsmouth-based ferries nine years later. Upon the arrival of the new **Netley Castle**, Red Funnel's original purpose-built car ferry, the **Carisbrooke Castle** dating from 1959, remained on standby for two months before being sold to Italian owners.

At the end of 1974, after her 25th year in operation, the **Balmoral** went to Dartmouth where the engineers at Philip & Son Ltd. had major work to do on her main engines and following lay-up there she was painted and had her survey done at Penzance.

This end of season photograph of the very rusty-looking **Balmoral** *shows the vessel approaching the Birnbeck Pier at Weston-Super-Mare (where it was said, that the tide never went out) in lively conditions in September 1974.*

Photo: Richard Winfield.

The 1976 annual trip to Cornwall and the Isles of Scilly left Penarth and Weston on 8th, and St. Ives on 9th October prior to sailing round Land's End and on to Penzance and St. Mary's. Here we see the **Balmoral** *berthed outside the* **Scillonian** *at the Lighthouse Pier, Penzance during that visit.*

Photo: Tim Cooper.

Every season (and Campbell's managed to make them quite long by running well into October) the **Balmoral,** now alone, covered the traditional sailings throughout the Bristol Channel and some special trips too. Calls at Bideford, Clovelly and Minehead or Tenby, Mumbles and Porthcawl on the other side were always that bit special. Also, she acted as tender to the **Kungsholm** at Llandudno and the Isle of Man and often managed some northern charter work too. Finally, the highlights of the seasons were her eagerly anticipated trips to Padstow, St. Ives, Newquay, Penzance and the Isles of Scilly and her Swansea, via Tenby, to Lundy cruises.

In 1975, it became known that the Isle of Scilly Steamship Company Ltd. with the aid of a substantial grant from the British Government, was going to replace the ageing **Scillonian**. Like the **Balmoral**, the **Scillonian** had been built at J. I. Thornycroft & Co. Ltd. She was their yard No. 4130 and was somewhat larger and newer, dating from 1956. In fact she was an altogether different type of ship and whilst able to carry 600 passengers on her Class IIA certificate, she was also a great cargo vessel with heavy lifting gear forward and a large hold in which she carried every conceivable item of cargo needed on the Islands.

Meanwhile the **Balmoral** was soldiering on alone and, to accommodate a charter voyage round Anglesey from Menai Bridge on Sunday 15th June 1975, had an interesting positioning run up from Penarth and Weston the previous Friday. Mr. Tim Cooper was aboard and he recalls that on leaving Penarth, the ship's Tannoy

The railway-owned vehicle ferry **Lymington***, which normally ran from Lymington to Yarmouth, was replaced by larger tonnage and sold in March 1974, for further service on the Clyde under the name* **Sound of Sanda***. Running for Western Ferries (Clyde) Ltd.'s service from Hunter's Quay, under her new name she continued for many years carrying passengers and vehicles, before becoming their freight-only vessel, finally to become redundant.*

Photo: British Rail.

came to life with the purser's announcement that the steamer was departing for Weston-super-Mare and Menai Bridge (twenty hours sailing time distant). It was announced so matter-of-factly as if such sailings were commonplace! So the same story goes, lunch on the way north included cabbage, that had been boiled in a bucket of seawater pulled from the over the side of the ship. Whilst that might save adding any salt, presumably the cook would need to have been fairly selective as to where he dipped his bucket!

Back at Southampton, in 1975 following the introduction of the new **Netley Castle**, plans were announced for both the **Cowes Castle** and the **Norris Castle** to be sent to Rotterdam to be stretched. When this work was complete, it quickly rendered the **Osborne Castle** virtually redundant. She saw a few days' service in the company of her former fleetmate the **Balmoral** at the June 1977 Fleet Review and did some work on the Cowes passage later that year. It was not until early 1978 that she was sold for further service in Canada.

The new Scillies vessel, aptly named **Scillonian III**, arrived on service in May 1977 rendering her former namesake redundant. Very pleasant news though it was, the ferry world was taken mostly by surprise when P. & A. Campbell Ltd. paid £150,000 for the outgoing **Scillonian** and she was immediately put to work. Mr. A.M.C. McGinnity was the Campbell's director who completed the **Scillonian** deal. He recalls that even whilst he was travelling to St. Mary's with the banker's draft with which to complete the purchase in his brief case, the Isles of Scilly Steamship Co. Ltd. still expected him to pay for his passage ticket! For now still bearing her old name and colours, although soon sporting a hastily white-painted funnel, the rather rusty looking **Scillonian** made her debut for Campbell's on the Bristol Channel following her delivery voyage from Falmouth. Campbell's had high hopes for the use of the vessel in the charter business generally and had at least one apparently lucrative charter signed up before, sadly, it came to nothing. They also hoped to negotiate with The Landmark Trust for the ship to be the principal Lundy Island passenger and cargo vessel and, if successful, they would have her in service all the year round. Whilst off duty on 27th June 1977, the **Scillonian** was physically renamed **Devonia** and registered at Bristol, her previous port of registry having been simply, Scilly.

So, with the timeous arrival of the **Scillonian** at Bristol, the **Balmoral** was able to go to the Silver Jubilee Review of the Fleet at Spithead on 28th June 1977, having also been at the previous one on 15th June 1953 in her early Red Funnel years. In true Campbell's tradition, they marketed the outward (only) trip as a public excursion taking place over three days, Tuesday 21st,

Wednesday 22nd, and Thursday 23rd June 1977, with tickets available to Southampton from Swansea, Ilfracombe, St.Ives and Penzance. £15.00 was the full fare for the single trip from Swansea to Southampton. Amongst a few others, Mr. Keith Adams and his father made the almost 400-mile trip.

Whilst the **Balmoral** was passing Portland Bill on her way from Penzance, they met up with a flotilla of Naval ships which was just leaving the Naval Base at Portland, bound for the Spithead Review. In Mr. Tim Cooper's reminiscences, he recalls that proud moment as the **Balmoral** sailed by, with the Naval squadron falling in astern for a while, presumably before overhauling her.

Later in the season the **Devonia** commenced running excursions for Campbell's on the River Thames. Whilst on passage up the Thames, between Gravesend and Greenwich on 18th August 1977, the **Devonia** suffered engine failure and could not get beyond Greenwich. The next day she collided with a barge and ruptured her hull above the waterline in the process.

At the end of the season, both ships went to Dartmouth for early winter lay-up. Encouraged by the previous season's performance, there was more than the scintilla of a plan that for 1978, the **Balmoral** would be the Thames-based boat and the **Devonia**, with her vast cargo space and deeper draft, would cover the hoped-for Lundy Island supply service and Bristol Channel sailings generally. Various alterations were planned to make the **Devonia** more suitable for excursion-trip business.

In January 1978, the **Devonia** went on charter to Chevron Oil Inc. in Scotland. At the time, following the collapse of her trade in the wake of the tragic **Wahine** disaster, the former New Zealand turbo-electric express steamer, **Rangitira,** of the Union Steamship Co. Ltd. was in use as a static accommodation ship for oil workers at Loch Toscaig. Part of the **Devonia's** work was to ferry personnel between the **Rangitira**, the shore at Kyle and the oil-rig being constructed at Loch Kishorn in the Sound of Raasay. The **Rangitira** then went on to Sullom Voe in the Shetlands for similar work and after some years of then being idle at Falmouth she

finally found work in the Mediterranean running as the **Queen M.** for Marlines Lines and, later, as the **Carlo R.** belonging to Alimar, Italy. As a result of the **Devonia's** charter in Scotland, Campbell's had to retain the **Balmoral** for use on the Bristol Channel and abandon their plans for a service on the Thames, which had been eagerly awaited by the excursion ship fraternity.

The **Devonia** was only working for the oil industry in Scotland a short while and even in that brief period had grounded, been towed to Greenock and taken out of the water at Lamont's Shipyard for inspection and repairs. It turned out to be quite a major job requiring a new rudder, rudder stock, steady bearing, reconditioned starboard propeller and repairs to her keel in four separate places. Fortunately for them (as the **Scillonian**, she had been built to dry-out at low water and was often previously seen high and dry) she was a very hardy specimen.

Sooner than had been hoped, on 8th May 1978, the **Devonia** was released from her charter and then returned to the Bristol Channel. So, during the main summer season of 1978, Campbell's unexpectedly and hurriedly re-cast their schedules and briefly resumed a welcome, if wholly unexpected, two-ship Bristol Channel service. This had last occurred in 1971 when, prior to her port engine exploding, the **Westward Ho** had partnered the **Balmoral**. In the main, the **Devonia** was based at Swansea and, in addition to visiting the usual harbours and piers, made some rare visits to Pembroke Dock.

Following an all too short season, the **Devonia** returned to Bristol on 4th September 1978, for laying-up.

The **Balmoral** finished that season alone, including the annual four-day Scilly Isles trip, which was accomplished in rough but often sunny weather. On 22nd October, the **Balmoral** reportedly ran her longest day excursion of the season. She left Princes Wharf, Bristol at 08.15 hrs. and Cumberland Basin half an hour later with 300 passengers aboard; she set sail for Ilfracombe and Lundy where she arrived shortly before 16.00 hrs. She left Lundy again two hours later and it was not until 00.45 hrs. the next day that

*The **Balmoral** is seen here rounding the notorious Horseshoe Bend in the River Avon on 14th May 1977.*

Photo: Pat Murrell.

she safely entered the docks and tied up at Princes Wharf. Shortly thereafter, she was laid-up for the winter alongside the **Devonia** at The Grove, in Bristol City Docks.

The economics of running the two-ship service cannot have been good. From September 1978 onwards, the **Devonia** remained tied up at Bristol and only the 30-year-old **Balmoral** was made ready for the forthcoming season. Again, there was no work for the **Devonia**.

The **Balmoral** began her 1979 season on 10th April with a poorly patronised sailing from Ilfracombe to Lundy carrying just

*On 17th April 1978, the **Balmoral**, dressed overall, took what appears to be a capacity crowd to Sharpness.   Photo: C.C.A. archives.*

*This photograph of the **Devonia** was taken at Southend Pier on 28th August 1977 when she was running in the Thames area for Campbell's late that summer. Whilst the ship had a certain muscular charm about her, as is clear from the photograph, she was not a natural excursion ship. Like her quasi sister the **Queen of the Isles**, she too had been designed for the all-year-round cargo and passenger, rough weather passage from Penzance to the Scilly Islands. For the following season, she received a black hull, French grey upperworks and looked good in the full livery of P. & A. Campbell Ltd.   Photo: Author's collection.*

29 passengers, certainly not enough to pay even for the fuel. Easter that year was warm and sunny and some good loadings were achieved. On 21st April, the **Balmoral** had plenty of passengers aboard for a rare trip into the north Somerset harbour of Watchet, the first since 1971. There, she disembarked a large number of railway buffs who then went by steam train to Minehead, where the **Balmoral** picked them up later before returning to Barry.

A month later, on Saturday, 2nd June 1979, the **Waverley** visited Ilfracombe for the first time ever. By way of an unexpected bonus for passengers aboard the **Balmoral's** advertised trip to Lundy (where, due to a very strong easterly wind a landing was impossible) they got a ringside seat when the two ships met for the first time and were alongside at Ilfracombe together. The **Balmoral** returned to Bideford and Swansea and Campbell's 60 passengers not able to be picked up at Lundy due to the weather that day, were

*On 10th April 1976, the **Balmoral** was on charter to the Coastal Cruising Association and she is seen here, well laden, arriving at Cowes on her sailing from Bournemouth. Next day, she was on charter at Plymouth for a cruise out to the Eddystone Lighthouse.*   *Photo: Edwin Wilmshurst.*

collected by the **Waverley** when she made an unscheduled stop for them the next day. This was of course, some years before the two ships would both be sailing together under the P.S.P.S. banner, but it provided a brief foretaste of things to come.

Early that October, beginning on Friday 5th, the **Balmoral** set out on her then annual pilgrimage to Cornwall and the Isles of Scilly, but as we shall see, nature took a hand in the proceedings. Mr. Keith Adams was aboard and he presented an interesting account of the trip in the January 1980 edition of *Cruising Monthly*, the journal of the Coastal Cruising Association. It was to be the last ever down-Channel sailing from Weston's Birnbeck Pier before its closure.

From Weston to St. Ives is a sea voyage of more than double the

70-mile range limit for a Class III licence. So for this leg of the journey, the **Balmoral** was specially issued with a Board of Trade Class IIA passenger certificate (issued for ships engaged on any voyages other than international voyages) for 218 passengers and crew, being the number for which she had lifeboat and raft capacity.

Their willingness to do this stemmed from the **Balmoral's** sturdy origins and the fact that she was built to a design that at one rather optimistic time, back in the days of Red Funnel's irrepressible Captain Clarke, had been hoped to permit Class II (cross-Channel) use. This part of the trip was made with only a moderate sea running even though gales had been forecast. That evening, the **Balmoral** dried out completely on the tide whilst alongside at St. Ives. During the night the weather blew up and sadly it was decided that the **Balmoral** should remain tied up for the day. A number of hardy travellers managed to get themselves across to Penzance for what turned out to be a very rough trip to the Scilly Islands aboard the new, purpose-built **Scillonian III**, proving how wise the **Balmoral's** captain had been to stay in harbour at St. Ives.

Next day, Sunday, the weather had worsened still further and the **Balmoral** had quickly to leave the harbour wall, where she was heaving up and down taking a terrible pounding, and anchor out in St. Ives Bay. This was despite some heavy-duty tyres providing a certain amount of cushioning for her belting. Monday dawned with far calmer conditions in prospect for the return trip up-Channel to Weston, which was accomplished without further problems.

The **Balmoral's** ten-year demise charter from Red Funnel Steamers was finally completed and, upon payment by P. & A. Campbell Ltd. of £1.00 on 10th October 1979, she passed into their ownership.

If the longest day trip of the previous season (22nd October 1978) set any records, her 24 hour marathon starting at 01.00 hrs. on 13th October 1979 from Bristol, Penarth (03.00 hrs.) and

Ilfracombe (07.30 hrs.) to Lundy and return must be doubly so and all credit to Campbell's for their willingness to put on such long trips. The landing at Lundy was not possible due to the bad weather so an unpleasantly rough cruise around the Island was substituted, following which, six hours ashore in a rather dreary, end-of-season Ilfracombe was the remaining highlight available. The trip back up-Channel was again rough and dense fog came down at Bristol to engulf the weary ship, her passengers and crew. Late that night the **Balmoral** ended her day and it was decided that on account of the danger posed by fog in the river, she would remain there for the night and not sail back down to Penarth as originally planned.

In the December 1979 edition of *Cruising Monthly*, there was published a round-up of the end of season's sailings for the **Balmoral** and the piece ended with the following succinct paragraph:

'On the credit side, the **Balmoral** has mechanically performed very well while most of her sailings have seen average patronage. However, special mention should be made of the high season day-trips from Bristol (not seen since the days of two vessels) which brought encouraging results and the excellent loadings from Minehead, which were well up on 1978. On the debit side was the appalling weather, which forced a fair number of trips to be lost, the disappointment of the **Devonia** not earning revenue and the end of Weston calls. Fortunately, such set-backs are not stopping the White Funnel Fleet sailing into the 1980s'.

In making that bold statement in his last sentence, its writer could be forgiven for expressing his hopes and aspirations; indeed, they were widely held throughout the coastal and excursion ship fraternity. Unfortunately they were not in accord with those of P. & A. Campbell Ltd.'s management nor, perhaps more accurately, those of its parent company, European Ferries. They really did not see the Company with any ship-operating future at all, but a compromise was reached.

Sadly, P. & A. Campbell Ltd. announced the cessation of operating pleasure steamers in their own right at the end of the 1979 season but said they would retain an involvement with the excursion ship business by entering a joint venture with The Landmark Trust. Since 1969, that trust had been responsible for the administration of Lundy Island.

A new company called White Funnel Steamers Limited was formed with Campbell's Mr. S. Clifton Smith-Cox as its chairman and managing director and Mr. J. L. E. Smith of The Landmark Trust as its other director. Having recently bought the **Balmoral** outright from Red Funnel Steamers, P. & A. Campbell Ltd. then

The brand new **Scillonian III** *and the* **Balmoral** *at St. Mary's in the Isles of Scilly on 16th October 1977. In those days, the* **Balmoral** *used to run a very popular annual four-day trip from Bristol Channel ports to Cornwall and the Scillies. It was always run either at the very beginning or the very end of the season, so was often subject to severe disruption by gales and stormy weather.*
Photo: R.B. Adams.

*Here we see the **Balmoral** on 1st April 1979, in the entrance lock at Barry Dock on charter to the Lea Valley Railway Club who had hired special trains to bring their members from London, Paddington, down to Barry. At Barry they boarded the **Balmoral** for a cruise to Watchet arriving at the former G.W.R. pier. At Watchet, the passengers disembarked and joined a steam train which took them to Minehead where they rejoined the **Balmoral** for the return trip.   Photo: Richard Winfield.*

WHITE FUNNEL FLEET

P. & A. CAMPBELL LTD.

Sailings from BIRNBECK PIER, WESTON-S-MARE

With special coach connections from Bristol (for particulars see back of leaflet)

By the Motor Vessels BALMORAL and DEVONIA

THE BALMORAL which performs most of these excursions is a large sea-going ship capable of accommodating nearly 900 passengers. The vessel has a restaurant and tea bar where meals and snacks can be obtained, also fully licensed bars. There are two lounges, spacious open decks and covered accommodation is available sufficient for all passengers.

AUGMENTED SAILINGS—Sunday, July 23rd until Monday, October 9th, 1978

Passengers should allow themselves 10 minutes from the Pier Gates to the embarkation jetty

Passengers wishing to travel to Cardiff via Penarth are advised that a regular bus service now operates between Penarth Pier & Cardiff bus station. Open top bus tours of Cardiff (Capital City of Wales) also operate from Cardiff bus station.

SUNDAY, JULY 23rd
9.50 a.m. Day Trip to ILFRACOMBE and LUNDY ISLAND (to land). Due Ilfracombe 12.50 p.m. Lundy Island 2.40 p.m. Leave Lundy 5.00 p.m. Ilfracombe 6.45 p.m. due Weston 9.45 p.m.
9.50 a.m. Combined Steamer and Coach Tour via ILFRACOMBE to EXMOOR. Outwards via Challacombe and Simonsbath to Withypool, then on to North Molton and South Molton (stop for tea). Homeward via The Bray Valley to Blackmoor Gate and Combe Martin. Leave Ilfracombe 6.45 p.m.➤ due Weston 9.45 p.m.
Coach leaves Ilfracombe 5.00 p.m. (Coach Station) at 2.15 p.m.
9.50 a.m. Single Trip to PENARTH.
Note: Steamer leaves Penarth 9.00 a.m. for Weston.

MONDAY, JULY 24th
PENARTH (for Cardiff). Leave Weston 9.50 a.m., 7.40 p.m. Leave Penarth 9.00 a.m., 10.45 a.m., 8.30 p.m.
9.50 a.m.   } Cruises across the CHANNEL, back about 11.30 a.m. and
7.40 p.m.   } 9.20 p.m. respectively.
9.50 a.m. Combined Steamer and Coach Tour of the WELSH MOUNTAINS via PENARTH and allowing approximately 2 hours at PORTHCAWL. Passengers travel to Penarth by steamer and there join special coaches which steamer to take them for a tour of the Welsh Mountains via Pontypridd, Porth, Rhigos Mountain, Vale of Neath and Porthcawl. Returning to Penarth in time to connect with the steamer leaving there at 8.30 p.m., due Weston 9.20 p.m.
11.35 a.m. Day Trip to ILFRACOMBE and Cruise to NORTH POINT. Due to arrive Ilfracombe 2.30 p.m. Leave Ilfracombe 4.30 p.m., due Weston 7.35 p.m.
Note: Steamer leaves Penarth 10.15 a.m. for Weston.

THURSDAY, JULY 27th
11.15 a.m. Day Trip to ILFRACOMBE and Cruise to BIDEFORD BAY. Due Ilfracombe 2.30 p.m. Leave Ilfracombe 5.35 p.m., due Weston 8.55 p.m.
9.00 a.m. Single Trip to PENARTH.
Note: Steamer leaves Penarth 10.15 a.m. for Weston.

FRIDAY, JULY 28th
PENARTH (for Cardiff). Leave Weston 11.10 a.m., 2.30 p.m. and 4.50 p.m. Leave Penarth 10.15 a.m., 12.05 p.m. and 3.30 p.m.
11.10 a.m. & 2.30 p.m. Cruises across the CHANNEL. Back about 12.55 p.m. and 4.20 p.m. respectively.

SATURDAY, JULY 29th
PENARTH (for Cardiff). Leave Weston 11.30 a.m., 3.15 p.m. and 5.45 p.m. Leave Penarth 11.30 a.m., 2.00 p.m. and 4.15 p.m.
11.30 a.m. & 3.15 p.m. Cruises across the CHANNEL. Back about 2.50 p.m. and 5.05 p.m. respectively.

SUNDAY, JULY 30th
2.10 p.m. Cruise passing CLEVEDON, PORTISHEAD and up the AVON GORGE, calling at BRISTOL (due Bristol 4.00 p.m.).
2.10 p.m. Single Trip to BRISTOL (due Bristol 4.00 p.m.).
6.10 p.m. Single Trip to PENARTH.
Note: Steamer leaves Penarth 1.00 p.m. and Bristol 4.05 p.m. for Weston.

WEDNESDAY, AUGUST 2nd
PENARTH (for Cardiff). Leave Weston 3.15 p.m., 5.15 p.m. and 7.30 p.m. Leave Penarth 11.00 a.m., 4.15 p.m. and 6.15 p.m.
3.15 p.m. & 5.15 p.m. Cruises across the CHANNEL. Back about 5.05 p.m. and 7.05 p.m. respectively.

THURSDAY, AUGUST 3rd
10.30 a.m. Day Trip to ILFRACOMBE and Cruise to BIDEFORD BAY. Due Ilfracombe 1.40 p.m. Leave Ilfracombe 6.45 p.m., due Weston 7.45 p.m.
Note: Steamer leaves Penarth 2.30 p.m. for the Cruise.
7.50 p.m. Single Trip to PENARTH.
Note: Steamer leaves Penarth 9.30 a.m. for Weston.

FRIDAY, AUGUST 4th
10.55 a.m. Day Trip to MUMBLES and a Cruise along the GOWER COAST, due to arrive Mumbles 2.15 p.m. Leave Mumbles 4.35 p.m., due Weston 8.05 p.m.
10.55 a.m. Combined Steamer and Coach Tour to PORTHCAWL via MUMBLES. Passengers travel to Mumbles by steamer thence by coach to Porthcawl where they will arrive about 3.30 p.m. Return from Porthcawl Harbour at 5.40 p.m. by steamer direct to Weston (due 8.05 p.m.) Inclusive Fare £4.90 (children half price).
8.10 p.m. Single Trip to PENARTH.
Note: Steamers leave Penarth 10.00 a.m. and Porthcawl 5.40 p.m. for Weston.

SATURDAY, AUGUST 5th
9.50 a.m. Day Trip to LYNMOUTH, ILFRACOMBE and Cruise to LUNDY ISLAND ROADS. Due Lynmouth 12.25 p.m., Ilfracombe 1.10 p.m. Leave Ilfracombe 5.15 p.m., Lynmouth 6.00 p.m., due Weston 8.30 p.m.
10.00 a.m. Single Trip to LUNDY ISLAND, due Lundy 3.00 p.m.
A steamer also leaves Penarth 9.10 a.m. for Weston.
A steamer also leaves Penarth 3.25 p.m. for Weston.

SUNDAY, AUGUST 6th
9.50 a.m. Day Trip to ILFRACOMBE and LUNDY ISLAND (to land). Due Ilfracombe 12.40 p.m., Lundy Island 2.30 p.m. Leave Weston 9.55 p.m.
6.45 p.m. due Weston 9.55 p.m.
9.50 a.m. Combined Steamer and Coach Tour via ILFRACOMBE to EXMOOR. Outwards via Challacombe and Simonsbath to Withypool, and then on to North Molton and South Molton (stop for tea). Homeward via The Bray Valley to Blackmoor Gate and Combe Martin. Leave Ilfracombe 6.45 p.m., due Weston 9.55 p.m. Coach leaves Ilfracombe (Coach Station) at 2.15 p.m.
10.00 p.m. Single Trip to PENARTH.
Note: Steamer leaves Penarth 9.00 a.m. for Weston.

MONDAY, AUGUST 7th
PENARTH (for Cardiff). Leave Weston 9.50 a.m., 7.35 p.m. Leave Penarth 9.00 a.m., 10.45 a.m., 8.30 p.m.
9.50 a.m.   } Cruises across the CHANNEL, back about 11.30 a.m. and 9.20
7.35 p.m.   } p.m. respectively.
9.50 a.m. Combined Steamer and Coach Tour of the WELSH MOUNTAINS via PENARTH and allowing approximately 2 hours at PORTHCAWL. Passengers travel to Penarth by steamer and there join special coaches which steamer take them for a tour of the Welsh Mountains via Pontypridd, Porth, Rhigos Mountain, Vale of Neath and Porthcawl. Returning to Penarth in time to connect with the steamer leaving there at 8.30 p.m., due Weston 9.20 p.m.
11.35 a.m. Day Trip to ILFRACOMBE and Cruise to BULL POINT. Due to arrive Ilfracombe 2.35 p.m. Leave Ilfracombe 4.30 p.m., due Weston 7.30 p.m.

WEDNESDAY, AUGUST 9th
PENARTH (for Cardiff). Leave Weston 9.50 a.m., 8.20 p.m. Leave Penarth 9.00 a.m., 10.45 a.m. and 7.30 p.m.
9.50 a.m. Cruise across the CHANNEL. Back about 11.30 a.m.
11.45 a.m. Day Trip to ILFRACOMBE, due Weston 2.45 p.m. Leave Ilfracombe 4.30 p.m., due Weston 8.15 p.m.

THURSDAY, AUGUST 10th
PENARTH (for Cardiff). Leave Weston 9.50 a.m., 12.10 p.m., 7.15 p.m. and 8.10 p.m.
9.05 a.m. Leave Penarth 9.20 a.m., 11.10 a.m., 1.15 p.m. and 8.10 p.m.
10.15 a.m., 12.10 p.m. & 7.15 p.m. Cruises across the CHANNEL. Back about 12 noon, 2.05 p.m. and 9.00 p.m. respectively.

FRIDAY, AUGUST 11th
10.40 a.m. Day Trip to MUMBLES and a Cruise along the GOWER COAST, due to arrive Mumbles 2.15 p.m. Leave Mumbles 4.40 p.m., due Weston 8.05 p.m.
10.40 a.m. Combined Steamer and Coach Tour to PORTHCAWL and MUMBLES. Passengers travel by steamer to Porthcawl (due 1.05 p.m.). Return from Porthcawl by special coach at 3.30 p.m. to Mumbles thence by steamer direct to Weston (due 8.05 p.m.) Inclusive Fare £4.90 (children half price).
8.10 p.m. Single Trip to PENARTH.
Note: Steamer leaves Penarth 9.45 a.m. for Weston.

SUNDAY, AUGUST 13th
11.40 a.m. Cruise passing CLEVEDON, PORTISHEAD and up the AVON GORGE, calling at BRISTOL, due about 3.45 p.m.
11.40 a.m. Single Trip to BRISTOL (due Bristol 1.30 p.m.).
4.35 p.m. Single Trip to PENARTH.
Note: Steamer leaves Penarth 10.45 a.m. for Weston. A Steamer also leaves Bristol 2.00 p.m. for Weston.

MONDAY, AUGUST 14th
PENARTH (for Cardiff). Leave Weston 9.50 a.m., 3.15 p.m. and 5.40 p.m. Leave Penarth 9.50 a.m. & 3.15 p.m. Cruises across the CHANNEL. Back about 3.05 p.m. and 5.05 p.m. respectively.

TUESDAY, AUGUST 15th
2.30 p.m. Afternoon Cruise passing CLEVEDON, PORTISHEAD and up the AVON GORGE, calling at BRISTOL. Due about 6.15 p.m.
2.30 p.m. Single Trip to BRISTOL (due Bristol 4.20 p.m.).
7.00 p.m. Single Trip to PENARTH.
Note: Steamer leaves Penarth 1.30 p.m. for Weston. A Steamer also leaves Bristol 4.30 p.m. for Weston.

FRIDAY, AUGUST 18th
10.30 a.m. Day Trip to ILFRACOMBE 4.30 p.m. due Weston 7.55 p.m.
Ilfracombe 1.45 p.m. and a Special Circular excursion to MINEHEAD, also to Butlin's Holiday Camp at Minehead. Passengers leave Birnbeck Pier Gates at 10.45 a.m. by special coach for Minehead arriving there about 12.45 p.m. Return from Minehead Harbour by steamer at 6.15 p.m., due Weston 7.55 p.m. Admission to Butlin's Holiday Camp payable on entry.
8.30 p.m. Single Trip to PENARTH.
Note: Steamers leave Penarth 9.30 a.m. and Minehead 6.15 p.m. for Weston.

SUNDAY, AUGUST 20th
9.50 a.m. Day Trip to ILFRACOMBE and LUNDY ISLAND (to land). Due Ilfracombe 12.40 p.m., Lundy Island 2.30 p.m. Leave Lundy 5.00 p.m., Ilfracombe 6.45 p.m., due Weston 9.55 p.m.
9.50 a.m. Combined Steamer and Coach Tour via ILFRACOMBE to EXMOOR. Outwards via Challacombe and Simonsbath to Withypool, and then on to North Molton and South Molton (stop for tea). Homeward via The Bray Valley to Blackmoor Gate and Combe Martin. Leave Ilfracombe 6.45 p.m. due Weston. Coach leaves Ilfracombe (Coach Station) at 2.15 p.m.
10.00 p.m. Single Trip to PENARTH.
Note: Steamer leaves Penarth 9.00 a.m. for Weston.

MONDAY, AUGUST 21st
10.25 a.m. Day Trip to MUMBLES and a Cruise along the GOWER COAST, due to arrive Mumbles 1.35 p.m. Leave Mumbles 4.50 p.m., due Weston 8.00 p.m.
8.05 p.m. Single Trip to PENARTH.
Note: Steamer leaves Penarth 9.30 a.m. for Weston.

PENARTH (for Cardiff). Leave Weston 9.50 a.m. and 8.35 p.m. Leave Penarth 9.00 a.m., 10.45 a.m. and 7.40 p.m.

FOR FURTHER SAILINGS, FARES, GENERAL INFORMATION AND CONDITIONS—see over.

This fascinating August 1978 photograph shows the **Balmoral** *anchored off the North Devon harbour of Clovelly at low water and landing her passengers by local tender.* Photo: Malcolm McRonald.

chartered her to the new joint venture company. The obvious problem with the new arrangement was that the **Balmoral** had no capacity for bulky cargo and supplies so, where once it was planned to utilise the former **Scillonian** for the carriage of passengers and cargo, now two vessels would probably be required - the **Balmoral** and another for supplies.

In a rare press announcement dated 20th March 1980, by European Ferries Ltd. about its subsidiary, P. & A. Campbell Ltd., they extolled the virtues of the new arrangements for the 1980 summer season, under which all profits from the joint venture (if indeed there were any) would accrue for the benefit of Lundy Island.

It was stated, *inter alia*, that they had been trying for some time to rationalise this smaller area of their operations and they were reluctant to deprive the Bristol Channel of a major tourist attraction and Lundy Island of its vital link. Their approach was one of a gentle let-down.

In the same announcement it was stated that the *Devonia* was available for sale or charter. The covert message underlying the press announcement was that minor outfits like P. & A. Campbell Ltd. were really something of a distraction, which these days European Ferries could now well do without. They certainly had no plans of their own to prolong pleasure steamer services in the Bristol Channel or anywhere else for that matter.

However, that year's events began hopefully enough with the *Balmoral* having been at Penzance that winter. Her season began at Bristol on 1st April 1980 with a trip from Ilfracombe to Lundy the next day with just 46 passengers aboard. Easter sailings were dogged by bad weather, which persisted throughout much of the season. Contemporary reports state that the general condition and visual state of the ship was not good, due to bad weather early in the season and the fact that her paint supply had been stolen from its store in the still idle *Devonia*!

The weather remained rough for much of the summer and, in mid-September, gales wreaked havoc with her efforts to close the season profitably. The 18th was a particularly bad September day and on leaving Ilfracombe, bound for Lundy, the *Balmoral* had to turn back and seek shelter because of the weather - and it does have to be rough for the *Balmoral* to admit defeat.

One bright event in an otherwise rather sorry season was on 27th September when the *Balmoral* sailed from Bristol to Steep Holm Island for the first ever White Funnel landing there. For the second year running, the weather was unkind for the planned annual trip to Cornwall and the Isles of Scilly which again only reached as far as St. Ives. Between Ilfracombe and St. Ives the weather was so bad her passengers had to travel by coach! For her final day's sailings of the season, supposedly to Ilfracombe and Lundy, strong easterly wind meant that once again a landing at Lundy would be impossible and was therefore not attempted.

Of all the years that the *Balmoral* desperately needed to make

a good impression, particularly with the new Lundy Island arrangements, nothing seemed to work in her favour. When the *Balmoral's* season closed on 14 October 1980, she sailed light from Penarth to Bristol for what everyone assumed was to be her normal winter lay-up and nothing that had been said would have prepared her loyal supporters for the news that lay immediately ahead. Indeed, Campbell's had by then drawn up their proposals for the forthcoming season necessitating a costly refit for the *Balmoral* (or the *Devonia*) but The Landmark Trust was not interested.

In fact, it transpired that Lundy Island had its own agenda, not involving the *Devonia* or the *Balmoral*, and was keen to get its own boat as quickly as possible. European Ferries and P. & A. Campbell Ltd. had, the previous year, made it quite clear that as far as they were concerned the only way forward was via The Landmark Trust arrangement.

Not surprisingly, it was said that the joint venture had lost a small fortune in 1980 so it ended abruptly after just that one, none too happy, season. Facing redundancy for the second time in her career, the *Balmoral* suffered the ignominy of being put up for sale once again.

Both the *Balmoral* and *Devonia* were laid-up, first at Bristol and later at Avonmouth where it was hoped that their proximity to the Channel, giving improved accessibility and security might help them find a buyer more quickly. Neither vessel was to prove easy to sell!

More than a whole year went by as both ships sank further into the seemingly inescapable morass of obsolescence and redundancy. They remained at Avonmouth, superfluous to their owner's needs. With no revenue-earning capacity, both vessels were now a drain on capital and, having no obvious suitors, their prospects could hardly have been worse.

At the end of 1981, salvation for the *Devonia* came rather unexpectedly from Torbay Seaways and Stevedores Ltd. who, according to Russell Plummer's articles in *Ships Monthly*, had been running a cargo service from Torquay to Alderney employing the coaster **Ontic** and excursion trips in Torbay using the **New Roseland**. Torbay Seaways bought her from P. & A. Campbell Ltd. at a price of £90,000 and she was to make her own way to Torquay via the Dart, following overhaul that December.

It was not until March 1982 that our ship, the **Balmoral**, finally managed to secure some sort of a future for herself but, this time, it was to be for static use as a floating public house and restaurant at Dundee. A new company called Craig Inns Ltd. bought her from P. & A. Campbell Ltd. for £30,000 (the same figure Campbell's had themselves paid for the ship some 13 years previously) and on 25th March 1982, she set sail under her own power for Dundee. Her delivery voyage took her south-west from Avonmouth, round Land's End and along the South Coast (passing all her old haunts en route) through the Straits of Dover before heading north for the Tay.

One member of her new owner's family was a qualified ship's master and despite encountering dense fog for much of the journey he safely delivered the **Balmoral** non-stop, Avonmouth to Dundee, four days later. This was a record for her, being by a considerable margin, her longest-ever continuous voyage. Various work was done on her in readiness for her new job, including the welding of some steel skids on her port side, to ensure that she rose and fell with the tide and remained safely attached to Dundee's none too salubrious dock wall.

Sadly, the venture foundered almost as soon as it had begun and after a few months, the **Balmoral**, then known as The Inn on the Quay, was boarded up and, *prima facie*, left mouldering. At the time, that area of Dundee was run down and hardly the place for a fledgling business to make a good, vibrant start as a floating night-spot aboard the **Balmoral**. As if Avonmouth was not a bad enough potential graveyard for the ship, at Dundee she fell to her very lowest ebb, from which few gave her any chance of resurrection.

Meanwhile, the **Devonia**, by then renamed **Devoniun**, had arrived at Torquay where she was repainted white and started her new service from Torquay to Guernsey and Alderney on 15th May 1982. She was a great success, too successful for her own good some would say, as she was replaced less than three seasons later, first with a hydrofoil carrying passengers only and a year later with a car ferry from the Western Isles. Originally, it should have been the **Clansman** from Caledonian MacBrayne, but Torbay Seaways, like others before them, came up against Torquay Town Council who really did not want to develop their harbour as a roll on-roll off port. So the **Clansman** was sold on to Malta and eventually her former sistership, the **Hebrides**, took up the service from Torquay to the Channel Islands loading vehicles via her hydraulic lift and ramps. Slow and cumbersome it may have been, nevertheless no linkspan was needed and therefore little interference came forth from the Town Hall.

Thereafter, the **Devoniun** briefly went north to serve the Orkney and Shetland Islands as the **Syllingar** (Norse for Scilly) where sadly, her new owners went into liquidation.

It was in May 1986 that the author was in Scotland at the Sheriff's Court in connection with the **Waverley's** now well-known and difficult sailing from Garlieston to Douglas in a gale, the previous April. It was the natural thing for him to detour from Stranraer to Greenock and pay his last respects to the now battered, former old **Scillonian**, by then flying the Greek flag prior to her setting sail for the Mediterranean on the night of 17th May 1986.

Renamed **Remvi** and registered in Piraeus, she was extensively rebuilt (increasing her tonnage from 921 to 1315 gross tons) before commencing operations for her new owners, Hellenic Cruising Holidays of Piraeus. Nothing has been heard of her for the last few years.

After almost 100 years of operations, P & A Campbell Ltd. had ceased all trading activity on 31st December 1981. There is little doubt that without the employment of the pretty little **St. Trillo** from 1963 and of the former Red Funnel stalwarts **Vecta** and **Balmoral** from late 1965 and 1969 respectively, for Campbell's, the end would have come permanently, far sooner.

The Balmoral in Partnership with the Waverley

Back in 1959, the formation of the Paddle Steamer Preservation Society, which was the first ship preservation society in Britain, got under way. Prior to that, a number of like-minded people, not all enthusiasts *per se*, but all with a common sense of purpose, had become concerned at the alarming rate at which paddle steamers were disappearing from our shores. They united to form the Paddle Steamer Preservation Society and to see what could be done at a practical level, by discussions with operators and if necessary by outright purchase of threatened ships, to draw a halt to the loss of all these fine old steamers. From those humble beginnings, the Society now has 3,500 members today and is responsible for the three historic vessels remaining beautifully preserved in regular operational use.

In 1962, they tried to make their first acquisition by bidding for the paddle steamer **Alumchine**, a 76-ton vessel recently displaced from the Pembroke Dock - Neyland ferry. Despite goodwill and effort on all sides, this fell through because of the impossibly high cost of towing the ferry to Southampton for restoration and preservation. Sadly, the little **Alumchine** was scrapped, but history will show her to have been the catalyst for even more concentrated preservation efforts in future.

The Society's first successful acquisition was the former River Dart paddle steamer, the **Kingswear Castle**, built by Philip & Son Ltd. Dartmouth in 1924 for the River Dart Steamboat Co. Ltd. She had been withdrawn from commercial service in 1965. For the princely sum of £600, she was purchased by the P.S.P.S. in 1967 and, after nearly four years berthed on the mud in the Isle of Wight, she began the journey that, eight months later, would see her safely to her new base at Rochester on the River Medway. First she was towed to East Cowes where she had some preliminary work done on

her to permit the long tow east to be undertaken. In June 1971, she was towed the rest of the way to the Medway for what was then described as 'a substantial refit'. This must rank as the most masterly piece of under-statement ever uttered!

It was fully thirteen years later, during which long period she was virtually completely rebuilt with tremendous care and passion by her supporters, that she was finally restored to her former 1924 glory. She underwent her first trials in November 1983 and began limited public sailings the following year. The efforts of all concerned will go down in the annals of history as being one of the great, but hitherto mostly unsung, success stories of the excursion ship business. These days, every summer, the **Kingswear Castle** operates a full season's sailings around the Medway and the lower Thames in mostly sheltered waters, with full passenger certificates for all her varied excursions.

Five years after the **Kingswear Castle** was acquired, the Paddle Steamer Preservation Society really went into pleasure steamer ownership in a big way with its second acquisition, which was the paddle steamer **Waverley**. Towards the end of 1973, it had been announced by the state-owned Scottish Transport Group that they would in future be operating just one big excursion cruise ship in the Clyde area, and this was to be the turbine steamer **Queen Mary II**, not the **Waverley**.

As a result, the last sea-going paddle steamer in the world, the **Waverley**, was taken out of service on 30th September 1973 and laid-up in James Watt Dock, Greenock.

Believing the **Waverley** to be the better all-round vessel (of which there was little doubt) and far more charismatic in terms of crowd-pulling ability, there were many who questioned the wisdom of that decision.

Above: Soon to be renamed **Prince Ivanhoe**, *the ill-fated former Portsmouth based ferry* **Shanklin** *is seen here with the* **Waverley** *at Stobcross Quay, Glasgow on 30th November 1980, just a few days after she had arrived from the South.*
Photo: Ken Angus.

Above right: Whilst coming up the River Avon to Bristol for the very first time, in the early hours of the 1st May 1981, the **Prince Ivanhoe** *hit a rock and holed the outer skin of her hull. As a result, she had first to go on to the grid-iron at the entrance to the Cumberland Basin for inspection (where she is seen in this photograph) following which she went into dry-dock at Barry for £20,000 worth of permanent repairs.*
Photo: Author's collection.

Right: Few ships have had more lives than the former 1931-built Red Funnel ferry **Medina**. *She was sold to Metrex Industries Ltd for breaking up at Denton Island in the back of Newhaven Harbour in 1982, where she is seen here in the photograph dated 22nd December 1982. Before breaking-up had commenced, she was then resold and had several more static uses until being finally broken up on the Tyne at the fine old age of 67, in 1998.*
Photo: Tim Cooper.

As things turned out quite quickly, preservationists were to be the ultimate beneficiaries. On 8th August 1974, (whilst technically sold for £1.00) the **Waverley** was donated by Caledonian MacBrayne Ltd. to the Paddle Steamer Preservation Society's new company, named Waverley Steam Navigation Co. Ltd., for preservation. Originally there had been little thought of returning the steamer to service, it having been contemplated that she would fulfil the role of museum ship and restaurant moored locally.

Immediately thereafter, the Society's fund raising machinery went straight into top gear and, after a lot of people, companies, local and other charitably minded bodies had been persuaded to dig deep into their pockets, sufficient funds were raised to enable the ship to go to sea again, on 22nd May 1975.

The Scottish Transport Group had shown considerable (some people might even say uncharacteristic) foresight in the paperwork that had been prepared for the gifting of the **Waverley**. However unlikely they may have thought the possibility that the **Waverley** could ever be restored to full working standard, they took the precaution of stipulating that the ship was never to be used in competition with their own fleet of ships.

On 15th July 1977, the **Waverley** *grounded spectacularly on the Gantocks Rocks, off Dunoon and was holed in several places below the waterline putting her out of action until 1st September. During that period, the little motorship* **Queen of Scots** *(built 1935) that was originally the* **Coronia** *of Scarborough was chartered. She became Croson's* **Bournemouth Queen** *during the period 1968 to 1974 when, in that October, she was sold to Sir Robert McAlpine & Son Ltd., Ardyne (who immediately renamed her* **Queen of Scots***) for ferrying construction personnel on the Clyde. If not a lot else, she proved to the* **Waverley** *organisation the need to have a back-up vessel.*

Photo: Author's negative library.

This meant that, once operational again, the paddler had to be based right down at Ayr or up at Glasgow, two places long since abandoned by Caledonian MacBrayne's predecessors as being totally uneconomic.

As we saw in the previous chapter, by 1979, the **Waverley** was getting around the British Isles quite a bit, including her first trip to Ilfracombe where she met up with the **Balmoral**.

The fleet of preserved vessels operating under the Paddle Steamer Preservation Society banner was never originally intended to include the **Balmoral** at all. As we shall see, the **Balmoral** joined the preserved fleet some years later. That may seem surprising to readers of this book who, these days, probably look upon the **Waverley** and the **Balmoral** as being virtually synonymous.

The third ship, **Kingswear Castle** is operated separately on her own very interesting timetable, based on Rochester and Chatham with additional special sailings from Strood.

The **Waverley** organisation had already had some experience of operating a second ship in support of the **Waverley** when they chartered the little **Queen of Scots** (ex-**Bournemouth Queen**, ex-**Coronia**) in 1977 after the **Waverley's** near-fatal grounding on the Gantocks Rocks off Dunoon. By 1980 they were therefore all too aware of the vulnerability of their own one-ship operation and wanted to find a suitable second ship as soon as possible.

They had already inspected the Portsmouth ferry **Shanklin** and had concluded that she would make an excellent ship for their fleet, should her purchase be possible in the future. In fact, they did not have to wait too long for their wish to come true.

The Sealink ferry **Shanklin** became available in the autumn of 1980 and, on the **Waverley** organisation's behalf, what was described as a group of Scottish businessmen bought the **Shanklin** and had her registered in the name of the Firth of Clyde Steam Packet Co. Ltd. This was before it had become known that P. & A. Campbell Ltd. were effectively finished.

At Portsmouth, Sealink had been considering employing two purpose-built fast catamarans for the Ryde passenger service and with this in mind, they had laid-up the **Shanklin** in March 1980 leaving the service in the hands of the sometimes hard-pressed **Southsea** and **Brading** (the **Shanklin's** elder sisters). The **Shanklin** had been chosen for lay-up as she was suffering from what they thought were major problems with her port main engine.

After obtaining the necessary paperwork for the voyage north, the **Shanklin** set sail on the afternoon of 13th November 1980 with just her starboard main engine in operation. A week later, after encountering storms and heavy seas on the way, she safely arrived at Helensburgh and then moved on up the Clyde to Glasgow.

What was then needed was a huge injection of time, energy and cash to get her into Class again so that she could get fresh passenger certificates for the year ahead.

Here we turn to the words of Mr. Nigel Coombes:

'Possibly the bleakest day in the **Balmoral's** *life was the 28th March 1981. It was also, paradoxically a moment of great optimism in the on-going history of Bristol Channel sailings, whose continuation had been suddenly rescued by the purchase of the* **Shanklin** *to be a running mate for the* **Waverley**. *The* **Shanklin** *was already undergoing overhaul in Glasgow and the* **Balmoral**, *with the* **Devonia** *alongside, was up for sale in Bristol's City Docks. In a gesture of goodwill Clifton Smith-Cox gave his permission for the* **Balmoral's** *buoyancy apparatus and life-saving equipment to be removed to the* **Shanklin**, *by now renamed* **Prince Ivanhoe**, *to assist the new project. A team, under the supervision of Capt. Murray Patterson, loaded the equipment onto a waiting lorry for the return trip to Scotland. When the task was finished I climbed aboard the* **Devonia** *to reflect on a job well done. My mood changed. Somehow, the* **Balmoral** *seemed suddenly empty - pillaged of everything which symbolised a useful career, a ravaged ghost of my happy days, a forlorn hulk fit only for the knacker's yard. Suddenly memories came flooding back . . . Idyllic Lundy afternoons and the heavy scent of spring gorse; wonderfully comfortable pints after the trip, at Birnbeck,*

These eight, superbly historic photographs were taken during 1985 and 1986. Above left: The **Balmoral** *in dry-dock at Dundee in March 1985, undergoing preliminary survey following her 'eleventh hour' rescue. Above right: The* **Balmoral** *passing the Stobcross crane in January 1986, en route from Anderston Quay . . .*

*. . . Glasgow to Clydedock Engineering Ltd. at Govan where she was to be substantially rebuilt. Above, and opposite page bottom: The **Balmoral** at Govan during the various stages of her major rebuilding and refurbishment. The quality of her restoration is a credit to all concerned.*   *All photos: Joe McKendrick.*

chatting with a few friends in front of a roaring log fire; Captain Jack Wide's peerless seamanship at Ilfracombe on a windy day when, surely we would have to go back up-Channel by coach. I honestly thought, then, that this was the end'.

Following the apparent end of the agreement between P. & A. Campbell Ltd. and The Landmark Trust, the Firth of Clyde Steam Packet Co. Ltd. offered to charter its new purchase (which was by then named **Prince Ivanhoe**) to them for use in the Bristol Channel, as she was then immediately available and not required elsewhere. Certainly, the newly restored ship would have cost much less to commission than either the **Balmoral** or the **Devonia** at that stage of the proceedings.

It quickly became clear that there was to be no commercial activity, competition or resistance from Campbell's ever in the future and with that, the **Prince Ivanhoe** started her second career, this time on the Bristol Channel directly under the auspices of the **Waverley** Organisation.

There were a few uncomfortable moments early in that first summer season of 1981 as the new ship and her men, became familiar with her various ports, harbours and piers, but this was only to be expected. Business had built up to generally good levels and there was no doubt that the **Prince Ivanhoe** was an excellent ship, now that her port main engine had been fairly permanently repaired. With her huge beam, she was as roomy as a paddle steamer, but as economic as the other motorships. Her future looked very bright indeed.

In order to benefit from this increased business, it had been decided to apply to the Department of Trade and Industry, for an extension to the **Prince Ivanhoe's** Class III certificate, to enable her to sail after dark. As we read earlier, there are a number of fair weather, range and distance qualifications attached to Class III certificates, including the fact that they only normally permitted ships with full navigation lights (as had the **Prince Ivanhoe**) to sail not later than one hour after sunset.

On 3rd August 1981 the **Prince Ivanhoe** was on her 14.15 hrs.

excursion from Mumbles to cruise along the Gower Coast due to return at 17.15 hrs. Captain Goldie was navigating the ship and was a fully qualified pilot for the voyage. Down below, the ship's own master, Captain David Neill and chief engineer Mr. Ian McMillan were discussing the extension to the ship's Class III certificate with the government marine surveyor, when disaster struck. Having rounded Port Eynon point at 15.35 hrs., the **Prince Ivanhoe** hit some uncharted wreckage or obstruction and tore a 60 foot gash in her hull, which breached adjacent watertight bulkheads. With her compartments flooding, tough though she was, from this there could be no recovery. Her situation was dire and it was clear that she was sinking. Her engines were stopped and she began to drift. Captain Neill immediately returned to the bridge and took control of the situation that instant.

Here we read the emotive words of Mr. Alan Brown, taken from his superb book entitled **Shanklin**, *Ill-fated Prince.*

*'Since the **Prince Ivanhoe** was taking in water rapidly the sole course of action was to beach the ship as quickly as possible, and fortunately the gently sloping sand bottomed beach at Horton was only about a mile away, but would the engines start - and continue to run? Then mercifully, the sharp hiss of starting air was heard, followed immediately by the continuous dull rumble and vibration of the diesels. Captain Neill first cautiously backed the ship, heavy with water and sluggish in response, to turn the head towards the beach. Then after a momentary silence, a column of black smoke erupted from the funnel as the throttles were pushed fully open and the two Sulzers, with only oily salt water for lubrication, pounded away on their final task. On the fo'c's'le a leads-man took soundings and as shallow water was reached, so the ship slowed and came to rest gently and smoothly on the sand, about 100 yards from the shore. Captain Neill's quick and correct actions and the dedication of the engineers, now almost waist deep in black sludge, undoubtedly averted what could have been a major disaster'.*

Whilst all 400 passengers managed to get safely ashore, sadly, one passenger passed away shortly thereafter.

It was reported that, dated 5th August 1981, Captain D.L. Neill made the final entry in the ship's log following which, the ship was abandoned to the underwriters as a constructive total loss.

During 1981, the **Waverley** first joined the elite band of vessels to have circumnavigated mainland Britain, no doubt enjoying the extra steam provided by her new £200,000 boiler fitted the previous winter.

With the sad demise of her new partner, the bereaved **Waverley** sailed on alone and her season ended on 28th September 1981. During the season, she had carried 194,000 people.

Terrible though her loss was, the **Prince Ivanhoe** had not died completely in vain as, during her all-too-short second career, she proved that with proper marketing and husbandry, the business to support the extra ship really was there to be developed to mutual advantage.

From then on, between 1982 and 1985, the **Waverley** maintained the main Clyde summer programme and fitted in sailings in various areas at other times. For each of those seasons, she managed about a month of sailings on the Bristol Channel and also elsewhere around the coast although not on the scale of the **Balmoral's** peregrinations these days.

Within most of the **Waverley** organisation, the need to restore the seagoing fleet to two ships was understood. Whilst the primary ship would always be the **Waverley**, another vessel was needed to act as back-up and to bring in extra revenue against which the fixed overheads of the whole operation could be partially set.

The marginal cost of the second ship, that is to say the extra cost of running two ships rather than one, makes it viable even though the second ship in isolation cannot hope to make much actual profit. Those who see the situation purely in cash terms will not see the logic for having the second ship, especially if it is not (even) a paddler. It needs to be remembered that there are other vitally important, non-monetary factors supporting the argument

for the second ship too. The greatest benefit is certainly gained by helping to preserve the infrastructure at piers and harbours. Local councils and authorities would otherwise not maintain these if the **Waverley** alone paid only ephemeral visits - the second ship potentially doubles the operational presence. To quote Mr. Terry Sylvester's now famous and oft-repeated phrase, *'Piers need pleasure steamers as much as pleasure steamers need piers'*.

Another reason for having two ships not one, concerns being taken seriously by the authorities. One old ship might simply be construed as an unwanted nuisance, whereas with two or three vintage vessels in the fleet, the organisation as a whole has much more influence on the Department of Transport, the Maritime and Coastguard Agency, licensing and port authorities around the coast. The regulations governing passenger ships are not made with veteran excursion ships in mind yet, to honour the spirit of the regulations (if not the letter) some considerable sympathy needs to be shown for the essential character of the old ships. Equally, the extra vessel provides a finite back-up in case of major breakdown or work having to be done on the **Waverley** during the season, thus maintaining continuity of life-giving revenue.

Looked at in terms of passenger numbers, there are only a certain number of customers likely to be inclined towards sea excursions and related pastimes during any given season. The maximum number of potential passengers is quite stubborn and hard to increase whatever the effort. The number will vary downwards from that potential maximum according to many things.

Variables such as:- the weather, suitability and availability of timetables, so that customers get to know and like what is on offer, the total price of the excursion, interesting places to go to, available extras such as horse tram and steam train rides, the success of competing attractions, and so on, all have a major effect. Like any other business, the optimum excursion ship operation is the one that attracts the highest percentage of the available business, at the minimum cost.

*The **Kingswear Castle** was the first outright preservation success for the Paddle Steamer Preservation Society. They bought her in 1967 since when she has been completely and beautifully rebuilt. With her skipper, John Megoran, in command, she now operates a full schedule of summer passenger sailings between Chatham, Rochester, Strood and occasionally farther afield too. This photograph, taken off Chatham, dates from 3rd October 1987. The **Waverley** had had to completely abort her South Coast sailings due to boiler trouble as a result of which, the **Balmoral** had stood in manfully and covered the entire programme. There have been a number of occasions since, when the virtue of having the dependable reserve vessel **Balmoral** to rely on has proved invaluable.*　　　*Photo: John Goss.*

The **Balmoral** *was just two months into her third career when she was photographed in Lundy Roads on 18th June 1986, in the company of the* **Waverley** *(built 1947) and Lundy Island's own supply ship, the* **Oldenburg** *(built 1958). This first meeting of the three ships had been engineered by Bristol Channel Agent, Comdr. Tom Foden and was marketed as 'The Three Ships Festival'.*
Photo: Tim Cooper.

Immediately after the first 'Three Ships Festival' on 18th June 1986, the **Balmoral** *then went to North Wales for a successful but very short visit (just over a week) based at Llandudno. It had been intended that the* **Balmoral** *would go on to Fleetwood and Barrow but unfortunately pilotage could not be arranged. Therefore, she remained at Llandudno for the final weekend before returning south via Swansea, where she met up with the* **Waverley** *on 30th June. The* **Balmoral** *is seen here a year later at Llandudno Pier on 8th June 1987.*

Photo: Author.

The belief was, and remains, that two coastal ships provide the optimum ratio of coverage : costs. More ships would increase operating costs without necessarily increasing that stubbornly set number of available passengers. Both the **Waverley** and the support vessel have roving commissions. The **Waverley** is very much the Scottish cruise vessel but sails elsewhere from time to time. The support vessel would find its main business in the Bristol Channel area but goes farther afield in search of passengers and also deputises for the **Waverley**.

And so, the search for a support ship, the new partner for the **Waverley**, gathered pace. Despite the advent of the new generations of vehicle and passenger ferries at Portsmouth, the late **Prince Ivanhoe's** elder sisters, the **Southsea** and the **Brading** were still in use there. However, by then the **Brading** was becoming unreliable and in 1986, had to be retired and parts cannibalised to help keep the **Southsea** running. The **Southsea** would not be available for a while anyway.

The only two relevant ships that were available, were the **Balmoral** (and she had been out of service at Dundee for almost four years) and her one-time old fleetmate the **Devonia**, the former **Scillonian**. Both vessels were by then, very much unknown quantities. The former **Scillonian**, with her deeper draft and vast redundant cargo space, was not likely to be suitable as a running mate for the **Waverley** without significant work being done on her. The **Waverley** organisation also briefly considered the former Red Funnel tug/tender **Calshot**, by then renamed **Galway Bay** and redundant in Eire.

So, undeterred, it was decided to approach the Bank of Scotland, which was selling the **Balmoral** as 'mortgagee in possession', with a view to inspecting the ship.

On 21st December 1984, Captain David Neill sent a memorandum to all Waverley Steam Navigation Co. Ltd. directors to the effect that he and **Waverley** engineers Mr. Ken Blacklock and Mr. Ken Angell had just visited the **Balmoral** at Dundee and to tell the board of their findings.

Mr. Blacklock was the **Waverley's** chief engineer and Mr. Angell was a former Campbell's man who fortunately knew the **Balmoral** and all her little idiosyncrasies well. Apparently, so the story goes, the Bank of Scotland bank manager accompanied them to the dockside to view the drab spectacle in which his bank had invested so heavily. The arrival of these three ship's officers to inspect the **Balmoral** must have appeared to him as a sign that Christmas had come early to his part of Scotland in 1984. Privately, he was probably praying earnestly for what had previously seemed the unlikely prospect of being able sell this rusting, rather forlorn piece of nautical security over which his bank was unfortunate enough to have a marine mortgage.

Fortunately for all concerned, one of the two engineers knew his way around the **Balmoral** well and, better still, not only did he know the necessary mantra with which to wake the sleeping Gods of Sirron but he also knew where the engine room light switches were!

When engineers Blacklock and Angell went below, they succeeded in getting a generator going and soon topped-up the starting-air tanks. Moments later, they let the sibilant blast of compressed air rush into the **Balmoral's** sleepy cylinders and with it, her main engines started-up thunderously and came reassuringly back to life. It is not difficult to imagine the bank manager's utter astonishment to find smoke pouring healthily from the **Balmoral's** dirty funnel and that her silent, empty decks, were now vibrating to the dull throb of her Newbury Sirron diesels as they settled down and rumbled away gently.

That was a very significant engineering success. Mr. Blacklock and Mr. Angell had proved that they were not buying just any old derelict hulk and happily were able to report that all was well down in the **Balmoral's** bowels department!

Presumably Captain Neill was able to speak for the rest of the ship as advocates Messrs. McFadyen and Semple were then instructed to make an offer of £20,000 for the **Balmoral**, on behalf of the **Waverley** organisation. This was accepted and a delivery date of on (or about) 22nd February 1985 was agreed. The acquisition was actually made in the name of an off-the-shelf company named Helseam Limited which shortly thereafter became Balmoral Excursions Limited. In a process that was to prove to be almost as divisive as it was well-intentioned, of which we shall read more a little later, the **Balmoral** was to remain separately registered in its name until 1991.

The first job was to put the **Balmoral** into dry-dock at Dundee on 7th March 1985 which would enable the necessary certificates to be issued for the voyage to the Clyde and for insurance cover to be effected for the trip. Considering her lack of maintenance of recent years, it was found that most problems were superficial and that the ship was in generally satisfactory condition. In the end, under her own power on 31st March 1985, she set sail from Dundee, round the north of Scotland, through the often wild Pentland Firth (but not so on this occasion) arriving at the **Waverley** Terminal at Glasgow, two days later.

Whilst the actual purchase price of the ship was modest enough, the real expenditure was yet to come. In order to make the ship fit for sea-going passenger service, it was estimated that well over £300,000 would have to be raised to cover the cost of the works. The estimated costs fell under the following headings.

Purchase, delivery and initial dry-docking	£ 61,000
Clydedock Engineering specification works	£141,500
Machinery/Engines overhaul	£ 34,200
Lifesaving and Fire fighting Equipment	£ 48,795
Galley and Lounge Refurbishment	£ 25,000
Preliminary Dept. of Trade and Industry work	£ 10,500
Total	£320,995

The Paddle Steamer Preservation Society and **Balmoral** Restoration Fund began fund raising in earnest, as the directors knew it would be irresponsible to start work until it was clear that sufficient funds would, in the end, be forthcoming to complete the whole job. Cruising enthusiasts were keen to help and the people of Ilfracombe in particular were quick to realise the true worth of pleasure steamer calls at the town. Local authorities and tourist boards of England and Wales all contributed with financial help, but inevitably it was slow coming and some had 'strings attached'. In the end and with more than a little help from the directors and others (without whose extra and quite substantial final contributions and loans, the project was close to foundering) it was decided that just enough funds were available to make a serious start.

In January 1986, the **Balmoral** moved to Clydedock Engineering Ltd.'s works at Govan to begin her rebuilding. Considering that J. I. Thornycroft & Co. Ltd. had constructed the **Balmoral** with raw materials available straight after the end of the War, they had done an excellent job.

Nevertheless, nearly forty years on, some sections of her hull were found to be badly corroded and had to be cut out. With riveting a long forgotten skill new plates were welded in their place. On this subject, director Dr. Joe McKendrick tells of how, on a working party in 1986 when clearing out the **Balmoral's** old Britannia lounge, he made an unfortunate start to the proceedings by putting his broom handle straight through the steel side of the ship!

Lifeboats, originally clinker-built, were replaced with modern fibreglass ones that could be used for landings by ship's boat at Lundy and elsewhere. The rather poky wheelhouse was completely replaced too. However, by far the biggest part of the project was the plating-in of the old car deck aft, enabling the construction of a large, new self-service cafeteria and galley within. The deck of the cafeteria remains to this day still constructed of the original teak planking of the old car deck. Immediately above, the open promenade deck was continued aft, to enclose the newly built cafeteria and galley. This reinstated the original car/sun deck space thereby given up for the new cafeteria and galley, one deck below. The new upper deck was built in steel and coated in a composition as to have sheathed it with teak or other hardwood

On 10th June 1987, the **Balmoral** *makes a wonderful sight approaching Caernarfon from Menai Bridge, on the first leg of a Round Anglesey excursion.*

Photo: Richard Winfield.

Despite sailing restrictions placed on the **Balmoral's** *visits to Lundy, there were a number permitted. On one of these in August 1986 the author, his son John and father-in-law Donald (prised away from his village shop and Post Office in St. Mabyn for the occasion) enjoyed a beautiful, hot sunny day trip from Ilfracombe to Lundy. On the same day, the author's other son, James and the rest of the family shivered in sea mist on the beach at Polzeath! One of the author's photographs of the occasion was used to illustrate the front cover of the March 1987 edition of the shipping magazine* Sea Breezes.

Above: At anchor off Lundy.

Left: Alongside at Ilfracombe.
Photos: Author.

would almost have doubled the cost. All the other passenger accommodation was refurbished to a comfortable standard with the former dining room/cafeteria forward becoming another lounge and bar. The forward observation lounge on the promenade deck was particularly tastefully finished too and where, within it, once there was a bar, the ship's souvenir shop was to be built.

Following all this reconstruction work, she was re-measured at 735 gross tons.

The **Balmoral's** publicity machine geared up alongside the fundraisers, describing the re-built ship with such words as 'the motor yacht', and 'her yacht-like lines'. This unnecessarily purple prose included so many references to the likeness of the **Balmoral** to Sir Bernard and Lady Docker's yacht **Shemara** (also built at Woolston but in 1938) that it seemed an action for breach of design copyright was just as likely to be attracted as a good crowd of passengers! In fact, the **Shemara** was a deep-drafted ocean-going luxury yacht having rather less in common with the **Balmoral** than many people liked to think. A more obvious visual comparison could be drawn between the **Balmoral** when she was at the design stage and the rather larger, luxury coastal cruise ship **Lady Enchantress** which J. I. Thornycroft & Co. Ltd. converted from the Royal Naval sloop/yacht **Enchantress** in 1946.

As if to emphasise what a few might have regarded as her yacht-like lines, she was given the full cruising treatment by

This fine photograph of the **Balmoral** *rolling lazily off Southend Pier was taken on 24th September 1987 during the ship's first ever visit to the Thames area. At the time, she was standing in for the* **Waverley***, which had severe boiler trouble and had suddenly had to conclude her season on 24th August 1987.*

Photo: Copyright: Telegraph Group Limited, London 1987.

being painted all-white with a primrose yellow funnel and bright, so-called 'Estuary' green boot-topping.

Whilst a lot of time and thought was put into devising the new livery, there was actually little wrong with either her original Red Funnel Steamers or Campbell's White Funnel fleet colour schemes. To many people, it was hard to understand the need for such a radical (and some would say inappropriate) change.

The all-white hull paint could, at best, only gloss-over the many previous years' dents and scratches and it proved difficult to keep clean and rust free. So over the years the *Balmoral's* livery has since been changed with various different combinations of boot-topping, hull and funnel colour being tried.

Those of us privileged to review the initial financial records fourteen years later, can only marvel at (and be thankful for) the dedication of those who came up with all the necessary money in the dark days of 1985, 1986 and 1987. Theirs were the devoted acts of the really faithful few. The predicament of the dour bank manager from the Bank of Scotland was positively joyous compared with those who had financed the *Balmoral's* resurrection. But money was to remain a pressing problem with Clydedock Engineering Ltd. at Govan needing to be paid £187,000 for all their work.

The *Balmoral* left Glasgow at 16.20 hrs. on 31 March 1986, which was Easter Monday. In true tradition she ran her trials on the Skelmorlie measured mile, the scene of so many vessels' speed trials. The *Balmoral* managed 15 knots with ease. The official *Balmoral* booklet (published by her operators from time to time) tells us that she then sailed on to Rothesay where she berthed in order that the officers and crew could obtain fish suppers, as the galley was incomplete. After dinner, she returned to Govan for further attention and then moved back to Anderston Quay on 4th April 1986.

Later that week, the Department of Trade and Industry trials with maritime surveyors aboard were run from Glasgow, down the Clyde to off-Greenock following which the *Balmoral* was certified fit and ready to re-enter passenger carrying service. Late on the evening of 10th April 1986, the *Balmoral* slipped her Glasgow moorings and set sail for Bristol, which was to be her new home.

In the early hours of the next morning, the *Balmoral* sailed south, quietly passing the Isle of Man well to the west. There, the author who lives at Laxey, high on the Island's opposite coast overlooking the Irish Sea, having witnessed her previous visits when tendering the *Kungsholm* all those years ago, was now able to certify that she had finally completed her full circumnavigation of Britain.

Whilst running for Campbell's, eleven years previously (and several times before that too), operating as a tender for the cruise ship *Kungsholm*, the *Balmoral* had come north to Llandudno and the Isle of Man before returning south again to Bristol. So at that time, Douglas was as far north as the one-time Red Funnel, Isle of Wight boat had ever ventured. When she was finally sold to Craig Inns at Dundee, she sailed from Avonmouth round Land's End before going the breadth of the South Coast and heading up the East Coast, all the way to Dundee. Happily, in the end, she was rescued from there, when Captain Neill sailed her back round the top of Scotland. Thus the vital final leg to complete her circumnavigation of mainland Britain was from the Clyde, south past the Isle of Man which she achieved on 11th April 1986.

By the next day she had made Barry where she unloaded the Lundy launch (named *Westward Ho*) and by later that evening she sailed up the Avon to Bristol, which was only now, her new port of registry. Right until this time, for the first 37 years of her career, she had remained registered at Southampton even though she had been running for P. & A. Campbell Ltd. at Bristol since 1969.

Hundreds of well-wishers turned out to greet the *Balmoral* upon her arrival, many having doubted that they would ever see the good ship again after she had sailed off into the fog to become a floating public house and nightclub at Dundee, four years earlier.

The *Balmoral's* official celebration excursion, her third quasi-maiden voyage, was on April 26th 1986, on which morning she left Bristol on an exceptionally high tide with Captain Steve Michel in

*In this photograph, the **Balmoral** is seen at Peel, Isle of Man on 4th June 1989 having just arrived from Warrenpoint in Northern Ireland. There is no doubting the amount of economic activity generated by the arrival of the **Balmoral** with so many passengers, ready to go off by bus and on foot, to sample the delights of the Island.*

Photo: Author.

*Right: 10th June 1990 is the day for this photograph showing the **Balmoral** arriving at Peel after a sunny but very boisterous passage from Warrenpoint. A 4½ hour sail in these conditions must be near the limit for most passengers' endurance!*　　　　　*Photo: Author.*

*Below: Is this winter on the North Atlantic? No, it's high summer off the coast of the windswept Isle of Man, as the **Balmoral** rolls her way down the coast towards the Calf, again on 10th June 1990.*　　　　　*Photo: Author.*

Against the backdrop of the famous Tyne Bridge linking Newcastle-upon-Tyne with Gateshead, this photograph is of the **Balmoral** *at Newcastle Quay, during one of her earlier visits to the Tyne, Tees and Wear.*   Photo: Edwin Wilmshurst.

command, sailed down Barry Roads in dense fog and arrived at Ilfracombe where the tide later went out farther than ever. Big crowds welcomed the vessel to glorious North Devon. Captain Michel was to remain her skipper for almost the next decade, safely taking the **Balmoral** to more ports, harbours and piers than any other excursion ship, ever.

Wherever she went, the message went out, *'It's the **Balmoral**, she's back!'*

But that is not to say that it was all, plain sailing. As we read in the previous chapter, when The Landmark Trust, who own Lundy on behalf of the nation, decided against any further joint venture with Campbell's, they were clearly after their own little passenger

ship - which was to be the **Oldenburg**. They placed severe access restrictions on other craft trying to visit Lundy and the **Balmoral** was to suffer greatly as a result. On one of her rationed trips, the **Balmoral** and the **Oldenburg** met in Lundy Roads for the first time on May Bank Holiday 1986, when the **Balmoral** brought 600 passengers down-Channel. Later, in June 1986, the **Balmoral** sailed north to Llandudno where she briefly re-instated the ever-popular cruises along the North Welsh coast and through the Menai Straits.

Captain Steve Michel says that, exacerbated by bad weather and the unwelcome restrictions at Lundy, 1986, the **Balmoral's** first season since her rebuilding, was a difficult one and money remained a big problem. She spent virtually the whole season on the Bristol Channel with just a week at North Wales and a short while at the end of the season on the Clyde. Business on the Bristol Channel turned out to be quite fickle and any success that accrued was as much a function of the odd day's good weather combined with the offer of a particularly interesting trip, rather than pure customer loyalty. Whilst the **Balmoral** did enjoy a certain following, especially from those whose memories went back to the golden days of the White Funnel fleet, clearly her nets would have to be cast much wider in following seasons, if she were to survive.

Clydedock Engineering Ltd. still had not had all their money and before long, the **Balmoral** would need her first overhaul and survey if she were to run in 1987. Fortunately, money came in from Bristol City Council and Somerset County Council and, with more help from the directors, it was possible to think about 1987. However, early in that year there were enquiries from several interested parties who wished to acquire the **Balmoral**, now that she had been returned to sea-going standard. The first offers were in the region of £150,000 to £200,000 (clearly an insufficient amount) and these offers were made for restaurant use and also for excursions out of Weymouth. Further serious enquiries came from Holland where £480,000 was the figure quoted for sale of the **Balmoral** and delivery in April 1987.

Fortunately for us, the directors took the bold decision to try again in 1987 to make that season even more successful than the previous one. The ship was therefore withdrawn from the market. If thereafter, a success could not be made of her, it was decided that would be the time to sell her and out of the proceeds, to pay off Clydedock Engineering Ltd., the loan received from Bristol City Council and any other debts due. It was planned that any surplus would be handed over to help rebuild the paddle steamer *Ryde*, by then in her mud berth on the Isle of Wight.

However, in May 1987, whilst the *Balmoral* was back in dry-dock undergoing her overhaul and survey, Clydedock Engineering Ltd. seized the *Balmoral* in order to secure payment of what they were owed. Thankfully, Mrs. Jenifer Leech, who with her late husband were solid supporters of the *Waverley* and *Balmoral* cause, was able to arrange a substantial loan from her own resources with which Clydedock Engineering Ltd. were paid-off. 1987 was a busy season with the *Balmoral* carrying just under 100,000 passengers. However, from July onwards, the paddle steamer *Waverley* was experiencing serious boiler problems which necessitated her withdrawal from service from 24th August 1987. She could not sail again that season and so the *Balmoral* was moved south to take over the *Waverley's* scheduled visits on the South Coast and the Thames. A hastily arranged bare-boat charter of the *Southsea* from Sealink (U.K.) Limited enabled the programmed sailings in Scotland to continue; save for trips to Ayr for which the *Southsea* could obtain no passenger certificate. She returned to her owners at Portsmouth at the end of September leaving the *Balmoral* to finish the season alone.

Whilst in the South, on 17th September, the *Balmoral* cruised right into Lulworth Cove. According to Mr. Tim Cooper who was aboard that sunny afternoon on 24th September, the *Balmoral* then made her debut on the Thames. Whilst sailing up to London's Tower Pier from Whitstable, she sailed close by the former *Vecta* (by then back down from Manchester) off Erith where, coincidentally, the author was born. Sailing on up-river, she then passed the old *Princess Elizabeth* laid-up in Gallions Reach and had distant views of the *Medina* at Canary Wharf. Down river, the *Balmoral* also met up with the preserved river paddler *Kingswear Castle* for the first time, presenting ship photographers with another golden opportunity to expose some more film.

Bad weather made the *Balmoral's* return voyage from the South Coast difficult and she had to seek shelter in Cornish waters off the Lizard, before returning to make her final trips on the Bristol Channel. Having ended her public sailings at midnight on Sunday 11th October, she left Penarth in the very early morning on Monday 12th October 1987 and returned to Scotland for winter lay-up.

There was good reason for satisfaction in the *Balmoral* camp at that time. Just two sailing seasons after her rescue from almost certain oblivion at Dundee and all the worry and heartache of trying to find £300,000 for her refit, everything was suddenly vindicated. Faith and hope had not been misplaced.

After all, this was the real reason for having acquired the *Balmoral*. She had acted as support ship for the *Waverley* in time of dire need such as had just occurred following the boiler of the paddle steamer giving out. The *Balmoral* had done everything that could have been expected of her, and much more besides, and in so doing had kept the flag proudly flying.

Modesty would preclude any thought by the following two gentlemen claiming for themselves merit for the reincarnation and survival of the *Balmoral* after her rescue in 1985. Happily, under the privilege of authorship, accessing the facts takes precedence over such self-effacement.

It can be fairly said that if any two personalities have contributed to the operational success of the *Balmoral* through all the trials and tribulations, the honour undoubtedly lies with her original master Captain Steve Michel appointed at inception, and her then chief engineer Mr. Ian McMillan who joined the ship in February 1988.

When asked by the author for details of any key events that had a bearing on the entire project or individual contributions that had

Above left: A relaxed moment in Loch Long in 1989. Captain Steve Michel and the Chief Officer, Kit Lee, on the bridge of the **Balmoral**. *Photo: Iain Quinn.*

Above right: A very happy ship's crew at Clevedon after a successful River Wye cruise on 22nd September 1996. Chief Engineer Andy Westmore (far left), Captain Gary Wilson (at wheelhouse door), Purser Neil O'Brien (holding life belt) and to the right of him, behind, Captain Steve Colledge (Chief Officer, later Master) and Comdr. Tom Foden, Bristol Channel Agent (tie and sunglasses right).

Photo: Nigel Coombes.

Left: 22nd September 1996 at Clevedon. Comdr. Tom Foden (Bristol Channel Agent) is on the left with Waverley Steam Navigation Ltd.'s Chairman Mr Terry Sylvester and his wife Anne. On the right is Mr. Ray Buck, Clevedon's remarkable ropeman with a seventy-year experience of deep sea and port work.

Photo: Nigel Coombes.

According to Cruising Monthly, *during her 1990 Spring Bank Holiday Clyde visit, the* **Balmoral** *became the first ship of any size to berth at Ormidale since 1939. Is this the* **Balmoral's** *'grassiest' pier?*

Photo: Joe McKendrick.

helped to turn the tide, Captain Michel responded in the way that is typical of him. He generously stated that the ship has survived because of the contribution of so many different people. That is certainly true and a book far larger than this one, relating details of all such good-deeds, could easily be written on the subject.

However, Captain Michel says:

'Because of the huge difference made by the arrival on the scene of Mr. Ian McMillan in 1988 his contribution is difficult to ignore. Gradually and methodically he transformed the engine room from a dark, dingy hole of regular mechanical misfortunes into the pristine, efficient and much admired space we know today. His influence spread to other parts of the ship during the winter refits in Bristol where with his boundless enthusiasm he brought so many improvements to the ship at the hands of his trusted band of volunteers. Today he oversees most of the ship refit work for both the **Balmoral** *and the* **Waverley**'.

Also, where money was concerned (or lack of it) very many people and organisations have helped out from time to time. However, it is clear from the records that the willingness of Mrs. Jenifer Leech to come to the financial aid of the **Balmoral** very substantially on several occasions must also rank very highly in the ship's Roll of Honour.

It speaks volumes for Captain Michel's affection for the **Balmoral** and desire to see her succeed that he stayed with her for almost a decade. When the time came for him to make the break, it was for the best of reasons so that he could have more time with his wife and young family. Fortunately, he still returns to command the ship from time to time. Readers of this book may not readily appreciate the fact that a season in the **Balmoral** is likely to extend for up to six whole months, with little time to get home to enjoy normal family life.

When the author visited Captain Michel aboard the **Balmoral** in Douglas Harbour one off-duty evening a few summers ago he found the Captain getting ready to welcome some of his young family aboard for a few days. Perhaps it should be mentioned that the Captain's cabin where they were all to live is down below the waterline, on the lower deck along with all the other crew accommodation. It measures no more than seven or eight feet square having room for just one none-too-large bunk bed and a small desk. It certainly puts a new perspective on the word 'togetherness'. Captain Michel also says:

'Another aspect of the **Balmoral's** *work from which I drew great enjoyment was her capacity to negotiate narrow stretches of navigable water with ease. This ability took us to some really fascinating and memorable places, which for my money sets the ship in a place of her own. Runs such as the Menai Straits, the Newry Canal, the Strangford Narrows, the Rivers Tay, Wye, Avon and Parrett. These cruises have proved to be exceptionally popular with the public and good sources of revenue for the preservation cause'.*

1988 found another financial appeal going out, this time to finance the repairs to the **Waverley's** boiler and the work was duly completed by 24th April 1988, giving the **Waverley** just enough time to get to Milford Haven for a quick dry-docking before her season got under way. The **Balmoral** was also there having her own overhaul and both ships left the West Wales port on 29th April.

21st May 1988 saw the **Waverley** at Padstow in Cornwall, a favourite haunt of the author. Passengers were taken off by the local cruise boat **Tri-Star** (since withdrawn and thought to be in Scotland). The June 1988 edition of *Cruising Monthly* tells us that this was the first call by a paddle steamer since 16th August 1967 although the **Balmoral** was there in 1972 when she paid her last previous visit with Campbell's on 23rd July. The **Balmoral** was back in the picturesque North Cornish port herself on 25th June with 300 passengers aboard for her cruise up the Camel Estuary.

Gradually, over the years, the team comprising the **Waverley** and the **Balmoral** has settled into more or less annual routines. It is not economic for the **Balmoral** to come into service at Easter as she then has too long a period unproductive, before the crowds begin to gather from Whitsun onwards. The **Balmoral's** season normally develops from around the middle of May, beginning in the North-West and with sailings throughout the Irish Sea for which the Isle of Man is a very attractive and convenient central destination. This is eminently achievable on her Class III passenger certificate in terms of range and distance and these sailings from Cumbria, south-west Scotland and Northern Ireland to the Isle of Man have proved to be amongst her most profitable ever.

No one would doubt the wisdom of controlling how far from land (and therefore from help should the need arise) an excursion ship should be permitted to sail. However, one problem the **Balmoral** encountered several years ago was that the Isle of Man Marine Administration decided it had no alternative but to flex its newly found muscles and to declare that voyages to the Isle of Man were now 'international'. That is to say, a Class III certificate issued in the United Kingdom would, by definition, no longer cover such a voyage. Previously, the issue of passenger certificates had been solely a matter for the British Government but with the advent of the Manx Shipping Register and associated activity things became understandably more complicated.

At this point, the author interceded on the **Balmoral's** behalf resulting in questions being asked in Tynwald, the Manx Parliament, and support being sought from interested parties. Eventually a compromise was reached under which the **Balmoral** sailed to the Isle of Man within British Class III limits and the 'internationality' of the voyage was disregarded. In return, the life-saving apparatus on board the **Balmoral** was greatly improved and enlarged to provide modern life-raft space for all passengers, without having to rely on flotation units which are only effective after the ship has gone down. It was a very practical compromise and one that the author was very happy to have helped to broke.

The Manx authorities have felt it necessary to exercise their control over the activities of the **Balmoral** and the **Waverley** in other ways too, the most noticeable being to ensure that the Calf

The **Balmoral's** *trips to Northern Ireland ports are always very popular. Of these many are run as local cruises whilst others often sail across the Irish Sea to Peel, cathedral city on the Isle of Man's west coast. Here we see the* **Balmoral** *at Portaferry (N.I.) jetty, on 17th June 1990.* Photo: Edwin Wilmshurst.

Sound (the strip of water between the main island and the adjacent Calf of Man) is specifically excluded from passenger sailing limits.

On one calm fine day, 30th April 1985 (and there may have been others, before the ban) the **Waverley** did sail through the Sound carrying passengers, much to their delight. However, the powers-that-be decided it was a manoeuvre that brooked no safety margin and as they thought it involved unnecessary risks the practice was outlawed. Since that time, the **Balmoral** has sailed through the Calf Sound on many occasions and in both directions, but never with fare-paying passengers aboard. On a trip from Douglas or Port

The author took this photograph of the **Balmoral** *at Bristol on 31st January 1991. Thick snow had fallen on that day, the 38th anniversary of the tragedy of the loss of the* **Princess Victoria**. *Being in the middle of winter, it seemed impossible to believe that in just a few months the* **Balmoral** *would be carrying trippers on warm, sunny excursions around our coast.* Photo: Author.

4th June 1991 found the **Balmoral** *running one of the longest-ever single excursions when she carried 219 passengers from Great Yarmouth to Tower Pier on a trip taking 9½ hours. Here we see her going through Tower Bridge which had raised its mighty bascules to let her through.*

Photo: Tim Cooper.

Left: This view, dated 15th May 1992, is of the **Balmoral** *at Newcastle-upon-Tyne Quay and was photographed from the famous Tyne Bridge. The former railway-owned Tilbury-Gravesend ferry* **Catherine** *is to be seen lying astern and she continues to run local trips on the River Tyne.*
Photo: Richard Winfield.

Right: The author and his wife made a start at 05.00 hrs from Laxey on 5th July 1992 in the hope of photographing the **Balmoral** *in the Calf Sound. It was a glorious, sunny early morning for the 25-mile drive and for sitting amongst the wild flowers on Burroo Ned waiting for the* **Balmoral** *to come into sight from Northern Ireland. Would she come through the Calf Sound or go the long way round to Port St. Mary? Just when it seemed that the journey had been wasted and that she was passing by, Captain Michel brought her sharply round to port, and through the narrow Sound she came at full speed, looking really splendid.* *Photo: Author.*

St. Mary to Ulster ports, taking the Calf Sound passage saves about 40 minutes - valuable time and precious fuel.

As her season progresses, having covered Northern Ireland, the Isle of Man, south-west Scotland, north-west England and North Wales, the *Balmoral* often heads off north to the North-East.

She may then work her way south towards East Anglia, London and the Thames ports before working her way back along the Sussex Coast to the Bristol Channel for the main summer season. Towards the end of the season, the *Balmoral* works on the Clyde whilst the *Waverley* returns to the South Coast.

The list of destinations for the *Balmoral* continues to grow annually so that there are very few ports, harbours and piers around the whole of our British coastline that have not played host to the visiting excursion ship. Her sorties take her to the upper reaches of far-away Scotland and out to some of the Western Isles. In the extreme West, she sails to the Isles of Scilly from Cornish ports and whilst in the East she sails right up the Thames to the nation's capital city. Some of the harbours she visits are so small or tidal as to require the services of small boats acting as tender to put her passengers ashore but, nevertheless, they feature in the ship's extensive and exciting itinerary. Without doubt, the *Balmoral* is Britain's most widely-travelled excursion steamer.

The scheduling of all these services takes a lot of organising and has to be dovetailed into the hours of daylight, suitable tides, shipping and traffic movements, pier availability and suitability, public and local holidays and other things going on. Competing events have to be turned to advantage by enabling boat passengers to sample the sea journey connecting with historic trips on land. Then there are one-off or irregular happenings such as meeting famous ocean liners, the Tall Ships and the start of Round the World and other important yacht races to witness. The printing and dissemination of timetables and local handbills, sailing instructions to masters, advertising of trips, booking local agents, liaising with harbour authorities and ropemen, bunkering, victualling and the like, all have to be arranged for the hundreds of voyages that take place every season.

Another happy event particularly close to the interests of the *Balmoral* and the *Waverley* occurs when a seaside pier is re-built or re-opened after a long closure. Millport and more recently Penarth and Clevedon are just three examples and the relationship between the vessels and piers is clearly symbiotic. Piers are very expensive pieces of historic architecture and there is a groundswell of opinion that wishes to see more of them saved and re-opened. Thankfully, Ilfracombe is the next pier to see a worthwhile amount of money being poured into its renovation, without which there would be no pleasure steamers. Maybe even the Queen's Pier at Ramsey in the Isle of Man, presently mothballed awaiting decisions as to its future, might one day host the *Balmoral* or *Waverley*?

Back in 1985 when the *Balmoral* was first bought for the *Waverley* organisation, it was perceived by some officials of the wider organisation as being desirable to keep the ownership and operation of the *Balmoral*, totally separate from the *Waverley*. This left many observers with a constant reminder of the then somewhat prevalent *'them and us syndrome'* that so often accompanies such man-made splits.

Incredibly, there were a few individuals and commentators who saw the *Balmoral* as nothing more than a time-expired example of motorised maritime elderliness, which was invested with so little charm as not to be worth reviving. Put bluntly (and some were very good at putting things bluntly) they said she was just a characterless, noisy, worn-out old diesel-powered ferry. Actually, what they really feared was either the remote possibility of another *Prince Ivanhoe* tragedy or that the ship they saw as the interloper would be a drain on their beloved *Waverley's* precious resources. That is to say, the *Balmoral* would only serve as a potential distraction, taking people's minds and their money away from the main purpose of the *Waverley's* preservation. Perhaps it never occurred to them that others would find the *Balmoral* to be a very attractive proposition in her own right? So, for those with open minds, it was easy to see that the *Balmoral* and her loyal team were occasionally left thinking that their efforts were not always appreciated, or were even unwanted. Fortunately, they remained undaunted and hopefully this book helps to set the record straight.

Justice was seen to be well and truly done following the 1987 episode when the faithful **Balmoral** held the 'maritime fort' so admirably whilst the **Waverley's** boiler was out of action. A lot of pride and harsh words had to be swallowed by those who suddenly realised the true worth of the **Balmoral**.

Back at Southampton in 1989, having fought off a previous hostile bid by Sally Line, Red Funnel Steamers were taken over by Associated British Ports PLC, owners of Southampton Docks, and with the take-over came many changes and also a welcome injection of much-needed new capital.

Happily, in 1991, ownership of the **Balmoral** was transferred to Waverley Steam Navigation Co. Ltd. resulting in an open acknowledgement that the **Waverley** organisation really was proud to embrace the **Balmoral**. In future, both ships would be more closely integrated in their operations and treatment and, at last, the economies of scale and full teamwork could begin to work to advantage.

At Penzance, the **Scillonian III** was having serious gearbox trouble in May 1991 and the **Balmoral** was chartered by the Isles of Scilly Steamship Company Limited to stand in for her for two periods on their island lifeline route to St. Mary's whilst they tried to cure the problems. During the second of the charters, the **Scillonian III** had a new gearbox fitted at Newlyn.

Mr. Lionel Vaughan (long-time shopkeeper, ticket collector, gangway man and general factotum aboard the **Balmoral** and the **Waverley**) rates the **Balmoral's** finest hour as occurring when she was deputising for the **Scillonian III** on the hectic Penzance-Isles of Scilly passage. He recalls that the **Balmoral** performed beautifully and earned generous praise from passengers, many of whom were surprised and delighted to find substantial cooked breakfasts available, even on the very early 06.00 hrs. Saturday crossings when the timetable calls for an extra double run for long

day-trippers. Another evening, standing on the quay at Penzance, a weather-beaten old Cornishman (sounding remarkably like the landlord of the Dolphin Hotel mentioned previously) looked from stem to stern of the **Balmoral** and exclaimed to Mr. Vaughan, *'Er's a lovely ol' girl'.*

Followers of the Bristol Channel pleasure steamer scene were saddened to hear of the death of Mr. Clifton Smith-Cox on 3rd August 1991. With his passing, Britain's coastal passenger ship business (and Britain's hotel industry within which he was a very senior director) was much the poorer.

In her refit in the spring of 1992 the **Balmoral** received a new livery comprising bright red boot-top, dark green hull with a gold strake line, off-white superstructure and a yellow funnel (darker than previously). Fitted in the Albion Dockyard at Bristol, she also received new propellers manufactured by Brutons. In the ensuing speed trials, run off Portishead, she made 15.87 knots on the first set of her trial runs and 16.86 knots on the second. The average of these, which were each run in both directions to eliminate the effects of the tide, was 16.36 knots being only fractionally less than her original trials average (16.55 knots) 43 years previously!

At various times later, experiments were tried out with different funnel colours and her yellow funnel received a painted black top and then it was bright red, white and black for a while, similar to the **Waverley**. The new livery and various adaptations of it that took place after could only be described as excessively ornate. It was not until 1996 that she was to return to one of her two traditional liveries, that of P. & A. Campbell Ltd.

The **Scillonian III** ran a special (overnight both ways) trip to Guernsey causing her to be away from Penzance for two days on 19th and 20th June 1992. The **Balmoral** was again taken on charter, this time for three round trips. Unlike the 1991 charters when the weather was kind, for 1992 the **Balmoral** had to contend with heavy seas and her proposed cruise round the Scilly Islands planned for Sunday 21st June, which had been so popular the year before, had to be cancelled.

*This fascinating photograph dates from 22nd September 1993. Here we see the **Balmoral** in the River Avon, about to pass under the Clifton Suspension Bridge, whilst she was running a charter for the Port of Bristol Authority from the Royal Portbury Dock (where she had just made her first call) up the River to Bristol. The white awning was provided by the Charterers to give shelter for their guests as they cruised up the River to the live music of Kenny Ball and his Jazzmen. The awning was erected the previous day whilst the **Balmoral** was anchored off Lundy. It was very unmanageable to erect and as it produced the effect of a giant wind tunnel it was quickly discarded.*

Photo: Richard Winfield.

170

This photograph, dated 10th June 1994, was taken from the castle ramparts at Scarborough and shows the **Balmoral** at Scarborough Lighthouse Pier during an excursion from Middlesbrough to Hartlepool and Scarborough. The **Coronia**, dating from 1935 (which, along with the **Regal Lady** dating from 1930) is operated by T. Machin, is also to be seen at the Pier. Both of Machin's vessels are Dunkirk veterans.
Photo: Richard Winfield.

Above: Incredible though it may seem, that a busy Clyde ferry terminal such as Gourock had not hosted the **Balmoral** *before, it was not until 13th May 1994 that she paid her first visit and was photographed there.*
Photo: Joe McKendrick.

Right: This interesting photograph dates from 16th October 1994. Especially for the occasion of the finale of the Penarth Pier Centenary celebrations, the **Balmoral** *came back out of winter lay-up at Bristol and sailed over to Penarth where she and the* **Waverley** *'posed' for photographers. Both ships then crossed to Clevedon where they berthed side by side at the Pier. The* **Waverley** *then set off for Bristol where she berthed at the Tongue Head, just outside the Cumberland Basin. The* **Balmoral** *followed the* **Waverley** *up the Avon and berthed at the nearby lock entrance. The* **Balmoral** *was temporarily given the* **Waverley's** *funnel livery for the day.*
Photo: Richard Winfield.

In response to European shipping rule changes, in 1992 the Merchant Shipping (Categorisation of Waters) Regulations were enacted. Under these new rules, the old Class V (smooth waters) and Class IV (partially smooth waters) were changed as follows:-

The description 'partially smooth waters' was replaced by the term Category D waters.

The description 'smooth waters' was divided into three separate categories where A denoted narrow rivers and canals where the depth of water is generally less than 1.5 metres, B denoted wider rivers etc. where the depth of water is generally more than 1.5 metres and where the significant wave height could not be expected to exceed 0.6 metres at any time, and C was for tidal rivers, estuaries and large, deep lakes and lochs where the significant wave height could not be expected to exceed 1.2 metres at any time.

Voyages on Class III certificates remain limited to operating in the April to October period during daylight hours (both sometimes

The harbour at Whitby, North Yorkshire is quite spectacular. Here we see the **Balmoral** *arriving on 14th May 1992.* Photo: Edwin Wilmshurst.

extended by arrangement to include Easter, if earlier, and evening trips). They are also subject to a sailing range not exceeding 70 miles from departure point, 18 miles' distance from the coast and Class III ships can only carry passengers when at sea in favourable weather. For the guidance of ships' masters, the word 'favourable' when used in official documents issued in connection with licences has been defined as follows: 'Weather, when the visibility is good and when the combined effects of wind, sea and swell upon the ship under consideration are never greater than those which would cause moderate rolling or pitching or result in the shipping of green seas on the weather deck'.

Following the welcome injection of capital emanating from the take-over of Red Funnel Steamers by Associated British Ports in 1989, five years later they began to introduce their new 'Raptor' class super-ferries on to the Southampton to Cowes route. It had been 20 years since the arrival of the **Netley Castle** and the stretching of the two earlier ferries. The new class commenced with the **Red Falcon** in March 1994 and the **Red Osprey** in October the same year, which then rendered the **Cowes Castle** and **Norris Castle** redundant. Within six months of each other, they both found their way to the Adriatic Sea, the **Cowes Castle** having been renamed **Nehaj** and the **Norris Castle** becoming the **Lovrjenac**.

On 30th April 1994, the **Balmoral** briefly became R.M.S. **Balmoral** again. Whilst sailing between Oban and Gigha the Post Office requested that the ship carry the Royal Mail and divert to Colonsay as they had missed the previous day's ferry service by Caledonian MacBrayne.

When the **Balmoral's** solid fibreglass lifeboats were finally removed and replaced with inflatable rafts, Mr Ron Sims tells us that the new davits were salvaged from old 'Ton Class' minesweepers being scrapped at Portsmouth. Fitted in 1994 and 1995 respectively, the port davit is of stainless steel but the starboard one is of mild steel.

1995 found the **Balmoral** making her first ever calls at Leith and Rosyth and whilst in the far North-East she had some very interesting work. She ran several cruises, some of which were a 'sell-out', in connection with the Tall Ships Festival and Race. On Monday 17th July 1995 she was under charter to Cunard firstly to convey H.R.H. The Princess Royal and invited guests from Rosyth Dockyard out to the **Queen Elizabeth 2** in the Firth of Forth, and to act as tender for the liner's passengers. Whilst under Red Funnel Steamers' and later under Campbell's ownership, the **Balmoral** regularly acted as tender to visiting liners and cruise ships, this was the first such occasion under the present ownership and earned the ship a useful £3,000 charter fee.

Because the liner was too long for Leith and too high to get under the two famous bridges between the entrance to the Forth River and Rosyth, Captain Michel tells us that the **Queen Elizabeth 2** moored on the buoys in Inverkeithing Bay, just east of the bridges. The **Balmoral** ran as tender between the **Queen Elizabeth 2** and Rosyth and, that night, with 578 passengers aboard, she also operated a fireworks cruise at 20.00 hrs. from Granton, returning at 23.05 hrs.

The next day was principally to see the preparations for and the start of the Tall Ships Race at 18.00 hrs. In the morning, the **Balmoral** was again on charter, this time to the Forth Ports Authority. In the afternoon and early evening, she had another cruise but, having hurried away with 500 passengers to view the Race, the organisers then announced that the start was to be put back two hours due to lack of wind. Dr. Joe McKendrick says what could have been a disaster turned into a magnificent evening. Captain Michel carefully explained the difficult situation to all the passengers and that he proposed to return an hour later than scheduled. Between then and the start of the race, he cruised up and down, round every Tall Ship, giving his passengers a perfect close-up view of the contenders in all their glorious magnificence.

Right on time, the **Balmoral** crossed the start line just as the sailing ships set-off on the Race and she was able to follow them well out to sea, before finally returning to base. So, Captain Michel and the **Balmoral** gave her passengers a really wonderful evening,

the purser's office was kept busy re-booking their connecting transport and the ship's catering department was called upon to produce hundreds of extra main evening meals. All in all, it was a first-class team effort. As the ship headed back to Granton with her 500 very satisfied customers, they spontaneously decided to give the captain and crew a standing ovation as a sign of their appreciation.

During his research for this work, the author enquired of a large number of people as to the times or events that they regarded as either the high or low periods in the **Balmoral's** career. Interestingly and totally independently, quite a number of those approached, including the ship's master, have all singled out that evening's sailing on 18th July 1995 to witness the start of the Tall Ships Race as being amongst the very best.

Captain Michel stated:

'At the end of the cruise, I do not believe I have ever seen a happier lot of passengers leave the ship. Each race has its own distinctive memories but for me the race of 1995 from Leith was just that little bit extra special. On this occasion the cruise earlier in the day to see the Parade of Sail was a bit of a disappointment. The sky was overcast, it was a little misty and there was very little wind. The Tall Ships had to motor round the parade course with their sails hanging limply. Because of lack of wind, the start of the race was put back by two hours. This was a seemingly easy decision for the race organisers to make but a nightmare for us with several hundred passengers with all sorts of travel arrangements to fulfil on completion of the cruise. The start line for the race was some seven miles to sea from Leith. As with most of these occasions, the main public interest is in visiting the ships alongside and then the Parade of Sail. The start of the race is sometimes far out at sea and missed by most. The weather on the run out to the start line on this occasion was a continuation of the earlier day but, as the time for the start-gun neared, the cloud began to break and a westerly breeze

*The Isle of Man has a population of 75,000, which for its land area of some 225 square miles is relatively few. By comparison, the Isle of Wight covers little more than half the area but has nearly twice the population. Nevertheless, when the weather is fine and an interesting trip is on offer, the Manx can be relied upon to produce a few hundred passengers for a trip off the Island in the **Balmoral**. Here we see her on 18th May 1995 at Garlieston on a day trip from Port St. Mary and Douglas, Isle of Man.*

Photo: Author.

*Left: When she was photographed on 17th and 18th July 1995, the **Balmoral** was in Scottish waters, tendering for the liner **Queen Elizabeth 2** in the Firth of Forth and running some very successful trips in connection with the start of the Tall Ships Race.   Photo: Stuart Cameron.*

The **Balmoral's** visit to Scotland towards the end of the 1995 summer season was dogged by some atrocious weather. In this dramatic photograph we see her on 26th September 1995 battling it out with the elements at Largs, where it took Captain Steve Michel several attempts before finally managing to bring her safely alongside.
Photo: Gordon Wilson.

sprang up. Then they were off! The wind was enough to allow them to set full sail and beat a course out to sea. Apart from the Balmoral, there was only a handful of small craft to witness this part. Our passengers were truly privileged. We ran with the Tall Ships for half an hour or so, weaving in and out of the ships with our decks crowded, cameras whirring and clicking, passengers cheering and ships' crews waving to our passengers, out to the front of the race. Then we had to turn for home. Just as we came round the sun broke through the cloud low on the horizon just above the Forth Bridges and directly behind the fleet of Tall Ships. It was a truly stunning sight as we picked our way back through the mass of billowing white sail and hissing, foaming wakes'.

In connection with these Firth of Forth sailings, Mr. Ian McMillan (now engineering superintendent amongst many other duties) has provided the following lovely anecdote. Both the **Balmoral** and the **Queen Elizabeth 2** required bunker oil whilst on the Forth and, since the Cunarder has been converted from steam power to diesel-electric, both she and the **Balmoral** need gas-oil for their main engines. After both vessels had been refuelled and sailed off on their respective voyages, Gulf Oil Bunkering Services, accidentally mixed up the two invoices and billed the **Balmoral** with the gas-oil pumped aboard the **Queen Elizabeth 2**.

Whilst Cunard might not have been too concerned about the £2,000 bill in respect of the **Balmoral's** modest thirst for diesel, the liner had taken £120,000 worth of fuel. Worse still, Gulf Oil had charged the **Balmoral's** bank account by direct debit! It was a case of almost instant bankruptcy for our little ship that in the course of a whole year only burns about £30,000 worth of fuel oil! Fortunately, the matter was soon corrected.

At Southampton, Red Funnel's latest 'Raptor' class ship, the **Red Eagle** came on service in April 1996. Mrs. Janice Whyte, wife of the present managing director, had launched her. Ferguson's at Port Glasgow had built all three of the new class on the Clyde. Her

arrival meant that the rather ugly, stretched **Netley Castle** could also be withdrawn and like her two older sisters she too went to the Adriatic Sea, being renamed **Sis**.

The International Festival of the Sea held at Bristol at the end of May 1996 was a tremendous success with historic vessels making the pilgrimage from all over the world. Both the **Balmoral** and the **Waverley** were there and the **Waverley** was acting as Festival Headquarters inside the docks whilst the **Balmoral** was ferrying-in passengers, 600 at a time, up the Avon. Thankfully, after no less than 10 years of experimentation with various liveries (the best of which was impractical and the worst of which was positively colourful) the **Balmoral** was repainted in the traditional White Funnel Fleet colours of P. & A. Campbell Ltd. in time for the great festival.

The French grey paint required for her superstructure is not a known fixed colour easily referenced on any colour chart, so this had to be done by eye, memory and with reference to old colour photographs of White Funnel Steamers. Apart from some minor fine-tuning to achieve the right shade of French grey, the **Balmoral's** livery now seems settled. The **Balmoral** now sports a splendid, rather deeper cowl top to her distinctive funnel than the somewhat flimsy, incomplete affair added way back in 1970. With it and her French grey upperworks being carried one strake lower, from certain angles she now resembles Campbell's magnificent-looking **Empress Queen**, in miniature.

During her career spanning half a century so far, the **Balmoral** has visited literally hundreds of harbours, piers and resorts right round the coast of Britain and of Northern Ireland too. However, in all this time, her peregrinations have only ever taken her out of British coastal waters twice, both occasions being in the month of June 1996.

The first of these unusual voyages was as a sequel to the Festival of the Sea on 6th June 1996, when the **Balmoral** made a single cruise down-Channel to Lundy. From there she continued 250 miles west, on a light sailing without passengers, across the southern end of St. George's Channel and the Celtic Sea to Bantry Bay in Eire. In very poor weather, the **Balmoral** spent that weekend running in and out of Bantry Bay and Castletownbere in the company of a number of the ships that had sailed there following the Festival of the Sea at Bristol.

At the end of that month, on 29th June 1996, for the first time in her entire career, the **Balmoral** carried passengers on an International Voyage. Her Class II passenger certificate issued by the Department of Transport Marine Office at Cardiff on 24th June 1996 was for 179 passengers and 21 crew. Having anchored off Eastbourne for the night of 28th June, she came alongside the Pier at 07.50 hrs. ready for her 09.00 hrs. sailing to Boulogne. The ship's log notes that clocks were advanced a further hour to G.M.T.+2 before setting sail. Thus it was with 200 souls aboard that the **Balmoral** set off from Eastbourne Pier to cross the English Channel. The 60-mile trip was accomplished comfortably, crossing the shipping lanes in strict accordance with the regulations. The Boulogne pilot was taken aboard at 13.59 hrs. and the ship made-fast in Boulogne Harbour at 14.25 hrs.

For the return trip, the **Balmoral** left Boulogne at 18.50 hrs., the Boulogne pilot was away at 19.15 hrs. and clocks were retarded 1 hour to G.M.T. +1. Having safely crossed the Channel, the **Balmoral** was back alongside Eastbourne Pier at 22.30 hrs.

So finally, on 29th June 1996, the **Balmoral** had achieved one round trip across the English Channel of the sort craved by Red Funnel's Captain Clarke all those years ago when he was arguing for the construction or acquisition of a long-distance and international excursion ship back in 1947.

There is little doubt that the willingness of the Department of Transport to help overcome the administrative problems of trying to arrange such an unusual trip stems from their knowledge of the high standards of construction to which the **Balmoral** was built by J. I. Thornycroft & Co. Ltd. during 1948 and 1949 and subsequently partly re-built at Clyde Dock, Govan in 1986.

Returning to Mr. Lionel Vaughan: he spends a lot of time each

season as shopkeeper aboard the **Balmoral** and this is something he has done for many years. Quite a number of volunteers do this throughout the season. When he is not doing duty in the **Balmoral**, he is just as likely to be in the **Waverley**, which is where the author last saw him at Kingswear on the Dart. The occasion was the **Waverley's** only 1998 River Dart sailing, being the memorable evening cruise across Start Bay to the Point, which the author, his wife and a near capacity crowd greatly enjoyed. 'Hello Lionel', the author called out having just stepped off the **Edgcumbe Belle** (ex-**Humphrey Gilbert**) ferry from Dartmouth, right by where the **Waverley** was berthed. *'Blimey, you're both a long way from the Isle of Man aren't you'* came back the instant reply from Mr. Vaughan who must see tens of thousands of faces in a year. What a wonderful ambassador he is for the two ships! He will comfort any passenger who is unwell or needs attention, or chat to them in quiet moments too. It seems to fall to Mr. Vaughan to hand out

On 4th June 1995, the **Balmoral** *paid her first call at Macduff, well up on the north-east of Scotland in Aberdeenshire.*   *Photo: Edwin Wilmshurst.*

*Above: These two sequential photographs were taken of the **Balmoral** in the River Camel on 25th September 1996 during her visit to Padstow, Cornwall. With Capt. Peter Tamblin in command, she was flying the Blue Ensign.*   *Photo: Author's collection.*

Below left: On a trip from Brighton to Bodmin, on 10th September 1996 the author and his wife detoured via Clevedon to see the newly re-built pier and for the trip up the Avon to Bristol. The Pier is now immortalised in Nigel Coombes' lovely book entitled Striding Boldly. *This was supposed to have been an excursion right up through the City Docks, but for operational reasons within the docks this was not possible. Having made the round trip up the Avon and back, Captain Michel substituted a very enjoyable cruise to see the newly completed Severn Bridge. The **Balmoral** did a couple of passes under the new bridge before returning her very contented passengers to Clevedon from where the sun could be seen setting peacefully, over the other side of the Channel.*   *Photo: Author.*

*Below right: Here we see the **Balmoral** on the grid-iron at Cumberland Basin, Bristol on 18th April 1996. Whilst by regulation, she only has to actually dry-dock every two years, she still needs to come out of the water somehow, to get the accumulations of weed and encrusted marine life off the bottom of her hull. In this photograph, the process of restoring her livery back to that of P. & A. Campbell Ltd. was well under way by the time this photograph was taken.*   *Photo: Philip Tolley.*

*On 18th May 1998, the **Waverley** paid her only visit that season to Kingswear on the River Dart. The author and his wife, together with a near capacity crowd, were aboard for a beautiful summer's evening cruise down the Dart and out across the Bay to Start Point. In times gone by, most vessels built at Philip & Son Ltd.'s Dartmouth shipyard ran their speed trials over the same course. Here we see the **Waverely** bathed in glorious evening sunlight with her navigation lights already on, steaming down the Dart.*

Photo: Jim Cozens Photography, 144 Victoria Road, Dartmouth. TQ6 9EG.

those hygienic little paper bags (the 'jolly bags') also for use when the going gets really tough!

An anecdote on that very theme (from the author's ditty box, not from Mr. Vaughan's as he is too much of a gentleman to propagate such a story) concerns an unfortunate passenger who was only just managing to cope with the pitching and rolling on one particularly rough trip. Finally in desperation he stood up to try to get on deck for some fresh air, but the movement was too much for him. Feeling the sensation of nausea sweeping over him, he reached for the nearest 'jolly bag', still hoping that he might just manage to get on deck. Unfortunately, any chance of his survival was quickly dispelled when he realised that he was not the first person to use it!

At times like that, it is as well to remember the old saying where seasickness is concerned that it is the hope of dying that is guaranteed to keep you alive! The **Balmoral** is a tough, reliable specimen and was well built. Even in poor weather she will protect her passengers and will get them home perfectly safely. Happily, most of the time the weather is fine and the sea calm. Under these conditions the **Balmoral** does what she does best every summer when she carries 100,000 people on memorable excursions all around the British coast.

One of the great strengths of the **Balmoral**, her camaraderie and brotherhood, manifests itself in the form of winter working parties made up mainly of volunteers, supervised by the ship's engineering staff.

*'As soon as the summer season is over,' says volunteer Mr. Richard Clammer, 'the **Balmoral** retires to her winter berth at Princes Wharf in the centre of Bristol's Floating Harbour. Securely moored with steel shutters over her saloon windows and a large 'No Entry' sign on the gangway, it might appear to the casual passer-by that the ship is in hibernation. Nothing could be further from the truth for, below decks, another unique aspect of the **Balmoral** story is taking place. Connected to a shore power supply and with*

her heating and galley in full working order, the ship continues to be a living and very busy community.

*It is no exaggeration to suggest that **Balmoral's** continued existence is due in part to the unseen winter work which is planned and supervised by chief engineer Mr. Andy Westmore and engineering superintendent Mr. Ian McMillan, and carried out by a team of volunteers supplemented by one or two paid professionals. Several of the volunteers live on board throughout the winter and the domestic needs of the workforce are looked after by Mr. Ollie Scott who splits his time between refit work and ensuring that everyone is kept supplied with a steady stream of hot meals and clean boiler suits.*

Work gets under way immediately. The decks and seating in the engine room alleyways are covered with sheets of protective hardboard, work benches are erected and work begins on dismantling the main engines. Because these are salt-water cooled, the cylinder heads have to be removed each winter and all the cooling water channels thoroughly cleaned. Work progresses methodically with each head, together with its associated injectors, pipe-work and other parts, placed in clearly labelled locations in the alleyways for further attention. The engines are cleaned, checked and reassembled by Mr. Andy Westmore and his 'weekday team' of volunteers most of whom are either ex-seagoing engineers or offer a range of electrical or mechanical expertise. Steering gear, pumps and auxiliaries are checked annually and refurbished on a regular rota to the survey requirements.

*The **Balmoral's** Sirron diesels are no longer in production, so these days, all spare parts have to be specially manufactured. This work takes place in an elderly railway carriage, now converted into a fully equipped workshop, which is shunted onto the quay beside the ship each winter. Containing lathes, power saw, drilling and shaping machines, the carriage is the domain of retired engineer Mr.*

Ray Eley who works tirelessly on all the turning, fitting, modification and manufacturing jobs which the ship requires.

The ship's passenger accommodation is left largely untouched until late December when, traditionally, a meal is held in the gaily decorated lower bar for the crew and regular volunteers, followed next day by a Christmas party for members of the Bristol Channel Branch of the Paddle Steamer Preservation Society.

With the festive season over, any major structural work begins. For instance during 1996/7 the whole of the stem and bow section was re-plated. The winter of 1998/9 saw the starboard hull belting strengthened, some hull plates renewed, the anchor windlass completely rebuilt and the forward end of the promenade deck observation saloon replaced. The latter also involved the construction of new teak window frames.

While the major welding work is being carried out by Mr. Nobby Clarke, the ship's professional welder, the weekend volunteers, many of whom travel long distances to help the ship, are busy with a wide variety of essential jobs. One of the least fragrant is the cleaning and repainting of the dark, cramped areas beneath the flooring of the lower deck - a task affectionately referred to as 'bilge diving'! Others include the cleaning and refurbishment of mechanical parts, decoration of the saloons, and a multitude of small but important jobs.

In April of alternate years **Balmoral**, her engines reassembled, makes the short journey down the Floating Harbour to the historic Albion Dry-dock. Here her bottom is thoroughly cleaned and re-coated with anti-fouling paint and all her underwater fittings are checked. The Maritime and Coastguard Agency requires the ship's hull to be ultrasonically tested for thickness every five years, but **Balmoral's** engineers prefer to exceed these safety requirements and test one third of the hull each winter. Any faults that are discovered are put right during dry-docking together with any other desirable periodic refurbishment. During the winter of 1996/7, for example, the starboard propeller and shaft were replaced, a task which involved removal of one rudder and considerable ingenuity on the part of the ship's engineers.

With dry-docking completed, **Balmoral** returns to Princes Wharf where all attention is turned to making her 'ship-shape and Bristol fashion' for the season ahead. A ship in the middle of a refit always looks so dirty and chaotic that it is impossible to imagine that she will ever sail again, but somehow order prevails! A week or two before the ship is due to enter service again the volunteers are joined by members of the deck crew, and the pace of work accelerates. The hull and upperworks are repainted, wooden brightwork receives several coats of varnish and the passenger accommodation is thoroughly cleaned. Curtains and soft furnishings reappear from store and life rafts are swung on board. Sea trials are carried out in the Bristol Channel before the ship returns to embark her catering crew and take on stores for the restaurant, bars and gift shop.

Finally, early in May, the great day comes when **Balmoral** slips quietly down the Avon and out to sea, bound for her first excursions in the North of England. The winter workforce watch 'their' ship go with a tinge of regret, mixed with tremendous pride at a job well done and the certain knowledge that in six months' time the whole task will begin again'.

* * * * *

Some of the other former Red Funnel ferries had remarkably long lives.

Having been towed across the English Channel at the end of 1987, the 1927-built paddle steamer *Princess Elizabeth* now flourishes as a floating museum and gallery, moored beneath Notre Dame in Paris on the River Seine.

Left: April 1999, sees the **Balmoral's** winter overhaul nearing completion at Bristol and a willing mix of Company personnel, P.S.P.S. members and winter regulars. From the left:: Captain Steve Colledge (Master), Mr. Mike Waterson, Mr. Ray Eley, Mr. Kevin Hopper, Mr. Andy Westmore (Chief Engineer), Mr. Nobby Clarke and Mr. Bob Flook.   Photo: Bristol United Press.

Bottom left: **Balmoral's** dry docking in April 1997 at Bristol. Engineering Superintendent Ian McMillan and Chief Engineer Jim Bullen (both in white overalls) and two other workers take a short break for a midday snack.   Photo: Nigel Coombes.

Bottom centre: New bow plates being welded into position by the **Balmoral's** own welder Mr. Nobby Clarke and engineering support staff.   Photo: Richard Clammer.

Bottom right: Part of the volunteer workforce that works so hard every winter to overhaul the **Balmoral**! Here we see Miss Clammer, wielding a brush-load of varnish onto the **Balmoral's** taffrail.   Photo: Richard Clammer.

Above: Immediately after the Festival of the Sea at Bristol on 9th September 1996, the **Balmoral** *sailed (light) to Castletownbere on Bantry Bay, Eire to run a short weekend's sailings in what turned out to be very inclement weather. Here we see the local ferry* **Misneach** *acting as tender for the* **Balmoral**, *which could not get into the harbour that day, as it was full of other craft.* Photo: Iain Quinn.

Above left: In Spring 1996, the **Balmoral** *commemorated the 40th anniversary of the final P. & A. Campbell Ltd. paddle steamer sailings to France. She arrived from North Wales to operate a Missions to Seamen charter from Littlehampton to the Isle of Wight on Thursday, 27th June 1996. Then, after spending the night at an industrial berth on the east side of the River Arun (astern of the vessel in this photograph) she has turned and is about to pass through the pedestrian and cycle swing bridge before taking on passengers for Worthing and Eastbourne on the Friday. Next day, Saturday 29th June 1996, she sailed from Eastbourne to Boulogne.* Photo: Keith Adams.

Left: The only time the **Balmoral** *has ever carried passengers on an International Voyage was on 29th June 1996 when she sailed from Eastbourne to Boulogne with 200 people aboard. Had he still been around to witness the event, Red Funnel's Captain Clarke would rightly have been very proud as it was he who, with Thornycroft's all those years ago, tried to give the* **Balmoral** *cross-Channel cruising capabilities. In this memorable photograph, the* **Balmoral** *is seen alongside at Boulogne* Photo: Keith Adams.

The former passenger ferry **Vecta**, later Campbell's **Westward Ho** which had become a floating public house and nightclub in Manchester in 1972, was towed via Bromborough, on the Wirral, south to London in 1985 where she then had various static uses in the old Docklands area on the Thames. Thoroughly dilapidated looking, she was finally towed to the Cornish side of the famous Devonport to Torpoint ferry where she was ultimately broken-up in 1996. She had a lingering death, the progress of which was watched in sadness by the author on his regular trips from the Isle of Man to Cornwall.

Of the three Torpoint chain ferries still in use today, just as the **Balmoral** was in 1949, two (the **Tamar** and the **Lynher**) were built at Woolston by J. I. Thornycroft & Co. Ltd. in 1960 and the third (the **Plym**) came from Charles Hill & Sons Ltd., Bristol in 1969. In 1986/87, all three ferries were 'stretched' to increase their capacity. The popular saying locally is that it is only the Torpoint ferry chains that attach Cornwall to the rest of England; the inference being that if they so decided, the Cornish could declare their independence, cast off and set sail to more amenable waters!

The former Red Funnel passenger ferry **Medina**, later **Mons Abyla**, was sold by her Gibraltarian operators in late 1971 for static work at London, Brighton, Lymington and elsewhere too. For these she had various names including **Moroccan Belle**, **Marilu** and she was also named **Take Two** at one stage. During her final years, her once stumpy but pleasing, almost homely shape became hideously defaced with the building of a massive and totally unsympathetic superstructure over virtually the entire length of the ship. It was not until 1998 that she was finally broken-up on the Tyne, by then named **Island Pride** and most recently having failed as a proposed Chinese restaurant. It was a sad end to this lovely little ship which, older travellers will recall, could roll and corkscrew her way across to Cowes and back in a manner never again equalled by any other such ferry.

The ex-landing craft **Norris Castle** was seized by Piraeus Port Authority around November 1988 whilst still bearing the name by which she was last known, the **Aghios Dionisios**. She was put up for auction on many occasions but they never managed to sell her. As recently as 1998, they were considering the possibility of her sale for breaking-up.

Following her sale to Tonga in 1970 when she was named **Olovaha**, the **Queen of the Isles** (chartered by Campbell's on several occasions in the late 1960s) has changed hands and had several changes of name. She became the **Gulf Explorer** in 1982, reverted to being **Queen of the Isles** in 1987 and became **Island Princess** in 1994. According to Lloyd's Register of Shipping, she was still Classed ✠100 AI until 19th March 1997, and as far as is known, she continues in the ownership of the Western Development Corp. Ltd. of Solomon Islands.

The Polygon Hotel in Southampton, once almost an integral part of the Red Funnel Steamers scene for Annual General Meetings, official gatherings and after-launch lunches, finally ceased trading as a hotel in 1998.

During 1998, according to the **Balmoral's** engine room logs, her main engines were running for 1,250 hours. If an assumption of speed averaging $13\frac{1}{2}$ knots is made and the whole is then converted from nautical to land miles, it follows that the **Balmoral** sailed almost 20,000 miles in that one year. This is quite typical of Britain's most widely-travelled excursion ship. The **Balmoral's** fuel consumption is about 45 gallons (or 0.17 tons) of marine diesel oil (M.D.O.) per hour of constant running. The cost of M.D.O. fluctuates with the world price of oil but, for guidance purposes only, in 1998 the cost per ton of oil averaged about £100.

Put another way, some £30,000 was spent on diesel fuel for the **Balmoral's** Newbury Sirron diesels in 1998. Theoretically, that would have sent her on the following 20,000-mile voyage, three-quarters of the way round the world. From Bristol across the Atlantic Ocean, through the Panama Canal to the American West Coast, straight across the Pacific Ocean, through the South China Sea and well on her way home across the Indian Ocean, heading towards Suez and the Mediterranean with some 7,000 miles to run!

Epilogue

So what lies in store for the future of the *Balmoral*?

As soon as the paddle steamer *Waverley* has completed her Millennium rebuilding with the aid of substantial financial help from the Heritage Lottery Fund, attention will need to be turned to the *Balmoral* to ensure her continued survival. She is, after all, now unique.

Throughout her long and sometimes illustrious career, the *Balmoral* has always suffered from one perpetual problem - or more precisely, her owners have suffered the problem. From even before the very first day she took to the water back in June 1949, none of her successive owners or operators has ever had any spare money to spend on the *Balmoral*. That she has survived these last fifty or more years at all is in itself a minor miracle.

The dire economic condition of Britain's coastal shipping straight after the War was felt by Red Funnel Steamers every bit as keenly as by others. In 1969, they disposed of the *Balmoral* but she raised only a tiny fraction of the cost of the new car ferry that was to replace her. Somehow Red Funnel managed, although at times their financial condition came uncomfortably close to being terminal. Nevertheless, under their stewardship, the *Balmoral* was properly maintained and kept in first-class order.

Ten years ago, in a world by then mostly dominated by shipping giants, the small size and independence of Red Funnel Steamers was so severely restricting their ability to raise the large sums of capital needed to finance their new fleet, that something had to be done. Happily in 1989, they then became part of Associated British Ports, the owners of Southampton Docks. Today they flourish and continue to run excellent high-speed and traditional ferry services from Southampton to Cowes.

In the hands of the penurious P. & A. Campbell Ltd., the *Balmoral* began the slow decline that was seemingly unstoppable. Theorists call this phenomenon 'the inevitability of gradualism'. It was not due to any lack of loyalty or desire on the part of her crew or the management and directors to do their level best for the ship (and her older consorts in their day) but was symptomatic of the total lack of money available for preventive maintenance. European Ferries, the parent body, were no longer in the business of presiding over the operation of old excursion ships in the Bristol Channel, or anywhere else for that matter. The continued running of Campbell's dwindling fleet of elderly cash-starved motorships for the final 18 years of its existence often called for acts of superhuman endeavour by its sea-going and shore-based staff at which the reader can now only marvel.

As her condition slowly but inexorably spiralled downwards, so too did her passenger appeal. It is axiomatic that thereafter there was even less money coming in. No doubt some readers will still recall the depressing sight and sounds twenty years ago, of the rusty looking *Balmoral* getting underway, belching oily black smoke and unburned fuel from her misfiring Newbury Sirron diesels that craved so badly some major care and proper maintenance. Things were no better inside the engine room either, where the air was filled with a pungent blue haze that pervaded every corner of her lower deck. In the end, P. & A. Campbell Ltd. sold their last two ships, the *Balmoral* and the *Devonia*, after which they withdrew from commercial activity altogether and their business was wound-up.

The *Balmoral's* emaciated existence at Dundee marked the lowest depths that she could possibly plumb and yet gradually she fought her way back to magnificent supremacy. At Dundee she had weeds growing in the joints of her rotting decks where the caulking had long since burst adrift and had never been replaced. Looking at her at that time was best done with the eyes firmly closed.

Few people witnessing the **Balmoral's** arrival at Clyde Dock in 1986 would ever have believed that having gone so far down-hill, she could be gutted and virtually rebuilt, then return to full, glorious, passenger-carrying service. Yet with a tremendous amount of hard work, much of it given freely by corporate supporters and her loyal volunteer labour force, what once was seemingly impossible has now been achieved. The result is a credit to everyone concerned. This book bears testimony to their magnificent efforts.

But keeping a fine and historic old ship like the **Balmoral** in full operational condition is no easy task and every year considerable sums of money have to be found to enable all the necessary work to go on. In a good year, the **Balmoral** will make a modest profit to go towards the ongoing maintenance programme. In an average year she will just about break even; she may even lose a little money, purely in cash terms. But all the while, she is proudly flying the **Waverley** banner, maintaining the back-up, sharing the costs and providing the presence all around our coastline and in our rivers and estuaries. Donations of money, work and specialist effort are always needed, even down to the begging of humble rags with which a volunteer might polish a copper tube in the engine room or mop up an oily spill when cleaning out the bilges!

*Having spent the night at Seacombe on the far side of the River Mersey, the **Balmoral** is seen here sharing the ferry berth, perched on the end of Liverpool's famous Landing Stage on 25th May 1997. A good crowd is about to board for her excursion from Liverpool to Llandudno and on to Menai Bridge.*

Photo: Richard Winfield.

*In this lovely photograph taken on 25th September 1998, a piper was on the quay at Rothesay to welcome the honourable **Balmoral** alongside. The **Balmoral's** livery is as she appears today.*
Photo: Gordon Wilson.

The main purpose of this book has been to arouse as much interest as possible in the **Balmoral** and in her history and achievements to date.

Throughout its lengthy research and gestation period, as every page and image evolved, more and more interesting facts were elicited. These facts form the backbone of the whole story from which the reader may enjoy and learn about the fascinating events of the last half-century in which the **Balmoral** and her peers have been widely involved. Splendid though it all undoubtedly is, nevertheless, it is now part of history. From this time on, the future success of the **Balmoral** will correlate with the degree of public awareness and support she receives around the British Isles. Happily, in this we may all participate and enjoy the **Balmoral** experience as a result.

Having read the book, the **Balmoral** now awaits you at a nearby pier, harbour or jetty!

Author's Thanks and Acknowledgements

A book of these proportions is very expensive to produce. Early in these proceedings I was able to arrange the making of a substantial donation towards its whole cost by a patron who has a love of all things old and mechanical. On behalf of everyone involved in these endeavours, I am proud to acknowledge our benefactor's generosity.

I have long been of the opinion that any serious book published on a particular subject has to add materially to the stock of knowledge generally in the domain of its readership. In writing this book and compiling its 192 pages, I have become acutely aware of the depth of knowledge that exists about the **Balmoral** and her peers. However, whilst some of this vast reservoir of knowledge is held reasonably accessibly in libraries, maritime museums and company records which need to be searched, much more is in private collections, people's memories, their scrapbooks and in tiny fragments spread widely across the world. Some of my happiest and most intriguing moments in producing *The Honourable* **Balmoral** *Her Peers and Piers* have involved meeting a lot of those people, discussing their connection with the **Balmoral** and the piecing together of what might be termed her 'maritime jigsaw puzzle' spanning well over half a century.

I have been privileged to be entrusted with the writing and production of this book but without the willing assistance of several interested people, whose knowledge and help has been liberally given, this celebration would not have been possible. Alongside the results of my own 45-year association with the **Balmoral** in all her various roles, the reader will also find the experiences of others too, amongst them the best names in the country. These people are truly the literati of the world of excursion ships and ferries. I appreciate and acknowledge wholeheartedly their help and assistance offered freely and copiously.

Indeed, given the opportunity, time and resources, there must be a small number of interested persons with the correct credentials upon whom could have fallen this happy and vital task and I am proud to name them throughout, alongside their known contributions. With their support and encouragement, nevertheless it is I who has readily and keenly accepted the challenge to produce this biography of the **Balmoral** and any mistakes are my own.

In addition to any mention made in the text, I wish to go on record and say that I am particularly indebted to the following people for all the encouragement, detailed help and in-depth knowledge they have provided:-

Mr. Tim Cooper (invaluable press files going back the whole 50 years, research, photographs, archives and anecdotes).

Mr. Keith Adams, well-known expert in his own right and son of the late Mr. R.B. Adams, author of the famous book *Red Funnel and Before* (photographs, research, anecdotes and archives).

Mr. Richard Winfield, publicity officer for the Coastal Cruising Association (research, photographs, copy documents).

Dr. Joe McKendrick, a director of the **Waverley** and **Balmoral** organisation (archives, log sheets, records, sailing information, photographs).

Mr. Bob Willatts (invaluable original research at the National Maritime Museum).

Mr. Nigel Coombes, author of fine books on the subject of the Bristol Channel and its steamers and piers (photographs, anecdotes and archives).

Mr. Edwin Wilmshurst (photographs).

Mr. Chris Collard, author of excellent books on the history of P. & A. Campbell Ltd. ships (photographs and research).

Mr. Alan Brown, author of very interesting books on the subject of ferries and excursion steamers (technical advice, copy documents).

Mr. Richard Clammer, author of quality books on paddle steamers (photographs, anecdotes and research).

Mr. Iain Quinn (photographs).

Mr. David Parsons, former editor of *Ships Annuals* (photographs and archives).

Mr. Terry Sylvester, chairman and Mr. Peter Reid, director of Waverley Steam Navigation Co. Ltd. (records).

Mr. John Edgington, now retired from the National Railway Museum at York (historic colour photographs).

Mr. Malcolm McRonald, stalwart of the Coastal Cruising Association and expert on coastal ships (photographs and archive material).

Mr. Mike Casey, former I.O.M. Steam Packet Company engineer superintendent (plans of the **Balmoral**).

Mr. Pat Murrell, long-term **Balmoral** and **Waverley** stalwart, ardent collector and archivist (photographs).

Mr. Richard Howarth (photographs).

The National Maritime Museum at Greenwich (photographs and engine plan).

Mr. John Hall of the Western Photographic Society in the Isle of Man (darkroom services).

Ms. Mandy Wheeler at the *Southampton Daily Echo* (photographs).

Mr. Alistair Whyte, managing director of Red Funnel Group (permission to research and reproduce the Red Funnel archives) and his secretary, Mrs. Jill Walker (who kindly copied key resolutions).

Miss Hazel Nicholson, the erstwhile company secretary at Red Funnel Steamers who kindly went through all their archives with me and turned up much interesting data, photographs and the **Balmoral's** original specification book and plans.

Ms. Anne Cowne at Lloyd's Register of Shipping (historic data).

Mr. Phil Fricker (photographs and research).

Ms Sonya Kemelmager at the *Daily Telegraph* (research).

Mrs Jane Macleod at Weymouth Library (research).

Capt. B. Fountain, Harbour Master, Shoreham (research).

I am indebted to my wife Patricia, Mr. Leslie Brown, Dr. Joe McKendrick, Mr. Nigel Coombes and Mr. David Parsons for reviewing the proofs - a necessary and onerous task that I appreciate greatly.

If through inadvertence I have omitted to mention the help of others, whether given directly or indirectly, I now do so most sincerely.

The **Balmoral** *was present at the start of the Tall Ships Race at Falmouth in July 1998 at which all the contestants set off on the first leg of the race to Portugal. The liner* **Queen Elizabeth 2** *and many local pleasure boats were also there to witness the great event.* Photo: Jim Cozens.

190

Bibliography

The author has, in his personal book collection, most of the major works (and hundreds of minor ones) ever written in the English language and published on the subject of British cross-Channel boats, ferries and excursion ships. From his whole library, the author has consulted the following books in the preparation of this work.

BOOKS

100 Years of Specialised Shipbuilding, by K. C. Barnaby (Hutchinson 1964)

A Pictorial History, by M. Archbold (Red Funnel 1997)

ABC British Railways Steamers (Ian Allan 1953)

ABC Coastal Passenger Ships (Ian Allan c1956, 1958, 1960, 1963)

ABC Coastal Ships, by H.M. Le Fleming (Ian Allan c1954)

ABC Excursion Ships and Ferries, by J.S. Styring (Ian Allan 1958)

Any More for the Skylark, by D.L. Chalk (Chalk 1980)

Balmoral Handbook (various dates Waverley/P.S.P.S.)

Birth of a Legend, by Armstrong, Brown, McKendrick and Robb (PSPS 1987)

Bland Gibraltar, by G. Somner (W.S.S. 1981)

Bridge Over Lyonesse, by D. Chudleigh (Isles of Scilly S.S. Co. 1992)

Bristol Channel Pleasure Steamers, by R. Wall (David & Charles 1973)

British Nationalised Shipping, by Clegg & Styring (David & Charles 1969)

British Paddle Steamers, by G. Body (David & Charles 1971)

British Pleasure Steamers, by G. Grimshaw (Tilling 1945)

Buff Funnel Book, by B.Cox (Bourne c1960)

Caledonian Steam Packet Co. Ltd., by I. C. MacArthur (C.R.S.C. 1971)

Campbells of Kilmun, by I. Hope (Aggregate, 1981)

Cardiff Queen, by N. James (James 1988)

Century of Progress (Philip & Son 1958)

Coastal Ships, by D.R. Chesterton (various dates Ian Allan)

Cross Channel & Coastal Passenger Steamers, by F. Burtt (Tilling 1937)

Decline of the Paddle Steamer, by R. H. Coton (P.S.P.S. 1971)

Denny 1844 - 1950 (Wm. Denny & Bros. Ltd. 1950)

Denny List Parts I - IV (National Maritime Museum 1976)

Directory of Shipowners, Shipbuilders & Marine Engineers (1956 onwards)

Dunkirk, by A.D. Divine (Faber 1945)

Early Solent Steamers, by Capt. F. T. O'Brien David & Charles 1973)

English Channel Packet Boats, Grasemann and McLachlan (Syren 1939)

Famous Paddle Steamers, by F.C. Hambleton (Percival Marshall 1948)

Farewell to the Floating Bridges, by J. Horne (Southampton 1976)

Ferries Forever, by D. Charters (Merseyside County Council 1984)

First Hundred Years, by G.W. O'Connor (Red Funnel 1961)

Gosport Ferry, by P.D. Childs (Portsmouth Harbour Ferry Co. PLC 1983)

History of Portsmouth Harbour and its Ferries, by J. M. Maber (Maber 1976)

Hythe Pier and Ferry, by A. Titheridge (Itchen 1981)

Instructions re Survey of Passenger Steamers (H.M.S.O. various dates)

Kingswear Castle Handbook (various dates, P.S.P.S.)

Little Ships of Dunkirk, by C. Brann (Collectors Books 1989)

Lloyd's Register of Shipping (various dates, Lloyd's Register)

Lymington, The Sound of Success, by A. Brown (Condie 1988)

Mercantile Navy List (various H.M.S.O.)

Mighty Mersey and its Ferries, by R. G. Danielson (Maritime 1992)

Nine Days of Dunkirk, by A.D. Divine (Faber 1959)

Paddle Steamers, by R. Clammer (Batsford)

Paddle Steamers of the 1970s, by R Plummer (Anglia)

Paddle Steamers at War, by R. Plummer (GMS Enterprises 1995)

Passenger Steamers of the Bristol Channel, by N. Coombes (Twelveheads 1990)

Passenger Steamers of the River Dart, by A. Kittridge (Tewelveheads 1987)

Passenger Steamers of the River Fal, by A. Kittridge (Twelveheads 1988)

Passenger Steamers of the River Tamar, by A. Kittridge (Twelveheads 1984)

Plymouth, Ocean Liner Port of Call, by A. Kittridge (Twelveheads 1993)

Portsmouth-Ryde Passage, by J Mackett (Ravensbourne Press 1970)

Railway and Other Steamers, by Duckworth & Langmuir (Stephenson 1968)

Red Funnel and Before, by R.B. Adams (Kingfisher 1986)

Red Funnel Steamers, Souvenir Guides (various editions 1953 onwards)

Red Funnel Stuff, by E. P. Leigh-Bennett (Red Funnel 1937)

River Ferries, by N. Martin (Terence Dalton 1980)

Round the Southern Fleet, by C. Grasemann Ian Allan 1946)

Royal Standard, Red Ensign, by D. Aitchison (Pall Mall 1958)

Royal Yacht, Britannia, by A. Morton (Orbis 1984)

Shanklin, Ill Fated Prince, by A. Brown (Waverley Excursions 1985)

Shipbuilding Industry, by L.A. Ritchie (Manchester University 1992)

Ships Annuals, all editions, edited by Carter, Clegg, Parsons (Ian Allan)

Ships of Southampton & The Solent, by L. Dunn (Adlard Coles 1964)

Ships of the Solent, by Rigby Watson Jnr. (Ian Allan c1950)

So Strong and So Fair, by R.G. Danielson (Maritime 1996)

South Coast Pleasure Steamers, by E.C.B. Thornton (T. Stephenson 1962)

Steamers of British Railways, Clegg & Styring (T. Stephenson 1962)

Steamers of North Wales, by F. C. Thornley (T. Stephenson 1952)

Steamers of the Forth, by I. Brodie (David & Charles 1976)

Steamers of the Thames and Medway, by F. Burtt (Tilling 1949)

Story of British Railways, by B. Tatford (Sampsom Low, Marston 1945)

Striding Boldly, by N. Coombes (Clevedon Pier Trust 1995)

Talisman, Solitary Crusader, by A. Brown (Aggregate 1980)

Thames Coast Pleasure Steamers, by E.C.B. Thornton (Stephenson 1972)

Trip Out, by G. P. Hamer (various editions)

Wahine Disaster, by M.Lambert and J. Hartley (Reed 1969)

Warships of WWII by H.T. Lenton and J.J. Colledge (Ian Allan 1963)

Waverley Handbook (various dates Waverley/P.S.P.S.)

Waverley, the Golden Jubilee (Waverley/Condie 1997)

West Coast Steamers, by Duckworth and Langmuir (T. Stephenson 1953)

West Country Passenger Steamers, by G. Farr (Tilling 1956)

White Funnel Handbooks (P.& A. Campbell Ltd. various years)

White Funnel Magic, by N. Coombes (Twelveheads Press 1995)

White Funnels (Book 1), by C. Collard (Baron 1996)

White Funnels (Book 2), by C. Collard (Wheelhouse Books 1998)

Whites of Cowes (J. Samuel White & Co. Ltd., Cowes)

NEWSPAPERS AND JOURNALS

Southern Evening Echo, Southern Daily Echo, Isle of Wight County Press, Daily Telegraph, The Times, Manchester Guardian, Bristol Evening Post, Sea Breezes, Ships Monthly, Ship Ahoy, Cruising Monthly, Ships Illustrated, Shipping Wonders of the World (Parts 1 - 55)

This photograph, the last in the book, is not included for its excellence or particular photographic charm of which it is notably devoid. What we see here is the **Balmoral** *at the end of the day. It could be any day but this happens to be 18th May 1995. Her passengers have all gone home having been well looked after on a lovely day trip from the Isle of Man to Garlieston in Southern Scotland and a cruise across Wigtown Bay. Young children will soon be in bed whilst parents sit by the fireside and talk of the events of the day. It is getting cold and is nearly dark; the* **Balmoral's** *navigation lights have been switched on. The wind has risen to near gale force and, before it, is driving heavy rain. The photographer has long since given up hope of staying dry whilst waiting, high on the exposed headland above the Calf Sound, for the ship. For the* **Balmoral**, *Captain Michel and his crew, they have another five hours' work ahead of them, pitching and rolling across the North Irish Sea as they take the ship back, through the Calf Sound, and north to Belfast. For them there is no alternative, as they have to be on station ready for the next day's excursions from Belfast's Pollock Dock and thence to Bangor. To everyone who works on the* **Balmoral** *or in support ashore, we owe them all a great debt of gratitude.* Photo: Author.

SUBSCRIBERS Lane - Shearer.

Lane, P.J.
Langford, M.J.
Larman, D.M.
Launder, K.R.
Lawrence, M.J.
Leary, N.
Lee, T.S.B.
Leech, J.
Leech, K.B.
Lehrian, P.
Le Jeune, B.
Lester, D.H.J.
Lester, J.C.
Lewis, A.
Lewis, M.
Liddle, E.
Littler, P.J.
Lloyd, E.K.
Lloyd, G.
Lloyd, R.A.
Lockwood, K.C.
Lodge, R.
Logan, J.A.
Love, B.
Lynch, D.J.
McCombe, A.
McCormick, W.B.
McCrorie, I.
McEwen, G.
McGinnity, A.M.C.
McGowan, D.
MacHaffie, F.G.
McIntyre, A.

McIntyre, C.
McKendrick, J.J.
MacKenzie, M.
Maclachlan, I.W.
Maclagan, I.
McLaughlin, I.
McLaughlin, M.
MacMaster, J.
McNab, C.
McRae, J.
Macey, J.
Maffey, W.
Mapledoram, T.
Marshall, G.
Martch, S.J.
Martin, B.
Mason, M.J.
Massey, P.K.
Matthews, P.
Matthews, R.D.
May, J.
Mayes, W.
Meacham, P. & Z.
Medway, K.F.
Menworth, J.P.
Miles, E.J.K.
Milford, R.B.
Mills, H.
Mills, H.R.A.
Mills, J.E.
Mitchell, R.
Moody, B.
Moore, D.

Morgan, B.J.
Morgan, D.
Morgan, H.R.
Morris, D.R.
Morrison, D.
Mortimer, I.
Moss, A.C.
Mowker, M.F.
Mullen-Curtis, F.
Munn, A.
Munnings, B.
Munro, I.
Murphy, G.
Murray-Lyon, N.
Murrell, P.J.
Mussett, T.
Neal, K.L.
Neill, R.M.
Nelson, M.
Newth, J.W.
Nichols, F.I.
Nicholson, I.S.
Nicholson, J.
North, P.
Oatway, M.
O'Brien, D.
O'Brien, N.
Offord, J.
O'Neill, H.
Page, C.G.
Pain, K.
Palmer, R.M.
Pankhurst, B.J.R.

Parkes, K.
Parr, R.
Parry, A.
Parsley, M.
Parsons, G.W.
Paterson, G.W.
Pearce, E.
Penrice, J.F.
Perry, R.J.
Phillips, C.J.M.
Phillips, P.
Pinfield, R.
Pledger, B.
Pomery, M.
Poole, A.
Poole, E.
Powell, C.G.
Preston, T.K.
Pullinger, A.
Purcell, R.S.
Ramsay, I.
Ramsay, J.
Ratcliff, C.
Ratcliffe, M.D.
Rawlings, R.W.
Rawlingson, C.S.
Ray, J.
Reading, B.
Readman, A.J.
Record, T.
Reed, C.G.
Reeve, D.
Renshawe, G.

Riley, D.W.
Riley, M.
Roberts, M.
Roberts, P.
Robins, D.W.
Robins, N.S.
Robinson, J.
Robinson, N.V.
Robinson, S.W.
Rolfe, D.
Rooke, H.
Rooney, A.J.
Ross, J.W.
Rowe, D.
Rumble, P.
Russell, A.R.
Sadler, P.J.
Salter, A.J.
Sammon, P.
Sankey, R.
Saunders, K.C.
Saunderson, B.
Sayer, P.
Scandrett, S.
Scargill, G.
Scott, O.J.
Seaton, C.
Semple, P.W.
Senior, S.
Sharman, S.
Shaw, G.J.
Sheach, L.
Shearer, D.C.

SUBSCRIBERS Shepherd - Wright.

Shepherd, N.A.E.
Shipstone, R.
Shore, B.
Siggers, K.
Sims, R.J.
Sinclair, D.
Sisson, J.D.
Slater, J.K.W.
Smith, C.J.
Smith, G.W.
Smith, L.J.
Smith, M.K.
Smith, N.
Smith, S.R.
Smith, T.R.
Snart, F.D.
Snellgrove, B. & M.
Sparks, H.
Spears, J.
Spells, J.
Stafford, P.M.
Stapleton, D.R.
Steeds, P.
Steere, R.
Stephens, G.P.

Stephens, P.J. & J.
Stockdale, N.M.
Stocker, P.A.
Stokes, A.J.
Stones, B.
Street, P.J.
Struthers, C.
Sudders, M.
Sweeney, A.
Sweet, F.
Tacchi, B.
Taylor, C.P.G.
Taylor, D.I.
Taylor, K.
Taylor, M. & C.
Taylor, P.
Taylor, T.W.
Tedstone, M.A.
Thomas, K.
Thompson, D.
Thompson, T.J.
Thorne, G.
Thorne, G.J.
Thornton, J.
Thurlow, M.

Tibbs, R.
Tighe, G.C.
Tilly, E.J.
Timms, A.E.
Tomlinson, P.N.
Train, G.C.
Tribe, D.
Triggs, R.
Trim, T.F.L.
Trott, G.M.
Tufnell, G.F.
Turner, C.
Turner, M.B.K.
Turner, R.
Turner, R.H.
Underdown, R.B.
Urie, T.
Urquhart, M.
Vaughan, L.
Verity, D.
Verrell, M.
Wade, J.
Wakelin, R.
Wakeman, A.
Waldron, M.B.

Walker, R.
Walker, W.M.
Ward, R.
Ward, T.
Warman, D.
Warn, A.B.
Warner, D.
Warren, G.C.
Wason, E.R.
Watkins, R.
Watts, M.
Weightman, D.
Westlake, A.C.
Westley, E.
Westmore, A.
Wheeler, G.E.
Whitaker, R.S.
White, J.
Whitelaw, R.
Whitmore, B.M.
Wield, D.C.
Williams, C.P.
Williams, D.
Williams, G.
Williams, G.S.

Williams, J.F.
Williams, M.J.C.
Williamson, J. & J.
Willis, G.
Wilson, A.
Wilson, G.S.
Wilson, H.
Wilson, I.
Wilson, R.M.
Windebank, W.
Winning, I.
Witt, T. & J.
Wood, R.
Woodham, M.
Woodhouse, G. & J.
Worley, M.
Wray, B.S.
Wright, D.
Wright, D.
Wright, H.
Wright, I.
Wright, M. & A.

As this, the first, edition of the book was closing for press in early September 1999, subscribers were still sending in their pre-publication orders for copies of the book. The publisher thanks everyone most sincerely for their support.